ERWIN PISCATOR'S POLITICAL THEATRE
The Development of Modern German Drama

ERWIN PISCATOR'S
POLITICAL THEATRE
The Development of Modern German Drama

C. D. INNES

Assistant Professor
York University, Ontario

Cambridge
at the University Press 1972

Published by the Syndics of the Cambridge University Press
Bentley House, 200 Euston Road, London NW1 2DB
American Branch: 32 East 57th Street, New York, N.Y.10022

© Cambridge University Press 1972

Library of Congress Catalogue Card Number: 72–183223

ISBN: 0 521 08456 3

Printed in Great Britain
by W & J Mackay Limited, Chatham

Contents

		page	
	Introduction	*page*	1
1	The Weimar Republic: Art and Environment		9
2	The Agitprop Theatre: Politics		23
3	Agitprop and Revue: Society		41
4	Documentary Drama: the Material		66
5	Epic Theatre: the Actor and the Structure		97
6	Total Theatre: the Audience		131
7	New Drama: the Author		152
8	Piscator: Contemporaries and Critics		181
	Notes		208
	Chronological Table		219
	Bibliography		227
	Index		237

Illustrations

Plates (*opposite page* 80)

1 Erwin Piscator at rehearsal, 1953.

2 *All the King's Men*. Multi-level acting area allowing simultaneous scenes, projection screen. Dramatic Workshop, 1948.

3 *Schweik* ('Off to Belgrade!'). Pallenberg as Schweik on outer band, officer-marionette (Grosz) on parallel band. Piscator-Bühne, 1928.

4 *The Fireraisers*. Set design, P. Walter. Placards and screens in auditorium, central and circling stage. Nationaltheater, 1959.

5 *War and Peace*. Pierre as commentator demonstrating the progress of a battle with toy soldiers on the 'Stage of Fate'. Schiller-Theater, 1955.

6 *War and Peace*. Russian battle orders and Napoleon's entrance on the 'Stage of Fate'. Landestheater, Darmstadt, 1955.

Figure

Despite All! Stage designs, John Heartfield, 1925   *page* 146

Introduction

There is considerable confusion today as to the proper function of the theatre. Its rôle in society, its relationship to the public and even its validity as an art form are questioned, since when reality is ignored or significant trends of thought are not reflected, art falls into disrepute. Traditionally the stage has been seen as a mirror of the world. But the individual actor is its prime constituent, which limits it to the particular, while the essentials of twentieth-century existence are abstract: power resides in bureaucracies not kings, and conflicts are between masses not duellists. This means that the theatre appears incapable of dealing with the significant aspects of life at a time when the demand is for relevance. Technology has created a new vision of the world. The internal combustion engine and the aeroplane have led to expectations of a comprehensive treatment of complex subjects, while radio and television have established new standards of immediacy and actuality. As a result conventional theatre has been relegated to 'entertainment' and there has been a tendency among *avant-garde* intellectuals (Abbie Hoffman is an example) to dismiss all formal definitions of drama. Such a rejection, however, is unjustified. The last fifty years have seen the transformation of stage conventions through a continual process of experimentation, ranging from the ritualism of Artaud or Grotowski and the formalized abstraction of the Bauhaus to the politically oriented theories of Meyerhold or Brecht. On the one hand there has been a retreat to 'pure' art, theatre for theatre's sake, on the other an attempt to adapt drama to the modern context, but in either case developments have been determined by a new awareness of the physical resources of the stage and its relationship to the audience.

It is normal to date modern drama from Ibsen, although Naturalism was actually the final phase of traditional theatre; but it is more accurate to take the Dada movement as the starting-point of these attempts to find theatrical correlatives for the new consciousness. It has been more a question of techniques than material, since the means of expression determine the range of possible subjects – and for this reason the major innovations have been the work of directors rather than playwrights. One of these, whose experiments have been seminal in the development of new stage-forms, is Erwin Piscator; and his productions which affected every aspect of the theatre offer an opportunity for evaluating the validity of the stage as a forum for contemporary society.

Anticipating Marshall McLuhan in his appreciation of the rôle played by technology in determining modern vision, Piscator introduced mass-media to the stage in order to make the theatre capable of handling twentieth-century issues. This raised certain basic questions about the nature of drama. The political situation immediately following the First World War discredited cultural traditions in Germany and prevented any compromise with former artistic conventions for reflecting society. Reacting against aesthetic criteria, Piscator attempted to represent current events or recent history in a direct manner, which necessitated reappraising the relative importance of the various elements of drama and spotlighted the difficulties of adaptation. His extensive use of mechanical aids drew notice to the balance between literary texts and theatrical performances and forced a re-evaluation of the part played by the actor vis-à-vis stage-effects and scenery, while his emphasis on recorded speech and documented fact focused attention on the author's position in reducing him from an imaginative creator to an organizer of given material. This led to a reassessment of the part played by the audience, exploring the different possibilities for imaginative receptivity, objective distancing or emotional participation.

Piscator, overshadowed by his contemporary Brecht, has been generally neglected. But his work provided models and standards for all *théâtre engagé*, shaping Communist propaganda plays, forming the distinctive elements of Brecht's dramaturgy and influencing Joan Littlewood, Roger Planchon and the American Living Newspaper as well as his German contemporaries. His career spans the whole period from 1919 to the plays of Hochhuth, Weiss and Kipphardt in the last decade, and his experiments were responsible for the major modern stage-forms of 'Agitprop' plays, 'Documentary Drama' and 'Total Theatre'. His ideas are still gaining influence, and the effect of his experiments can be seen today in

London, New York and Toronto as well as Berlin. His productions were consciously intended to provide examples which would frame practical foundations for a new kind of drama, and the sources of the dramaturgical forms that came from his work can be traced by following his personal involvement in Dada and his commitment to Communism.

Born in 1893, Piscator gained his experience in conventional production as a student at the court theatre in pre-war Munich, as an actor in an army theatre group where he played stock parts in popular comedy from 1917 until he was demobilized, and as a director when he opened the Central-Theater with Hans José Rehfisch in opposition to the Volksbühne. His involvement in politics was equally important. When he arrived in Berlin in 1918 Wieland Herzfelde, with whom he had acted during the war, introduced him to the Marxist core of the Dada movement, and in an emotional reaction to the murder of Karl Liebknecht and Rosa Luxemburg after the abortive Spartacist revolt he joined the Communist Party.

The contrast between the Flanders front line and the assumptions behind the entertainment put on for the troops led Piscator to reject the traditions of Western culture and to demand relevance in art. Dada, with its iconoclasm and its standards of active involvement and verisimilitude, confirmed this view. But by its nature the movement was incapable of establishing coherent artistic principles and when Piscator founded his first theatre, Das Tribunal, at Königsberg in 1919, his radicalism was limited in practical terms to Expressionist plays like Strindberg's *Ghost Sonata*. However, returning to a politically tense situation in Berlin and without funds, he went back to the first principles of drama when he opened his Proletarisches Theater in 1920, playing without a proper stage, costumes or lighting, in the meeting halls of industrial districts, and relying on amateur, working-class actors. The short scripts he produced under such conditions, designed to make an immediate propaganda impact, initiated the Agitprop movement in Germany and formed the basis of his mature work. Four years later he returned to this political type of theatre with all the resources of the professional stage, producing two propaganda revues designed for specific occasions, *The Red Revue* and *Despite All!*, which provided alternative dramatic models to conventional plays and set the form for all subsequent Agitprop performances. Normal artistic criteria were inapplicable to these experiments, which contained qualities that Piscator was to develop into the conflicting genres of Documentary and Total Theatre, and their major significance was to force a complete re-examination of drama's function and the relationship of the stage to society.

Relevance and political meaning were not enough for Piscator, who experimented with various ways of representing the modern environment. In 1919 he had attempted to rewrite Toller's *Transfiguration* as a vehicle for depicting reality according to his own war experiences, but Das Tribunal closed before it could be put on. When he first took over a proper stage in 1922, the Central-Theater, he tried a dirt-and-degradation extreme of Naturalism, and the climax of his 1928 production of *The Adventures of the Good Soldier Schweik* approached the vicious commonplaces of the *Neue Sachlichkeit* movement. He later referred to the three plays that he staged in the Central-Theater as a regression. But apart from winning critical recognition which made the next step of his career possible since he was offered a position as a guest director at the Volksbühne, these conventional productions were in line with his development. It was this impulse to realism that led initially to his use of film in stage productions – first for *Despite All!* in 1925 and Paquet's play, *Tidal Wave*, at the Volksbühne in 1926, then in all his most significant work.

Fusing film into a dramatic action was Piscator's decisive innovation. Backed by exposed and elaborate machinery it acted as a correlative for the modern context as well as gaining a new level of authenticity. But with simultaneous stages, symbolic acting constructs and such equipment as the 'treadmill' constructed for *Schweik*, film also altered the nature of the theatre. It allowed an apparent liberation from the temporal and spatial limitations of the stage and made it possible to shift viewpoints, so that the action could be extended to global scope and gained the 'epic' ability to comment on itself. It was film too, though Piscator preferred to give political reasons, which enforced a redefinition of the actor's function, and its intrinsic qualities reacted as a catalyst on the other elements of performance, setting new standards of precision, actuality and impersonality for sound effects, movements, scenery and particularly speech.

To make appropriate film sequences for his productions, to train actors to conform with the new conditions, to compose incidental music suitable for the mechanical nature of his stage and to provide scripts which he could use, Piscator – who had opened his own theatre in September 1927 – founded a teaching studio. This brought every aspect of drama under his direct control, which made it possible for him to produce practical examples of the ways modern technology could represent contemporary existence in its range and complexity, opening fresh areas of experience to the stage and providing it with new means of expression.

The five years between his appointment to the Volksbühne in 1924 and the closing of the Piscator-Bühne was the most fruitful period of Piscator's career, culminating in four brilliant productions, *Hoppla, We are Alive!* by Toller, Alexei Tolstoy's *Rasputin*, *Schweik* which broke box office records with Max Pallenberg in the title rôle, and Leo Lania's *Economic Competition* (*Konjunktur*). These were complex productions, combining the most extreme elements of Total Theatre with fully developed documentary techniques; contradictory innovations which were only later developed into antithetical types of dramaturgy for Piscator formulated his theory by observing the effects of his practice. This makes it impossible for any sequential account of his career to do justice to his work, particularly since his techniques raise so many basic questions about the nature of drama.

By any standards the Piscator-Bühne productions were successful: they dealt with political issues in a comprehensive and appropriate way, returned the stage to its Schillerian position as a moral tribunal, provoked a public discussion about the nature of art, influenced contemporary playwrights and directors, and acted as a truly representative social forum, attracting the artistic and wealthy as well as proletarian organizations. Yet they failed the basic test of theatre – survival. Each of Piscator's ventures was short-lived, which was partly due to his constant experimentation and his exorbitant use of machinery, but mainly the result of the situation in the Weimar Republic. Such radical experiments naturally aroused artistic and political opposition, making Piscator a lightning-conductor for scandal. His Dadaist principles and the criticism of local figures in a play programme had incited a riot which caused the Königsberg authorities to close Das Tribunal. A flagrant disregard for the author's rights in rewriting Ehm Welk's *Storm over Gottland* as Marxist propaganda split the Volksbühne and raised a vicious critical battle in the press which resulted in his dismissal as a guest director. *Rasputin* led to libel suits by the ex-Kaiser and a Russian financier, his version of *Schweik* broke copyright laws, and he was prosecuted on a criminal charge of blasphemy for Grosz's satiric cartoons. Financial pressures added to his difficulties. Economic depression closed the Central-Theater; and the popularity of *Schweik* paradoxically bankrupted the first Piscator-Bühne when a second theatre had to be hired to fulfill obligations to the subscription organization.

But in the final analysis it was Piscator's transformation of the theatre into a political institution, bringing the stage into the ideological arena and intensifying the political situation, which caused his difficulties and closed the second Piscator-Bühne in 1929. Resurgent Nationalism protested against Walter Mehring's treatment of the Jewish problem in *The Merchant of Berlin*, and there was a violent revulsion to one scene in which a street-cleaner, singing 'Muck – Away with it!' swept up the corpse of a soldier lying in the gutter. Piscator, relying on his acting troupe rather than machinery, continued his development of techniques to depict modern realities, but in January 1931, after the success of Karl Credé's § *218* which attacked the criminal code on the issue of abortion, Piscator was arrested on a trumped-up charge of tax evasion, while Credé was imprisoned for illegally procuring abortions. Both were released a month later after a public outcry, but Piscator left for Russia later in the same year, and his acting troupe, who also went on tour abroad after police action, finally disbanded in June 1932.

For Piscator the concept of 'political theatre' embraced sociological issues in their broadest definition and he had to defend his productions continually against ideological attacks from Communist critics. While in the U.S.S.R. he directed one production, which was banned at the dress-rehearsal, and filmed Anna Segher's novel, *The Revolt of the Fishermen*, which was suppressed. He was elected secretary of the International Revolutionary Theatre Association in 1934, an organization of Agitprop troupes which he expanded to coordinate the various efforts of all left-wing and liberal theatre groups, but left Moscow for Paris in 1936. Here he worked with Alfred Neumann on his first version of *War and Peace*, which he eventually produced at New York in 1942. He left for the U.S.A. in 1938 and worked at the Dramatic Workshop of the New School for Social Research, directing over a hundred plays, establishing a theatre centre which trained a whole generation of American actors and playwrights including Marlon Brando and Tennessee Williams, and encouraging the development of off-Broadway stages. He only returned to Europe in 1951 when summoned to appear before the Committee on Un-American Activities, although East Berlin had approached him through Brecht, who invited him to direct Nordahl Grieg's *The Defeat* (later transformed into *Die Tage der Commune*) in the Theater am Schiffbauerdamm. But Brecht's letter, written from Zürich in March 1949, contained a warning:

You would be received with the greatest warmth, and everybody will understand completely if you were somewhat uncommitted at first and stepped around the china shop with a certain caution. I myself have not spoken publicly, never, have not expressed myself publicly at all but simply gone on with my work

– and Piscator, whose exit from the U.S.S.R. has been described as 'fugitive', had no wish to work under a Communist dictatorship again. For the next decade he lived from hand to mouth as a free-lance director in the Bundesrepublik, and this restricted his influence on the development of post-war drama since he lacked a fixed base, a trained ensemble and often the machinery he required. But in this period he brought his style to a new precision with two simple innovations, setting part of the acting area aside as a 'Stage of Fate' and lighting the stage from beneath through a glass floor to integrate individual characters into the wider patterns of historical events; and in 1962 when he was appointed director of the Freie Volksbühne in West Berlin a young playwright submitted his first script, which Piscator recognized as the type of drama for which his productions in the twenties had been designed. This 'epic play, epic-scientific, epic-documentary, a play for the epic, "political" theatre for which I have fought for thirty years; a "total" play for a "total" theatre' – as he described it in a foreword he wrote for its publication – was *The Deputy* by Rolf

Hochhuth, and its production in February 1963 marked the foundation of a new dramatic genre.

Hochhuth's second play, *The Soldiers*, was written specifically for Piscator's stage and dedicated to him, but Piscator died before the text was fit for rehearsal. In 1964 and 1965 Piscator worked with Heinar Kipphardt and Peter Weiss, and since then the leading German dramatists have all written plays which show his influence – even unlikely authors, satirists like Günther Grass whose study of Brecht, *The Plebians Rehearse the Uprising*, appeared in 1966, or Absurdists like Tancred Dorst whose portrayal of individual commitment in a revolutionary situation, *Toller*, was produced in 1968.

This new drama was the fulfilment of Piscator's work, designed as it was to encourage playwrights to deal with the significant issues of contemporary existence by developing techniques to open up new subject matter for the stage. The German dramatic tradition and the atmosphere of the Weimar Republic gave him an incentive and certain advantages, and his direct influence is most obvious in modern German plays. But his experiments are not only of interest to students of German literature, although his career does provide a guideline to the development of German drama. His productions raise questions which are significant for the contemporary theatre as a whole – the relative claims of utilitarian and aesthetic principles, the criteria of relevance and the limits of theatrical realism, the value of classical revivals, the use of evidence (Documentary Theatre) as against imagination, the effectiveness of audience-involvement (Total Theatre) or distancing (Epic Theatre), and the nature of propaganda. His work records the effect of modern conditions on stage conventions, illuminates the nature of drama as literature or a synaesthetic performance, and provides a basis for critical standards to replace those which, drawn from traditional plays, are no longer applicable.

1 The Weimar Republic: Art and Environment

German theatre: the break with tradition

Cultures can be defined by the continuity of their artistic tradition, and the development of a civilization is reflected in the continual modification of artistic conventions. These not only echo any alteration in the way men see themselves, so that art conforms to changing conditions, but also adjust the picture of man's relationship to his world. The history of art is a chronicle of perception; an archive of changes of vision recording the self-appraisal of the individual in the context of his environment as the accepted views of reality are modified by major scientific or mechanical advances which increase man's control over his physical surroundings. Even in the fine arts, periods of stylistic experiment follow significant technical innovations in order to discover a fresh visual order that is capable of expressing the new approach to reality in terms of linear design, colour and texture. Developments within a civilization are more obvious in the theatre than in any other art form, since – unlike painting or literature – the speaking and acting man is its primary means of communication. Human relationships are its basic material, and these are portrayed against a representation of environment which depends for its form on the adaptation of the available technology to the stage. The theatre therefore becomes a seismograph recording changes of consciousness.

Up to the twentieth century the traditional heritage of philosophy and ethics maintained its authority in European civilization through a process of gradual transformation. With the First World War, however, there came a dramatic expansion of horizons, an increase of knowledge and an acceleration in the tempo of life. Since then the speed of change has constantly superseded modes of vision before they could be accepted and form the basis of a new tradition of artistic expression. As a result contemporary art is eclectic; characterized by violent and impermanent stylistic revolutions. These are generally, like Dada, Futurism or Panderma, of

9

aggressive modernity and take novelty and originality as their criteria. Alternatively, dramatists as different as Brecht and T. S. Eliot have made comparable attempts to form images appropriate to our age from fragments of extinct conventions – one has borrowed techniques from the Greek, Chinese and pre-Elizabethan stages, eighteenth-century operetta, nineteenth-century music hall and Chaplin's films, modelling his speech forms variously on the Bible, the Japanese Haiku and pseudo-American slang. The other has shored fragments of Kyd, de Nerval and Dante against his ruin, and made use of Sophocles, Euripides, medieval mysteries and drawing-room comedy.

Already at the end of the nineteenth century we can trace the intuition that tradition was breaking up under the pressure of social change. But the necessity of finding new artistic methods for ordering reality first became compelling as the Great War dragged into its final phase and the social order in the defeated lands – Russia, followed by the Germanic Alliance – disintegrated. In England the abdication of the old order was neither immediate nor obvious. In Germany, however, the sudden collapse of the Prussian régime brought its cultural values and traditions, already discredited by the war, into open disrepute. By 1919 Germany was a fully industrialized country. Yet since the process of industrialization, which had taken place almost a century later than in England, was not accompanied by any significant shift in the structure of power, fewer traditional assumptions had been questioned and the arts had remained more conservative. The disappearance of the old social order thus revealed an unbridgeable gap between art and actuality: a gulf that had already been exposed in the plays and operettas put on for the troops. The official cultural values appeared hypocritical in the context of trench warfare. The Classics and conventional comedies ignored reality and disguised the brutalization of the individual. By contrast, the machinery of mass-destruction and the headlong wastage of men and materials provided an eidetic image of the mechanization and tempo of modern life. The extent and inhumanity of the cataclysm exposed the inadequacy of traditional artistic responses.

Two factors accentuated this contrast for German artists. Unlike their English counterparts, they served in the ranks and were sensitized by their lack of responsibility as well as the degradation of defeat to the moral aspects of the catastrophe. In addition, the word 'art' had acquired connotations of divinity in Germany, due to the comparatively late development of a national culture. Art on a pedestal inevitably seemed irrelevant to the crude existence of the common soldier.

All compromise with pre-war aesthetics was barred by the consciousness that 1914 was the culmination of the past social evolution, not a break in it. Culture, associated with the upper classes who were held responsible for the war, was condemned as 'the whole literary rubbish-heap of a generation,...whose cowardice and thoughtlessness helped to drive us into the trenches'.[1] Consequently, novel methods were developed to express the new vision imposed by war, instead of attempting to adapt techniques that had been appropriate to outdated circumstances.

In the drama this development of new conventions was encouraged by the special position of German theatre. Since Lessing, German literature had had the acknowledged cultural purpose of unifying the country by spreading common moral and social standards, and the theatre in particular had been approached as an educational institution. The influence of the stage as a 'moral tribunal', acknowledged from the time of Goethe and Schiller, had established drama as the primary artistic means of social criticism. The theatre was therefore taken more seriously by the public than in other European countries, instead of being regarded primarily as a means to satisfy a demand for distraction; and was the natural outlet for the social criticism of German radicals – as it still is today.

Equally, however, the significance of the stage had given drama a solemn artistic character. Therefore when contemporary morality was attacked through the abolition of aesthetic values this was bound to arouse violent opposition – and not only from conservatives. Even *The Red Flag*, the official Communist newspaper, occasionally condemned propaganda plays on aesthetic grounds.

The cultural significance of German drama was merely a realization of the theatre's intrinsic potential for disseminating new ideas. In contrast to other art forms, the theatre addresses the community rather than the individual, and it appears to do so more directly because there is no printed page or painted canvas to interpose between the artist and his audience,[2] while its impression is more forceful because it can use any of the techniques available to the other arts. Being more transient than literature or painting and more subject to daily events, since a play, which only reaches complete artistic expression in performance, must be recreated nightly, the theatre seems more topical. Yet paradoxically it is less easily adapted to changing conditions. Its external forms are more traditional, since the building that decides the actor-audience relationship and the machinery that determines stylistic possibilities are products of the past – and at the close of a war that had accelerated technological advance and social change the theatre seemed only too obviously outmoded. Its plush and gilt and boxes were reminiscent of the monarchy, and its machinery had not been improved since the turn of the century. Regarded as a focus for public consciousness, the German theatre seemed more like a mausoleum to left-wing artists than a mirror of the contemporary world. Any attempt to create relevant drama therefore involved demolishing the ruins *à la* Jarry, so that even the 'revolutionary' art of the pre-war Expressionists and their followers during the war, the Young Germany movement, was condemned as a retreat from reality.

The rejection of tradition is therefore more noticeable in the German theatre than in other European countries between the wars. It was characterized by a more radical experimentation, which questioned the premises of drama as well as the nature of society in the search for a valid relationship between art and the modern environment. This process of experimentation continued longer and was carried further because society remained in upheaval throughout the Weimar Republic. Time was given to formulate the aims of the experiments, and their results could be evaluated. In consequence new methods of representing reality were developed into coherent systems which are still influential today.

Dada and the destruction of conventions

The first step in creating new techniques, the destruction of the old conventions, was admirably accomplished by Dada. With its spontaneity and individualism, this was more an activity than a movement, since it attracted many artistic rebels whose essential differences were at first disguised by their common rejection of traditional forms. The left-wing founders of Dada, Hugo Ball,

Tristan Tzara, Hans Arp and Richard Huelsenbeck, even included Marinetti[3] in their early exhibitions and appropriated some of the principles of Futurism before their ideological rationale became clear – so that in 1933 one has the incongruous picture of Kurt Schwitters, whose 'Merz' art was destroyed by the Nazis, and Moholy-Nagy, who fled Germany the very next day, attending an official banquet to honour Marinetti as the exponent of Fascist culture. Dadaist aesthetic theories were equally ill-defined because they produced a plethora of manifestoes while rejecting the concept of a programme – and the consequent confusion can be measured by the 1923 performance of Tzara's *Coeur à Gaz* in Paris. By this time André Breton, Francis Picabia, Louis Aragon, Paul Eluard and Tzara had each developed their own concept of Dada, and the stage became a battlefield where the supporters of spontaneous expression, the exponents of Abstraction and the Surrealists fought all against each over the definition of Dada. Breton was thrown bodily out into the street, one of Picabia's followers had his arm broken, Eluard was knocked off the stage, shattering the footlights, and the actors' costumes were reduced to rags before the police closed the theatre. The difficulty of categorizing the Dadaists, who deliberately avoided logical expression and rational definitions, has led critics to emphasize the purely negative aspects of their work. This has diverted attention from their motives to their tactics. The real importance of the movement, however, lay in the reasons behind the ostentatious moustache painted on the Mona Lisa and the insolence offered to their audiences: not in the shock effect.

The artists who produced the first Dada evening at the Cabaret Voltaire in Zürich in July 1916 were refugees from the various warring nations, and they shared a hatred of militarism. Their iconoclasm was a declaration of war on the civilization that made the 1914–18 holocaust possible and on the ethos that had welcomed it. Their violence was an expression of disgust at the respect paid to the priests, philosophers and artists, whose works were the expression of that civilization and whose standards had strengthened it. The basis of Dada was set out clearly by Tzara in one of the many manifestoes of 1918.[4] Logic and morality are condemned as the foundations of social slavery. Philosophy, psychoanalysis and all systems of thought are outlawed as systematizing bourgeois life. Rational explanations or theories are not to be expected from a movement which frequently avoided comprehensible grammar and legible typography as symptoms of systems. Even mental ability was blacklisted on the grounds that it was produced by and perpetuates bourgeois values, since 'the intelligence is an organization like every other. Like the social organization. . .it serves to create orders and to bring clarity where there is none . . . it serves to create a class structure in the state'.[5] Against such uncompromising radicalism, the rejection of the family as 'a comfortable compromise' is hardly more than an incidental consequence.

In the absence of any positive political creed, this denial of all forms of established order found expression in Abstraction. In Switzerland, cushioned against the immediate impact of the war and the following social chaos, Dada kept its anarchic character. But in Berlin it was exposed to the conflict and was politically committed before the November Revolution. While Tzara could still write that 'Dada ne signifie rien', the Berlin Dadaists had already embraced Marxism, since the news of a Bolshevist state in Russia seemed to offer a viable alternative to capitalism; a blueprint for an utopian future. Dada remained 'the negation of all previous values for life',[6] but had gained a positive viewpoint from which to mount its attacks: 'Communism is the Sermon on the Mount, organized in a practical way. It is a religion of economic justice.'[7]

Huelsenbeck later claimed that the Dadaists were apolitical anarchists – a view that has superficial truth in the light of their inability, with the exception of George Grosz, to express their political convictions comprehensibly in their art. This negative impression was accentuated by the antics of Baader, who called himself the 'Supreme Dada'. He was arrested for indecent exposure, caused a riot during a church service and interrupted a parliamentary debate by throwing leaflets (entitled *The Green Corpse*) into the Chamber, demanding a referendum to give the 'Supreme Dada' dictatorial powers and promising, 'we will blow Weimar into the air'. But the First International Dada-Fair disguised a clear political standpoint beneath its bizarre inconsequence. Baader's 'Montage', which occupied the whole of the Galerie Burchard, devoted the fourth floor to the World War and the fifth to the World Revolution. The message that 'Dada fights on the side of the revolutionary proletariat!' was placarded in gigantic (but distorted) letters diagonally across one wall of the exhibition; and the title-page of the catalogue carried the slogan 'the Dadaist man is the radical opponent of exploitation' (even though it was upsidedown and camouflaged by one of Heartfield's montages). Walter Mehring, the founder of the Political Cabaret, and the Herzfeldes, who counted Levine, the professional revolutionary, as a close friend, were among the earliest members of the Berlin Dada group.

Like its political implications, affirmative qualities lay concealed behind Dada's flagrant denigration of aesthetics. The demolition of cultural values which was intended to raze Parnassus to a *tabula rasa* carried a programme for rebuilding within itself. The attack on art as the expression of 'eternal verities' implied a demand for involvement. The avoidance of convention removed the barriers between direct experience and art, which was identified with illusion, and linked to this rejection of artificiality was an attempt at unmediated communication.[8]

From this viewpoint, the four artistic forms that Dadaists claim to have invented are not merely intended to 'épater les bourgeois'. In negating the concept of 'beauty' in art they define a particular relationship to their environment. 'Bruitism', as a tonal concatenation using everyday objects as musical instruments, applied undisguised sounds to force the audience into a fresh perception of their surroundings. Marinetti, for example, used a collection of typewriters, kettle-drums, motor-horns, bells, baby's rattles and saucepan lids to present 'the awakening of a city'. 'Collages' incorporated objects as individual entities into pictures and used fabrics, glass, metal, paper and wood as things in themselves (whereas the schools of abstract art used them as materials to form a design; as means to express a higher meaning). 'Montage' juxtaposed photographs, in other words recorded events, in unusual combinations. 'Simultaneity', the verbal equivalent of Montage, was designed to show different aspects of life at the same time, so giving a truer picture of existence than is normally possible in the simplifying, single dimension of poetry. The aim of these techniques can be seen to be actuality and completeness. Even the outward confusion inherent in rejecting sequence and intelligibility had a positive value insofar as it reflected the superficial chaos and the complexity of life. Dada art was intended to have an immediate and actual effect on the public.

Active involvement and authenticity were the criteria of Dadaism, and its characteristic sensationalism and aesthetic brutality were correlatives for the tone of contemporary events:

Art is dependent for its execution and direction on the age in which it lives,...the highest art will be that which presents the thousandfold problems of the times in its conscious content and which reveals that it allowed itself to be marked by the explosions of last week, which continually has to gather its elements together again after the blows of the last few days.[9]

The majority of the younger creative artists were exposed to Dada before it lost cohesion under the pressure of political events, and its continuing influence on art can be seen in such modern phenomena as Panderma – an experimental literary and theatrical movement founded by Carl Lazlo in the 1950s.

Berlin, as the centre of imperial government, was also the cultural centre of Germany – and just as it was natural that Dada found its major support in the capital, so it was inevitable that men like Brecht and Piscator gravitated there after their demobilization, instead of returning to their homes in Augsburg or Marburg. Theatrical reputations could be made in Berlin, the workplace of Otto Brahm and Reinhardt, where critics were arbiters of taste for the drama. But the city held additional attraction for the politically conscious in 1918. In the decisive hours when the government disintegrated after defeat, events in Berlin had determined the political fate of the rest of Germany, and it was reputed to be the stronghold of Bolshevism. It was this that drew Piscator, who has left a lasting impression on German drama by his conscious attempts to adapt the theatre to modern conditions.

Piscator's debt to Dada

As a student, Erwin Piscator had worked at the Court Theatre in Munich, which played classical dramas in a traditional style, and during the war he had been seconded to one of the army acting groups which entertained the troops with popular comedy, crudely performed. His subsequent principles were based on these early experiences. The elevated sentiments of the classical plays contrasted with the brutality of the trenches, and the comedies were overtly designed to distract the soldiers from an awareness of their true position. In reaction he rejected all art which had no direct relevance to the real conditions of life and no aim but amusement. Piscator's poetry, published in *Die Aktion*[10] in 1915 and 1916, indicates a political position similar to that of Wolf, Wangenheim and Brecht, whose standpoint during the war was one of pacifism rather than directed social criticism. Society was held responsible for the holocaust, but the style of these poems is conventional, their tone is one of hopelessness and a typical subject the waste of death. When he arrived in Berlin at the beginning of 1919, however, his attitude changed. Wieland Herzfelde, with whom he acted in the army, introduced him to his brother, John Heartfield, who had anglicized his name in protest against Germany's part in the war, George Grosz, Richard Huelsenbeck, Franz Jung, and Walter Mehring – the inner circle of Dada, whose various talents Piscator was later to use for his productions. He took a minor part in Dada demonstrations, motivated by his war experiences which had revealed that 'A deep chasm, far too deep, separated art from life',[11] and their political discussions convinced him that art could only have meaning as an instrument in the class struggle.

Recollecting his post-war experiences, Piscator emphasized the effect of political events on his development, and minimized the artistic influence of Dada. But Dada was an important transitional period, and the most striking effects of his later productions formed part of the Dada repertoire. The extent of Piscator's debt to Dada can be demonstrated by a glance at the theatrical techniques used by Ywan Goll, one of the leading Expressionists who also joined the Dada movement. Although Goll is chiefly known today for his poetry while his significance as a theatrical innovator has been ignored, his attempts to create a 'superdrama' by using 'all technological props' to create effective images of contemporary life had considerable influence at the time. Brecht admired his farces and Piscator later considered two of his plays for production. Commenting on his staging of Paquet's play, *Flags*, in 1924, Piscator claimed that 'this was the first time to my knowledge that slide-projection had been used *in this fashion*'.[12] But Goll had broken out of the accepted stylistic conventions of the theatre as early as 1920 in *The Chaplinade* and *The Immortal* by dovetailing photography into the stage action.[13] *The Immortal* made use of film and the projection of placards, newspaper cuttings and photographs – as

Piscator was to do increasingly after his production of *Flags*. Goll introduced grotesque masks which exaggerated physical characteristics – as Piscator, with the help of George Grosz, was to do in *The Good Soldier Schweik* in 1927. He experimented with gramophones – as Edmund Meisel did for Piscator's production of Toller's *Hoppla, We Are Alive!*, also in 1927 – and he deliberately broke illusionistic conventions in a way that anticipates the 'alienation effect', which Piscator later claimed to have discovered by accident.[14] Goll's intention, however, was to 'objectify' his characters and their actions and, by revealing the banal as unreal and the monotonous as extraordinary, to create a world of imagination truer than the appearances of everyday life. Piscator used the same means to extend the spatial and temporal limitations of the stage, to document the events portrayed in a play and to comment on them.

Incidental Dadaist effects continued to appear in Piscator's work until the 1930s. For instance, his use of sound to portray 'the awakening of a city' in his adaptation of Gorki's play, *The Lower Depths*, was directly comparable to Marinetti's 'symphony', while the kicking of a soldier's body by a street-cleaner during the song 'Muck – Away with it!' in the production of Mehring's play, *The Merchant of Berlin*, was the exact equivalent in nationalistic terms of the moustache on the Mona Lisa. But Dada's importance for his development lay in the standards of realism and immediacy, which became Piscator's criteria for judging his work, rather than such incidental stage effects.

Berlin 1919: the effect on the theatre

The excitement of the atmosphere in Berlin and the impact of political events, however, were certainly as formative for Piscator as the artistic achievements of the Dada dramatists. The context of the November Revolution determined his approach to the stage. Dada had confirmed his conviction that art should be more than amusement, that involvement in current events and the activation of the audience justified the existence of the theatre. Dada proved unable to influence the public, since its esoteric methods had only a minority appeal, but it had introduced him to Marxism; and after the murder of Liebknecht and Luxemburg, Piscator joined Spartacus, the most radical of the German left-wing parties, together with many other Dadaists. From then on Communist theory provided him with guide-lines for his work. It gave him a rationalization of the unformulated Dada attitude to society and a definite task which supplied the incentive for a systematic reconstruction of the theatre.

Continual crises made political extremism a compulsion in the first years of the Weimar Republic. The actual results of the November Revolution disappointed the euphoric expectations of the radicals, while the fact that it had occurred at all drove the moderates toward a militant (and mainly militaristic) right-wing. This centrifugal movement, which eventually destroyed the Republic as repeated inflations swelled the ranks of the discontented and dispossessed, was already visible in 1918.

When the moderates manoeuvered the more extreme socialists out of power in the *ad hoc* parliament, Spartacus took to the streets: and the more violent their demonstrations, the further the moderates were driven to rely on the traditionalist army. The extreme left practised revolution, and the extreme right incited to assassination. Violence was reciprocal and retaliation led to terrorism. Politics were open and dramatic. The attempt of two sergeants and a handful of soldiers to arrest the *ad hoc* parliament and to proclaim Ebert, the moderate leader, President, was even played out in a theatre building which had been improvised as a debating hall. The incident illustrates the essentially theatrical nature of public life at this time, and the way in which the theatre reciprocated is indicated by the fact that Piscator later staged a re-enaction of these events in the same building.

As well as producing histrionic material, the crises moulded the audience, who came to the theatre in a state of excitement. The violence in the streets gave them standards to judge artificial conflicts on the stage, and the tension caused by the unrest was carried into the auditorium. Personal antagonisms between the leading critics accentuated the political enthusiasms of the public, and premières provoked demonstrations. Culture, like science and sport, became an acknowledged political factor. 'Pure art' acted against the interests of the radical left by avoiding involvement in topical issues and representing a view of life in which ideals were more important than materialist idealism. Conversely, art which dealt with current 'affairs, even when not open propaganda, contained an attack on the Establishment in rejecting traditional aesthetic standards. In the tense situation, art could not remain neutral. As Thomas Mann pointed out: 'Politics are latent in every intellectual attitude.' Communism appropriated certain art forms while others rapidly became associated with Fascism. Above all, the temptation of 'single formula' solutions to explain the political and economic confusion of the period gave Weimar intellectuals a tendency to think in slogans. The eventual result was that 'these catchwords ('cultural Bolshevism' and 'cultural Fascism') have made themselves independent and act like poison-gas. Intellectual conflict has become impossible. Denigration has stepped into the place of argument; denunciation into the place of justification.'[15]

The audience and the events together forced dramatists and directors into political commitment. The contrast between comedies and the actual environment, where 'thirty million human beings – peasants, factory workers, children, women – hunger, starve, die', or the immediate past, in which a complete generation had been massacred, acted as a moral imperative for the left-wing artist: 'Up! paint, compose, write! And singer, sing! And orator, shout! Until every eye sees and every ear understands.'[16]

Piscator's first theatre, Das Tribunal, founded in the winter of 1919 in Königsberg (which Jessner, the leading Expressionist director, had also used as a springboard to the Berlin theatre), formed part of a general theatrical movement. Its name and its programme of Strindberg, Wedekind and Kaiser echoed Die Tribüne, which Karlheinz Martin, another Expressionist, had opened earlier in the year. Like all the other Communist troupes (Joan Littlewood's Theatre Workshop, for example, which began with a repertoire of Ibsen and Shaw, or the English Workers' Theatre Movement which opened with one of J. M. Barrie's plays), Piscator's amateur group staged progressive plays written for the commercial theatre. Lacking more relevant texts, they produced Expressionist dramas in which the breaking of artistic forms was at least representative of the destruction of the social order, and the revolt against paternal authority symbolic of the revolution against the bourgeoisie. But these plays stressed the conversion of the individual through the power of emotion and sacrifice, instead of the inversion of the social order by the activation of the working-classes and the use of force. Their visionary idealism was unsuited for political application, their methods delusive by Marxist standards. (Almost all the Expressionist authors were socialists – but the distance between their political position and the Communist line can be seen by the contrast between Levine, the professional revolutionary who organized civil war, and Toller, who, as President of the short-lived Bavarian Communist Republic, tore up hostages' death warrants and ineffectually attempted to sabotage the fighting.) In addition, the form of these plays needed material conditions and expertise for their successful performance which Piscator's group lacked.

The audiences who came as agitators were (and in spite of Piscator's efforts, remained) the traditional theatre-patrons, the middle-classes. The Volksbühne, a theatre for the working-classes under Otto Brahm, attracted predominantly cultured audiences in the 1920s; while Karlheinz Martin's Proletarisches Theater (which survived only a single performance), like Max Reinhardt's 'Theatre of the Five Thousand', attempted to educate the workers to appreciate the art that the bourgeoisie enjoyed. The theatre was accepted (or rejected, in the case of the class-conscious proletariat) as a bourgeois institution, and it was to be Piscator's continual complaint that the proletarian public showed little interest in his work once it was produced in a proper theatre.[17] 'A revolutionary theatre is absurd without its most vital element, the revolutionary public',[18] yet Piscator's later 'political' productions proved to be a magnet for audiences in décolleté and dinner-jacket. Dada had gone out onto the Kurfürstendamm, the café centre of Berlin, in search of bourgeoisie to provoke when they stopped coming to the Dadaist 'expositions'. Similarly, politically consequent theatre (in a Marxist sense) aimed at activating the proletariat and had to take its productions to the industrial slums. The intention of the Communists was to improve not the minds but the material conditions of the workers – who had shown themselves uninterested by 'Art' or Expressionist abstraction in any case. Therefore when Piscator returned to Berlin in September 1920 his next theatre was different both in form and style from Das Tribunal. Its title, the Proletarisches Theater, was also taken from Martin, but the programmes addressed audiences militantly as 'Comrades!' – a sharp contrast to Das Tribunal's expressionist 'Brothers'. Instead of having a fixed base Piscator's group played in beer-halls and workers' meeting-rooms, and instead of producing established plays they acted out scripts that they had written themselves or borrowed from similar organizations. Artistic elements were abandoned in the search for impact on actual events, and drama was limited to 'a political tool. An instrument of propaganda, of education'.[19] From Expressionism Piscator had found his way into the Agitprop movement. This was an essential preliminary for his later achievements since it prevented him from basing dramaturgical experiments on his training in the conventional theatre; and the ways he attempted to implement Agitprop principles, together with his reasons for discarding them, spotlight various problems concerning the relationship of the stage to twentieth-century realities.

2 The *Agitprop* Theatre: Politics

The determining factors in proletarian drama

Agitprop – short for 'Agitation and Propaganda' – was theatre at its most primitive. There was nothing dramatic about this when it first began in the U.S.S.R. after the Revolution as a means of communicating news to a largely illiterate population. It was similar to the earlier European tradition of the town crier. Bulletins were transmitted by telegraph to the towns and villages and read out by political officials through megaphones to local inhabitants gathered in the central square. The doctrinal nature of Communism and the fact that the majority of workers were neither Marxists nor revolutionaries led to this type of factual broadcast being combined with political exhortations and discussions conducted by the news-reader; and since the aim was not only to inform but to arouse enthusiasm, these public meetings were rounded off by playing the Communist anthem, the *International*. The basic elements of theatre were there – a speaker, an audience and emotional involvement as well as rational communication. When music was added to underline points of importance and news-readers began to 'exhibit' events with bodily movements, it was a short step to a more formal kind of performance, and the first regular Agitprop troupe, the Blue Shirts, was founded by the National Institute of Journalists in Moscow in 1923. They toured the country, playing without costumes, curtains or scenery, using speech, song, dance and gymnastics to dramatize texts taken from leading articles. The link between Agitprop and the news media is clear from the genesis of this troupe, but the relationship to conventional drama is indicated by their choice of subject matter. The reported incidents they acted out illustrated those personal characteristics that the Party had designated as 'harmful', and the hallmark of their style was satiric caricature. Concentrating on personal reactions to social contexts, demonstrated in individual cases, they had in fact returned to traditional dramatic themes. By

1924 the Party had realized how effective Agitprop could be as an instrument for political persuasion, and the Trades Union Council of the Moscow Department of Culture proceeded to standardize performances. The form of a 'living newspaper' production was laid down for imitation: a parade march-in was followed with a lecture illustrated by the performance of short scenes, and a commentator, who linked the various scenes, summed up the political meaning at the end.[1] A new theatrical genre had been evolved from dramatizing news reports.

Although the general concept of Russian Agitprop was known in Europe, there was little opportunity of seeing a performance or learning about the practical details of productions. No report of any Soviet version of Agitprop was published in Germany until 1927,[2] when the Blue Shirts made a guest appearance in Berlin. The first workers' theatre-groups in Germany, which came into being between 1919 and 1923 and formed a spontaneous and sporadic movement, were amateur ensembles or *Sprechchöre*. Piscator's group was the forerunner of a mass phenomenon – by 1928 every town in Germany had one or more Agitprop troupes, and the movement spread to England in the 1930s – and the style of performance that he developed acted as a prototype for his imitators. It was only after Piscator had proved the practical use of the theatre as an instrument for propaganda that the K.P.D., the German Communist Party, began to sponsor permanent Agitprop troupes. Piscator was therefore breaking new ground with his Proletarisches Theater in 1920.

The Dadaist rejection of all established artistic forms as the residual expression of anachronistic social orders, which Piscator had adopted in theory, was enforced in practice by the conditions of performance. The dramatic tradition, which had increasingly separated the actors from the audience, was necessarily discarded in the beer-halls. There the stage was (at best) a low platform, the whole machinery of illusion that had been developed in the professional theatre was absent, and the only entrance for the actors was often through the audience. In effect, Piscator returned to the first principles of medieval drama. Throughout the 1920s Piscator continued to stress that his primary intention was 'the ideological, dramaturgical, spatial and technical abrogation of the bourgeois theatre'.[3] But this explanation no longer applied to his later dramaturgical experiments. It was more a defence against political attack on the popular grounds of 'formalism' than a description of his real aims, since his Agitprop work had already achieved this abolition of traditional theatrical values and conventional practices. From the Proletarisches Theater on, Piscator's career was constructive rather than negative. His aim was not simply to abrogate the bourgeois theatre, but to supersede it by more appropriate methods of portraying reality.

To reform the drama – or rather to return to the imagined relationship between the ancient Greek stage and its public, to make the theatre the cultural centre of society once more – was a common factor shared by many of the theatrical innovators between the wars. It unites Piscator with such different figures as Yeats and Antonin Artaud and Gordon Craig. Piscator, however, identified culture with politics not aesthetics and intended his theatre to be ideological instead of mythological, working on the principle that: 'The play on the stage should act as an advance-guard action in the Proletarian war of liberation... The theatre of the Proletariat must be a theatre of class – of class-warfare.'[4]

The framework for his Agitprop style was formed from the search for technical substitutes for specific dramatic effects denied him by the impromptu nature of the performances; backed by the notion that only 'proletarian' art could have social relevance in the predicted Marxist millennium and that this should embody working-class experience and spring from the capabilities of 'the people'. However, the opportunities for developing new stage techniques or for creating a uniquely Communist form of drama were limited in Agitprop production by three major conditioning factors. The audience – exclusively proletarian, since the plays were aimed at the raw material of the Marxist revolution and even theatre critics were excluded if they represented moderate or right-wing newspapers – were unfamiliar with theatrical conventions, uneducated and uninterested in 'art'. The actors – normally amateurs – were frequently unrehearsed and often unskilled. And the stage-equipment was moveable – to avoid the attention of the police and because the desired type of audience could only be reached on their home ground – and therefore makeshift. The scripts had to be easy to learn, the characters had to be open and without subtlety, and the performance had to be of less than thirty minutes duration to be within the actors' capabilities. The contents had to be striking, immediately relevant and easy to understand if the play was to engage the attention of the audience. The results were a simplicity of language, gesture and action which promoted caricature instead of characterization, while the subjects of the plays were restricted in practice to the representation of familiar material by the audience's narrow range of interests and limited imagination. These crude conditions of performance were aggravated by poverty. Working-class audiences after the war and during the subsequent depression were too penniless to pay for the support of a stage which was (in Piscator's case) unsubsidized, so that the technical materials were rudimentary.

These limitations were accentuated by a narrow approach imposed by the political aims of the Proletarisches Theater. Themes had to be suitable for awakening the audiences' awareness of the class-struggle, or for clarifying the official Party line, which in effect meant that plays had to deal with social injustice in general terms and end with a call to revolution. In the U.S.S.R. the function of the Agitprop theatre was the opposite – to help establish the new government in power and to prevent any action against intolerable conditions. The difference can be illustrated by comparing the elaborate and officially organized parades in modern Moscow with the simplistic clichés of anti-Establishment demonstrations in Western capitals.

Such material and ideological restrictions determined the nature of Piscator's first attempts to develop a new type of drama, and inhibited the growth of any individual style of production. Primitive conditions enforced what was applauded as 'concision and clarity' for political reasons, and this became the keynote of all Agitprop plays – whether in the Living Newspaper of post-revolutionary Russia or capitalist New York, in the Workers' Theatre Movement of literate London or industrialized Manchester – where exactly the same formal characteristics recur as a response to similar circumstances. Piscator's formula for experimentation, that 'theory can only evolve out of practical work',[5] is paralleled by a statement from the United States' Workers Theatre: 'We cannot wait or look for a ready-made style...we have to develop the style of the workers' theatre by bringing it in conformity with its tasks and its means of expression.'[6]

Agitprop plays

Very little Agitprop material has been preserved. The scripts were provisional and unpublished, the troupes were short-lived, and the Nazis destroyed all the records of Communist agitation that came into their hands in Germany and France, while the improvised nature of performances and the barring of professional critics and photographers contributed to the absence of records. Only one of the plays performed by Piscator's Proletarisches Theater has survived,[7] *Russia's Day*, staged in the autumn of 1920, but its qualities are representative of Agitprop work. It was a short sketch, worked up from a script by Lajos Barta, and it formed part of a triple bill with *The Cripple*, which protested against the treatment of wounded veterans, and *Before the Door*, a crude melodrama calling for mutiny and murder as an answer to the military repression in Hungary. Piscator later claimed that these plays were collective creations, produced during rehearsal; but all three were in fact the work of individual authors, and this claim was due to his wish to emphasize the difference between Agitprop 'scripts' and conventional plays.[8]

The setting for *Russia's Day* was plain: a simplified map of Europe acted as a backcloth, and the borders of the acting-area were marked out by frontier-barriers, each painted in the national colours of one European nation. The costumes were simple, being either uniforms or everyday clothes. The lighting was crude, and the stage was a section of the floor at one end of a hall.

The opening scene acted as a brief overture which stressed the irrelevance of moderate compromise to an extreme political situation. A professor of sociology, accosted by three separate proletarians, each crying 'Help!' and 'the White Terror!' pedantically recommends parliamentary democracy as a panacea. This is shown in the subsequent scene to be a weapon of the forces of repression. The relationship of propaganda to politics is well illustrated in the first and third scenes which demonstrate the Communist arguments against democracy and show the complete rejection of the Republic and its socialist government by the K.P.D. The actual political effects, however, did not necessarily correspond to the intention of such propaganda. In 1918 the left wing in Germany was already split and the K.P.D. attempt to draw support from the democratic socialists eventually prepared the way for Hitler.

The Establishment is then introduced, represented by burlesque caricatures of a diplomat, an officer and a priest, all of whom are presented as servants of 'World-Capital' (depicted as a paunched money-bag wearing a stockbroker's top hat and addressed as 'Your Majesty'). They reveal their supposed plans and motivations in simplified terms:

WORLD-CAPITAL   The state...
OFFICER   ...must restrain and enslave.
WORLD-CAPITAL   The church...
PRIEST   ...make blind.
WORLD-CAPITAL   The schools...
DIPLOMAT   ...make stupid.

And the figures exit shouting 'Crush! Blood-bath! In the name of the Father!' In the next scene, a German worker reads aloud from a book on socialist theory and class reconciliation which he has been given by the professor, while three other proletarians cross the stage to give up their weapons in accordance with the principles expounded in the book.

SECOND WORKER   It has been demanded of me in the name
                 of World Order.
FIRST WORKER   And who determines the World Order?
SECOND WORKER   World Capitalism.

Then the war widows and the war wounded enter to blame capitalism explicitly and repetitiously for their sufferings in a simple formula of question and answer. A voice representing the Russian Revolution exhorts the Germans through a megaphone to destroy capitalism by violence as the only way of ending 'the terror', and the war cripples turn this call into an impassioned plea with the repeated 'Proletarians of all Nations, listen to this...to our voice!' From this point the emotional content is steadily heightened. A victim of the Hungarian counter-revolution enters to describe the thousands of fathers massacred, mothers imprisoned and sisters or wives raped, and dies with the cry: 'Comrades, don't let Russia be beaten down!' This sensational catalogue of horrors is given a spurious appearance of truth and its effect increased by the entry of a second dying Hungarian, who repeats the speeches of the first word for word – except that the thousands of victims have become tens of thousands. The final tone of this passage is one of religious fervour with an evangelical exhortation from 'the Voice of Russia': 'Proletarians of all Nations, listen to the voice of these who have been tortured and destroyed, the voice of *the martyrs of our Holy Cause*'[9] – a voice with which the audience are invited to identify through the example of one of the proletarian characters: 'Witness! I swear by these pallid Martyrs in my arms...that all my strength shall be at the service of the international World Revolution forever.' In the concluding scene the representatives of the Establishment re-enter. They admit that they are powerless against historical forces and that all hope of power in the future lies only with the masses! On this note the German workers storm onto the stage, describing themselves as: 'The pivot of the World Revolution... The eyes of all who fight for the Proletariat are on us. And the light of Freedom gleams in them', and the orders of the Officer are drowned by the Voice of Russia: 'Proletarians, up and fight!' Cries of 'Fight, fight, fight!' come 'from all directions', and the figures of Capital, the Church, Learning, the Military, and Diplomacy are driven ignominiously and easily off the stage by workers rallying to 'Everything to Russia! Everything for Russia! Up Soviet Russia!' The closing stage direction reads:

Voices. A roaring chorus repeats the battle-cry. Masses appear on the stage...crowds rush from every direction onto the stage, breaking down the frontier-barriers with the cry of 'Brothers, Comrades, Unite!' The German worker recites the first verse of the International, a trumpeter in Russian uniform steps forward, blows the International, the chorus on the stage join in, *as do the audience*.[9a]

The nature of propaganda in Piscator's work

A bare summary of Agitprop scripts such as *Russia's Day* reveals a sharp contrast between the intended and the actual effect of propaganda. This reflects the distinction between 'propaganda' and 'agitation' – that is, the difference between the machinery for distributing information and the state of social disturbance aroused by exciting the emotions. Piscator defined his intentions as an appeal to 'Reason. It [the new type of drama inaugurated by *Russia's Day*] should not only transmit excitement, enthusiasm, passion; but rather enlightenment, knowledge, recognition.'[10] The script, however, hardly calls for a cerebral reaction. The facts are vague and exaggerated, the social criticism is presented at an emotional level, and the theme is handled with fervent sensationalism. The word 'Agitprop' itself, a fusion of the antipathies of intellectual 'propaganda' and emotional 'agitation', is a symptom of the Communist confusion of thought that was unsure whether Marx's *Manifesto* was a prophecy or a prognosis and was therefore undecided about the relative merits of rational persuasion and oratorical (or even apostolic) conversion. The root of this confusion lay in the dual rôle of the Communist Party. As a revolutionary élite it attracted the intelligentsia, who were influenced by the logical aspects of Marxism as a critique of history. As a mass-movement is represented the proletariat, who mistrusted intellectuals and were profoundly suspicious of education, which was by definition bourgeois.[11]

If historical materialism was an empirical method, then the Marxist interpretation of history was a scientific prediction and it would be enough to present the facts rationally for the conclusions to be accepted. This is the position that Piscator takes whenever he discusses the propagandist aims of his productions in the 1920s. The only bias (*Tendenz*) he acknowledged was the urge to portray the truth. Propaganda was identified with elucidation (*Aufklärung*). Its intention was to cause the audience to consider their social environment critically, and this postulated a degree of thoughtfulness (*eine gewisse Nachdenklichkeit*) which presupposed that the audience would be able to preserve its emotional independence. Analysis of the meaning of social phenomena would convince an audience of the justice and practicability of the Communist cause. The purpose of the theatre was to awaken consciousness and to provide proof; and from this standpoint Piscator criticized an essay by Eisenstein, who claimed that the intention of his film, *Battleship Potemkin*, was to shake and electrify the masses. Piscator commented that this aim was equally well achieved by boxing-matches or horse-races, declaring 'we don't just want to enthuse, we wish to transmit clarity and recognition',[12] and his production methods (at least in theory) mirrored his concept of propaganda: 'The style... must be completely concrete in nature...similar to the style of a Lenin Manifesto, which creates a powerful effect even on a purely emotional level from its simple, calm flow, and from its unambiguous clarity.'[13]

Behind this view of propaganda as a rational appeal to the intellect lies not only the conviction that Marxism is susceptible of proof, but also a misplaced confidence in the objectivity and reasoning capacities of the uneducated public. Piscator later blamed the failure of the sober approach on a general insensitivity to the sufferings of others[14] – but he never in fact tried it in his Agitprop work. The overheated atmosphere of the time and preconceived ideas derived from Communist propaganda made objectivity impossible, as an ancdote told by Karl Radek, one of the Party spokesmen, shows:

A huge workers' gathering. . . Instead of speaking about the great victory of the Russian Proletariat, I told them of their sufferings, of the civil-war and starvation, of the road to victory. Suddenly someone shouted 'How much have they bribed you to slander Soviet Russia?'[15]

In spite of his intellectual claims, Piscator's Agitprop techniques are clearly irrational. The speeches of *Russia's Day* achieved ideological clarity at the expense of logic, and were comprehensible because they were crude. The ideal of simplicity became simplification. Character, emotions and ideas were sacrificed to tempo and the aim of a performance became to involve the audience in the action – which was made easier by the absence of proscenium arch, footlights or orchestra pit.

Piscator worked on the premise that the inevitable result of rational enlightenment would be 'to kindle the flame of revolt among the workers'.[16] This, however, was a misjudgement. When thought is aroused, theories or interpretations of events will be criticized or queried – nothing but emotion, which submerges individuals into the group, can evoke such a total commitment. It also produces a more immediate and satisfyingly obvious response than intellectual conviction. So, since he considered that every production should be a public demonstration, Piscator's simplicity of style was not aimed at lucid exposition but at 'a clear and unmistakable effect on the feelings of the worker-audience'.[17] Even in his comparison of his style with Lenin's, it was the emotional effect of the apparently logical qualities that he had stressed. In practice the overt appeal to reason was merely a disguise for the attack on the emotions. Here Piscator anticipated modern advertising techniques, the effects of which have been analysed in a similar way: words engage the attention while the real message is carried at a subliminal level by the picture.

This dichotomy between agitation and propaganda became more obvious when Piscator acquired a fully equipped stage and began to apply its complex machinery of illusion to representing reality. In his Agitprop productions, however, the conditions he worked under made a factual analysis of events as difficult as intellectual dialogue with the audience. They necessarily reduced his practice to emotive rhetoric – as a glance at the characterization of *Russia's Day* demonstrates. Lacking all mechanical aids and any but the simplest of stage-properties, Piscator was limited to the human figures on the stage as a means of interpreting the environment. But the unskilled actors and ignorant audiences, made it 'impossible' (as all Agitprop directors found) to use 'complicated structures of ideas and refined intellectual language',[18] and reduced the speeches to slogans. The characters, who were only capable of expressing themselves in exaggerated and oversimplified terms, since they had to be crudely drawn, fall into two categories. Figures from social spheres outside the working-class actors' personal experience (such as the Diplomat) or those representing social abstractions (like the Church) are portrayed as black and white grotesques. Those, on the other hand, with whom the untrained imaginations of the actors and the audience could easily identify – the representatives of their own class, worker and workless – are more credibly and naturalistically presented. 'World-Capital', a caricature lacking not only humanity but also human shape, contrasts vividly with the figures of the German workers, who are all recognizably persons, even if generalized and nameless.

Character-types are not new to the theatre. Nineteenth-century melodrama was notorious for its type-casting of juvenile lovers, comic foreigners and villains, and the Expressionist play used depersonalized concepts such as the Father, the Mother or a Christ-figure. Here a new element was introduced. The old stock characters had retained a conventionalized appearance of individuality, and Expressionist figures contained a complex nexus of meanings as psychological symbols. But Agitprop characters tended toward complete nonentity because they were differentiated only by their economic functions: the worker, the tradesman and the capitalist. Virtue was measured solely in inverse ratio to salary, and vice was presented unmistakably in caricature. This cannot be entirely explained by the conditions under which Piscator had to work. Ideology as such is simplistic and encourages emotionalism. Appeals to the emotions tend to reduce subtleties of feeling to a common denominator, and the vulgarisation of sentiment in turn leads to the adoption of oversimplified positions and artificial expression. All didactic art is liable to this danger.

Plays as propaganda: the techniques of persuasion

A similar abstraction in characterization and the same contrast between naturalistic and grotesque figures recurs in Agitprop plays in every country. In *Where's that Bomb?*, which was one of the scripts circulated and produced in the English Workers' Theatre Movement, the hero, who is the only character to be individualized by having a name, and his landlady, who is carefully differentiated by a Yorkshire accent, are intended to be real people. 'Money-Power', on the contrary, introduced as that economic abstraction, a 'Captain of Industry', is represented as a pantomime devil with cloven hoofs and a tail – and with a glowing telephone, in order that there should be no possibility of mistake: 'Hello! is that Hell Gates? The Boss speaking...' This glaring difference in characterization was a means of channelling the audiences' sympathies – although with a more sophisticated public the lack of subtlety would be likely to have the opposite effect. The only characters with whom the audience can identify are those who are human, and not only familiar in dress and speech, but also claiming as Communists to represent them as a class. Assent to the Communist position is therefore gained without any appeal to their conscious reason, and they are made automatically receptive to the evangelical nature of this type of drama. This play, however, shows a revealing awareness of the artificiality of such techniques. A 'Bolshy', who is introduced as a caricature carrying a bomb (symbolizing the popular fear of Communists which is attributed in the play to capitalist propaganda), strips off his beard to reveal himself as an ordinary, 'respectable trades-union member'.

The narrow range of realistically portrayed personae indicates the limited variety of dramatic material that could be effectively staged in the Agitprop theatre. Each of the plays performed by

Piscator's Proletarisches Theater had urban workers as their central figures so that the action was restricted to the present and to an industrial environment. *Russia's Day* is atypical insofar as it has an international background – although the Workers, who were played with Berlin accents, anchored the action in the audience's experience.

This close relationship between life on the stage and the audience's immediate environment was characteristic of Agitprop drama, even where the technical aims were different. It was the result of political considerations, not the practical effect of a theoretical transformation of the theatre. Joe Corrie – a Fifeshire miner who wrote for the Scottish Community Drama Association, which played to the small mining towns of the Lowlands – used characterization in a remarkably similar way to his German and eastern European counterparts, in spite of working on opposed theatrical principles. Unlike the majority of Agitprop playwrights, Corrie was neither a professional nor an experimental writer. Instead of the continental Marxist view that traditional methods as the expression of bourgeois society could only transmit a traditional message, he rejected experimentation and called for 'old technique' to be applied to working-class themes. Yet his plays were equally limited. He took miners and rural life as his only subjects and depicted everyday scenes, which always had a political message but often lacked a plot, in broad Scottish dialect. This made his plays too parochial to be performed even in England (although some were translated and performed in Germany in the late 1920s). Few Agitprop plays were tied to a particular locality as closely as Corrie's work, but immediate relevance was always the primary criterion and any figures outside the audience's personal knowledge were always caricatured.

The exaggeration of caricatures tends towards the burlesque, however sinister they may be; and comedy might be expected to undermine the Agitprop theatre's evangelical approach to its political themes, since this depended on seriousness for effect. But the strict division in the characterization allowed this element of humour to be turned to advantage. Knock-about farce not only relaxes the onlookers' 'defences' and makes them receptive, it also gives them an euphoric sense of power. At the risk of making the hostile representatives of the Establishment figures of fun instead

of foci for hatred, Agitprop productions could apparently demonstrate that Marxist predictions were true. Audiences could be persuaded that the established order of society had outlived the sources
of its strength and that a working-class movement would sweep its
dominance away with the same effortlessness with which their proletarian protaganists in the play drove the caricatures off stage. It
was possible to convince an audience the more easily because the
lack of characterization avoided the involvement of their ethical
sense. It was implied that the revolution would be bloodless since
capitalist and military figures had no human reality and could be
removed by kicks and shouts alone. Therefore there was no moral
bar to the audience's assent or to their participation.

The danger in this use of parody was that the grotesques tended
to appear too funny or too fantastical to act as objects capable of
absorbing and holding the emotion directed against them. This
happened only too often in English Agitprop plays, and can be most
clearly seen in the numerous caricatures of Hitler during the
Second World War, the best of which are Joan Littlewood's
Shakespearean parodies – *The Strange Case of Sigismund McHess
and the Weird Sisters*, or *The Sleepwalker* (where Hitler was treated
as a Marx Brothers' Lady Macbeth).

To make the satiric characterization more than merely visually
and emotionally satisfying it was often reinforced by a specifically
evangelical tone: a tapping, for political ends, of the religious sentiments that had been fostered by the church. This provided a satisfactory balance to the broad comedy, and became characteristic of
the Agitprop theatre in Germany. Images were transferred wholesale from religious myth to ideology in order to draw on the
Christian teachings of sacrifice and upon the emotional reservoirs
of adoration and reverence. As a technique of persuasion, this frame
of religious reference was so effective that it spread to political
pamphlets and poetry, and was so widely exploited by both right
and left extremes that a decade later it was common for Hitler and
Stalin to be proclaimed openly as saviours in biblical terms.

Russia's Day is the first propaganda play in which this technique
was deliberately used, although here the perversion of images is not
so blasphemous, nor are the references so specific. Communist
doctrine is revered as if it were Holy Writ. The ideal and example
of Soviet Russia fills much the same rôle as the Holy Grail,

consecrating acts of civil violence. Class war is a crusade and victims of the counter-revolution are reverenced with the explicit title of martyrs. Indeed, the borrowing from Christianity is not limited to a matter of general tone. It includes the precise methods that had been developed to manipulate a congregation. The formal details of *Russia's Day* are largely modelled on the church's techniques of worship and exposition, and its similarity to a medieval morality play is pronounced. The theme demonstrates the relevance of doctrine to the human situation and the audience are exhorted by example to good works. Only the message and the reward have changed – the October Revolution has been substituted for the Passion, civil violence and revolutionary action have taken the place of charity and neighbourly love, and a paradisal utopia in the historical future has superseded the hope of heaven after death. The figures representing the forces of social repression are portrayed in the tradition of the comic devil, and 'the Voice of Russia' has replaced the voice of God. The Jesuits of the German Counter Reformation had discovered the possibilities that lay in secular drama for gaining religious converts, and their ecclesiastical plays are counted as the earliest 'political theatre' in a modern sense.[19] Agitprop theatre shows a reciprocal awareness of the ideological effectiveness of the order of divine service. The formula of question and answer, in which the question was often rhetorical and repeated in full in the answer, is that of the catechism. The stereotyped replies and affirmations evoked by 'the Voice of Russia' from the actors imitate the liturgical responses. Later plays added to these techniques. The ritual forms of prayer, exegesis and exhortation, confession and absolution, choral and congregational singing were all used. Agitprop troupes even adapted the formal sermon which was (as a static monologue) surely the most undramatic of the church's techniques, in their search for ways of influencing an audience. The popularity of even this form is indicated by the wide distribution of one script, *The Fire Sermon* by Sergei Funarov, a poetic harangue on the text of 'let us now praise famous revolutionaries and our engineers who built the Dneiper Dam', which was performed in Russia, England and the U.S.A. This aspect of Agitprop drama both aroused and reflected the secularized religiosity, the fanaticism that set the red and brown battalions marching in the thirties; and the ecclesiastical formalization of language introduced in *Russia's Day* was later applied in Party meetings and even affected the everyday speech of Party members.[20]

Pseudo-religious qualities are present in all Piscator's work before his exile, although they were progressively disguised beneath an apparent objectivity as he developed and applied his theories of pedagogic drama. The choice of ecclesiastical means to manipulate an audience is symptomatic of a crusading mysticism in his approach to politics. It is obvious in *Russia's Day* in the simplicity of the presentation and the singleness of Piscator's intention to exploit the stage for purposes of propaganda. But it continues to persist even when camouflaged by sophisticated stage techniques. As a reflection of the contemporary scene, this early play demonstrates the sensitivity of Piscator's stage to his environment, but the element of political fanaticism must call his aim of adapting the theatre to conform to contemporary reality into question. Religious fervour – and still more the articles of faith to which it gives rise – tends to distort observation.

Communism claims to be an empirical method of interpreting history. This claim is not only given a superficial semblance of truth by its emphasis on the science of economics and by its limitation to the material aspects of existence, but also gains plausibility by the breadth of its theories and attraction from the justice of its social programme. However, it is not the validity of Marxist theory, but the fidelity of Bolshevist practices to truth that is relevant here, since it was this that affected Piscator's stage experiments. The universality of the Marxist interpretation of history formed the rationale for the Communist attitude to reality and sanctified the divergence of propaganda from fact. It was the apparent all-inclusiveness of Marxism that seemed to make logical proof unnecessary and naturally lent itself to a religious interpretation: 'The Revolution is everywhere and in everything; it is without beginning and without end... The law of Revolution is not social but much wider – a cosmic, a universal law like the law of conservation of energy.'[21] By 1919 Communism already possessed inspired scriptures and elaborate dogmas, and faith rather than reason provided it with converts. As Bertrand Russell acutely observed,

Bolshevism as a social phenomenon is to be reckoned as a religion, not as an ordinary political movement. The important and effective mental attitudes to the world may be broadly divided into the religious and the scientific...By a religion I mean a set of beliefs held as dogmas, dominating the conduct of life, going beyond or contrary to evidence, and inculcated by methods which are emotional or authoritarian, not intellectual. By this definition, Bolshevism is a religion...Those who accept Bolshevism become impervious to scientific evidence, and commit intellectual suicide. Even if all the doctrines of Bolshevism were true, this would still be the case, since no examination of them is tolerated...[22]

The psychological effect of Communism as a religion and its claim to be a scientific method of interpreting social phenomena are irreconcilable and, since Piscator used ideology to explain the complexities of the modern world, both elements colour the new theatrical forms that he created.

The influence of Marxist theory was reinforced by the actions of the K.P.D. on a more immediate level. The Party exercised a certain control over the subject matter of the plays that Piscator staged, sending an officially approved author, Felix Gasbarra, to help him rewrite plays and organize dramatic material into a politically acceptable form. It tried to regulate the way in which his stage reflected current events by criticizing his productions solely according to the political impressions desired by the Party line of the moment. It also moulded his aims by its standards of expediency, and so affected the basis on which he built his style. Ends justified means because the Party was both morally infallible, since its aims were in accord with 'the Dialectic of History', and logically infallible as the proletarian vanguard, since the proletariat were defined as the embodiment of 'the active principle' in history. Communist theory claimed to give a true interpretation of events, but in political practice 'truth' was an instrument of policy – and policy demanded that the stage should propagate a myth, applying realistic techniques only as a method of persuasion. The K.P.D. followed Lenin's advice: 'One must accept each and every sacrifice and even – when it is necessary – be ready to adopt all possible trickeries, deceits or illegal methods, and *to suppress or distort the truth*.'[23] Piscator's productions were criticized as 'negative' in their effect, because they kept too closely to history, and because portraits of such revolutionary heroes as Liebknecht and Luxemburg were not idealized enough to correspond to Party hagiography.[24] One play even had to be radically altered after the dress-rehearsal, to which representatives of the K.P.D., the Soviet Embassy and the

Russian Trade Mission had been sent, because Party officials protested that there were 'political limits to objectivity'. The religious inspiration of Communism which discredited its claim to scientific enlightenment, was thus reinforced by a deliberate disregard of factual reality.

Art, like mathematics, may be pure or applied. Goya's etchings are not inferior as art although they have a clear political intention, and Picasso's *Guernica* was deliberately painted as a weapon against barbarism not as a decoration. Expedience and utility are legitimate aims, and the pressure of events in the first years of the Weimar Republic had made it impossible for the theatre to distance itself from the contemporary situation. But dogma encourages declamation. Art that is to be of any stature must make its concern reality (in the deeper sense of imaginative truth, not a superficial accuracy to facts) and the stage in particular must have relevance for its audience if it is to have cultural influence. The danger of a quasi-religious inspiration is that the reproduction of doctrine will replace insight into reality. Alternatively, missionary zeal may centre attention on the effect of the message instead of on its quality. In either case the result is the oversimplification of slogans and the use of emotional clichés which lack objective correlatives. This is especially so where all means are justified by an idealistic aim, or when truth has no absolute value and emotions are deliberately exploited for immediate ends. The crude conditions of Agitprop drama made it prone to the most flagrant faults of propaganda, while the fact that the K.P.D. found it particularly suited to their needs hindered it from evolving in subtlety of approach, variety of material, or even technique.

In 1925 the Tenth Party Congress of the K.P.D. passed a resolution to encourage Agitprop troupes and by 1929 no Communist meeting or demonstration took place without an Agitprop performance. But there was no development after Piscator introduced the revue-form. Brecht's 'teaching-plays' had only a limited influence at the time, and performances were produced according to basic pattern determined by Party directives.

The line taken by recent Communist critics is that Piscator's work can only be explained by reference to ideological developments within the Communist movement during the twenties.[25] Behind this lies the spurious contention that only a Marxist can evaluate art produced under Marxist influence – in other words, that only those opinions which are preconditioned to approve are valid. This view is perhaps justified as far as Piscator's early work is concerned, because of the extreme and open political nature of Agitprop theatre. But Piscator rapidly came to realize the limitations and shortcomings of the Agitprop stage, which prevented it from reflecting its environment. It could not be a sensitive enough instrument to reproduce contemporary realities. In order to evolve a style which would have more than a narrow political application and which would fulfil his intention to create stage conventions appropriate to modern conditions, Piscator had to distance himself from the Agitprop movement – and in 1922 he transferred his work to the professional theatre.[26]

3 Agitprop and Revue: Society

A return to Naturalism becomes apparent in Germany between 1920 and 1924. Some of the Expressionists turned to writing social comedies, and a new phase, 'brutal' realism, opened with Brecht's *Drums in the Night* in 1922. Stanislavski's production of *The Three Sisters* appeared on tour in Berlin, and revivals of the works of Ibsen, Hauptmann and the early Strindberg dominated the German stage. John Heartfield, who had provided Piscator with the diagrammatic scenery for *Russia's Day*, designed a brilliantly realistic factory-setting for Toller's *The Machine-Wreckers*; and Piscator's direction also shows the influence of the time. The final and most competent of his three productions in the Central-Theater, Leo Tolstoy's play, *The Powers of Darkness*, demonstrates his developing experience in handling the conventional apparatus of the stage. The acting style was underplayed and exaggeratedly natural, and critics complained that so much emphasis was placed on physical detail, scenery and stage-properties (as in the Moscow Art Theatre) that attention was diverted from the psychological force of the play. But they also acknowledged that Piscator's repertoire 'overpowers the onlooker with *legitimate* effects'.[1] Piscator had proved himself a capable producer even by conventional standards, and when he was forced to sell this private theatre in 1924 he was offered a position as a free-lance director in the Volksbühne, one of the leading Berlin theatres.

From his first production for the Volksbühne, *Flags* by Alfons Paquet, Piscator began to develop a characteristic style which reached its fullest expression when he once again acquired his own theatre in 1927. During this time he also completed his work in the Agitprop theatre, and it can be clearly seen that his professional achievements were based on his amateur Agitprop experience. With technical equipment and rehearsal facilities at his disposal he had the opportunity to expand and refine the techniques that he had created for his Proletarisches Theater. Now, with the help of

Gasbarra, he put together two revues of such spectacular effect that they acted as models for all subsequent German Agitprop productions.[2] *The Red Revue* (*Revue Roter Rummel*) of 1924 was a direct continuation of his earlier work. Like *Russia's Day* it played in meeting-halls of the Berlin working-class districts and the scenery had to be simple (indicative rather than representative). But a transportable stage was constructed, lighting was available, projection-slides and music were used, and the actors were professional and properly rehearsed. *The Red Revue* was looked on as the epitome of Agitprop theatre, but his second revue, *Despite All!* (*Trotz Alledem!*, words spoken by Karl Liebknecht), produced in 1925, showed how far Piscator had actually moved from this primitive form. The same techniques had only to be expanded to be effective in the Theatre of the Five Thousand, where Reinhardt had staged such overblown illusionistic spectacles as Vollmoeller's *Miracle*, and where the size of the auditorium, the complexity of the stage-machinery and the special difficulties of masking and voice-projection peculiar to the arena form created very different conditions of performance.

These productions were both commissioned by the K.P.D. for particular occasions – the parliamentary elections of December 1924 and the Tenth Party Congress of July 1925. Neither normal plays nor Agitprop material satisfied the K.P.D. requirements and a different form had to be developed.

Conventional full-length dramas were obviously unsuitable. Their formal artistic qualities associated them with entertainment, while traditional dramatic construction had been evolved for the picture-frame stage and emphasized characterization. They therefore lacked the impression of objectivity and simple directness that had proved successful for propaganda, since they tended to stress the imaginary nature of stage reality and insulated the action by enclosing the narrative behind the invisible wall of the proscenium. Above all, the time needed for writing or adapting a full-length script necessarily meant that any factual subject would be outdated – even if only by a matter of months – so that direct relevance to contemporary events could only be accidental. The sole K.P.D. aim was propaganda and they had no intention of relying on chance effects such as had aroused the audience at the première of *The Machine-Wreckers*, which took place six days after the assassination of Walter Rathenau. (The public identified Rathenau with the socialist martyr-figure of Jimmy. This was accidental since Toller undoubtedly intended Jimmy to be a symbolic personification of himself.)

At the same time Agitprop sketches were inadequate for the needs of the professional theatre. They were too short and could not be satisfactorily expanded, while their techniques, effective in their own context, lost their impact without gaining credibility when thrown into relief by the machinery of stage illusion. Piscator chose the revue-form as a solution to the technical problems which could also answer the demand for efficient propaganda.

Agitation programmes: *The Red Revue*

As election propaganda *The Red Revue* had the double task of presenting the Communist critique of society in general terms and giving tactical arguments in detail by extending the ideological rejection of the Republic into particular examples, interpreting current events in the light of political theory. The script had to be designed to allow the insertion of the latest news, and for the first time Piscator's key concept of 'actuality' enters his vocabulary. The requirements were complicated by a reversal in Party policy. Spartacus had relied on weapons instead of votes, and the K.P.D. had boycotted elections up to 1920 when – due mainly to their previous rejection of democracy – they gained a bare four seats in the Reichstag. Anti-parliamentarian propaganda had not abated, but the unsuccessful uprisings in 1921 and 1923 had exhausted the Communist strength, while the U.S.S.R. discouraged open revolution in Germany after the secret treaty of Rapallo, when Germany agreed to send officers to train the Red Army in exchange for arms which the peace terms of Versailles had forbidden them to manufacture. Arguments therefore had to be aimed at Party members which counteracted the effect of previous indoctrination as well as providing electioneering material for the 'politically unaware'.

What was needed was a theatrical convention capable of uniting heterogeneous themes and effects, and a basis was found in the music hall. This already incorporated a diversity of techniques, a tradition of social criticism and ideological justification as a popular art form. The revue had established itself as a vehicle for political satire in the tradition of Villon and Rabelais since the foundation of the Chat Noir in Paris in 1881, and was the natural choice for Piscator. Wedekind had introduced it to the German theatre at the turn of the century; the Cabaret Voltaire in Zürich had been one of Dada's most effective weapons; Walter Mehring had opened the Political Cabaret in Berlin in 1920; and Erich Mühsam's *Eleven Executioners* was one of the satirical successes of the time.

Piscator had already experimented with a similar type of dramatic construction in *Flags*, which had the characteristic Expressionist structure of short, semi-independent scenes aptly named 'pictures'. Now he deliberately reorganized the traditional two hours' traffic of the stage. Instead of being divided into acts marking the logical sequence of a unified plot, *The Red Revue* was formed of fourteen separate scenes. These varied widely in style. Music and song, slide-projection and action-painting, acrobatics and sport, statistics and rhetoric, film and dance and acting were promiscuously mixed. The hallmark of post-war cabaret in Berlin was just this type of formal medley, which made changes of tone and atmosphere possible at will. It was used by Kästner, Mehring, Mühsam and Tucholsky to juxtapose morality and disillusion or contrast sympathy and cynicism. This familiar mixture tended to dissipate the audience's attention, and Piscator changed its character by adapting the eclecticism to focus emotion. The scenes, each designed to arouse a simple and specific reaction, shared a common message, so that the diversity of techniques was linked by a single theme.

The first scene – after an overture by Edmund Meisel which introduced the theme of social conflict and set the tone with proletarian battle songs – portrayed an 'electioneering rumble' (*Wahlrummel*) where bourgeois candidates in caricatured costumes shouted out distorted socialist or contemptuously hypocritical election programmes. The second scene, entitled 'Class Justice' (*Das Klassengericht*) was designed as a contrast. Here a K.P.D. candidate, already in prison dress, was tried and condemned for 'agitation'. This is followed by 'Club-swinging Practice', an aggressive gymnastic dance accompanied by a 'cudgeling song', to symbolize the proletarian spirit of rebellion. Evidence in favour of the Communist position is offered by scenes where a factual example of the exploitation of the working-classes taken from the newspapers is balanced against a fantasy, intended as an objective commentary, of an incredulous Martian reporting, 'that there are beings on earth, who sweat and starve so that others can earn money'. Then a naturalistic argument between a Communist and his wife as to whether he should go to the polls emphasized that the K.P.D. expected its members to vote in this election, before the final scene of the cycle showed an utopian wish-fulfilment in the exhilarating symbol of a 'Boxing-match Election'. Recognizable caricatures of the right-wing and social democrat leaders pulled their punches in an arranged fight until – as the drama critic of *The Red Flag* reported with evident euphoria – a Communist made up as Max Hölz (an escaped murderer turned professional revolutionary who led various Communist uprisings and proclaimed the short-lived Workers' State in Sachsen-Thüringen) stepped into the ring and knocked the candidates of all four democratic parties into a heap. The victor then followed up his pugilistic prowess with an election manifesto detailing the K.P.D. platform of promises and radical reforms.

After an interval during which political slogans were projected on the screen, the same theme – class injustice in contemporary Germany, leading to a prophecy of effortless Communist victory – was repeated twice in increasingly violent terms. In the first, 'All in Rubble', a proletarian is invited into a nightclub by a member of the bourgeoisie. Here he observes the habits of the rich (who are presented as ugly, stupid and immoral) and is shown an opulent and indecent cabaret. The porter throws out a war-crippled beggar – despite the protests of the proletarian who then leads a revolt of the workers to storm the nightclub and demolish it. In the second variation, 'The Revenge of the Bourgeoisie', projected slides of executions and military repression, a film of the 'Noske Atrocity', and short historical scenes played with melodramatic pathos for emotional effect were interposed with impassioned speeches by actors representing Lenin, Liebknecht and Rosa Luxemburg, the heroes and martyrs of the revolution. These speeches, exhorting solidarity and inciting to active revolt build up to a final tableau, the 'Victory of the Proletariat', which is presented in much the same terms as the last scene of *Russia's Day*; and the revue ends with the communal singing of the *International*.

The versatility allowed for repeated demonstrations that emphasized the single sociological thesis and at the same time lent it an impression of universality. It also made it possible to find examples that would be relevant to the different experience of individuals without losing the interest of the audience as a whole. Each impression was isolated by changes of idiom and media, while the shortness of the scenes and the speed of transposition prevented any reflection on the contents, so that the sketches could be mere suggestions without losing impact or credibility. In this way the advantages of galvanizing tempo and striking theatricality associated with the naivety of Agitprop productions were adapted to the larger, more complex scale of the professional theatre without creating stage illusion.

To link the disparate episodes Piscator made one decisive innovation to the normal revue-form by adapting the traditional Compère and Commère from operetta (modernized as 'Bourgeois' and 'Prole'), who remained on stage throughout the performance. These figures provided a constant and unifying frame for the kaleidoscope of scenes and styles, they could be used to interpret the action, standing outside it, and also to involve the audience by acting as their representatives on the stage, when (as in 'All in Rubble') they became protagonists.

As the lights dimmed an argument over social conditions broke out between these two figures, contrastingly dressed actors seated in the auditorium. The bourgeois invited the proletarian to spend an evening with him and, still arguing, they left their seats, made their way through the audience and climbed onto the stage as the curtain rose. As observers they continued their quarrel between the scenes, taking the incidents as examples for their arguments; and in this opportunity for commentary the groundwork can be seen for Piscator's later development of 'Epic Drama'. Through these figures the audience's reactions could be controlled – with a consequent gain in the effectiveness of the propaganda. Both sides of an argument could be presented to give an impression of objectivity without endangering the desired response. A working-class audience would naturally identify with the figure of the proletarian and the scenes presented only evidence in his favour, which made the bourgeois arguments appear hypocritical. The commentary also gave the additional advantage that material could be used which would otherwise have an ambiguous effect, or which was good theatre but prohibited by political considerations. Thus the sensual excitement of a strip-tease show in the nightclub scene could be justified as edifying evidence for a moral theme which would otherwise have excluded it. The Communists disapproved of entertainment (in particular sexual titillation) as frivolity symptomatic of the decadence of capitalism. Even the fox-trot and tango were prohibited in Russia on the grounds that they were corrupting, and the contrast between puritanical Party directives and the need for colourful entertainment to draw the public caused constant difficulties for Communist producers. This attitude stunted the Agitprop movement by limiting it to scenes of persecution and spectacles of violence for emotional and visual excitement – but Piscator had provided a way round it. His Compère and Commère figures allowed a significant expansion in Agitprop material.

Play programmes: the signs of Piscator's development

Compared to *Russia's Day*, Piscator's use of the stage was far more precise in *The Red Revue*. The introduction of commentary, and the ability to repeat and vary a theme made the production more exact in operation, since complex issues could be highlighted from different angles. (A bonus was the impression of veracity on the dubious principle of 'what I tell you three times is true'.) This repetition also intensified the force of the statement, so that the culminating appeals to physical violence appeared a natural means of releasing the emotional tension. Piscator's awareness of this gain in control can be measured by the change in the pamphlets printed as programmes.

These were always elaborate booklets, containing critical essays and commentaries as well as a cast-list, and their contents reflect Piscator's estimation of his ability to communicate with the audience. The later ones deal with general issues, but the programmes to *Russia's Day*, *The Cripple* and *Before the Door* betray a lack of confidence that these one-act plays would be self-explanatory in performance. The simple plots are summarized, and explicit morals drawn from them: 'The White Terror is as much a necessity for the bourgeois social system as the World War. The Proletariat removes the cause of the White Terror, since it roots out the bourgeois social order.' The stories are declared to be typical occurrences as well as illustrations of political theories, and the

Party's attitude to the ethical questions raised by the action is explained: 'Even revolutionary action which takes life is sanctified...and such deeds alone, for which the deed of the soldier [the particularly brutal murder of an officer in *Before the Door*] is only a symbol, can save us.' Above all, the emotional reactions desired from the audience are carefully defined: 'Either Socialism or a decline into Barbarism' – their relationship to the actors is spelt out to prevent any mistaken alignment of sympathies: 'Feel with the raging cripple! He is You, You...' – and they are encouraged to participate in the action: 'Demonstate that you want to join with the German worker in aiding our Russian comrades by singing the *International*' (and the *International* is printed in full).

By contrast the programme published for *The Red Revue* is a far less impassioned document. Allegiance to the K.P.D. is affirmed, but the only direct exhortation is to support the Agitprop theatre financially. The description of the play is a plain list of the order and titles of the scenes and, instead of interpretation or audience-manipulation, factual evidence is quoted to support the theme. Piscator had space to include a theoretical article on the importance of the theatre as a means of influencing politics, and the tone of the writing is more subtle, indicating that propaganda could be entrusted to the stage. It is clear that Piscator was confident in the actors' capacity to transmit the meaning of a scene; that the projection of photographs as backgrounds – the Kurfürstendamm, the Reichstag, a tenement or the Supreme Court – automatically gave the scenes relevance; and that the capacity for comment during the performance meant that he could be certain what effect the action would have on an audience. Here, in contrast to the scepticism implicit in the programmes for his Proletarisches Theater, there is a feeling of assurance in the potential of drama as a instrument of propaganda.

Theatre programmes always had a particular importance for Piscator as a means of extending the effect of a performance.[3] While Agitprop productions had to be supplemented at a crude level by clarifying the message, the later programmes could be used to familiarize audiences with the factual background to a play so that they might have their attention free to focus on the consequences which were drawn from the action. Alternatively space could be given to intellectual issues arising from the play, or the theatrical implications of any new technical experiment could be discussed. A theoretical essay on 'Drama and Society' was printed in the programme to *Rasputin* (Piscator-Bühne, 1927), for instance, while the programme for *The Good Soldier Schweik* (Piscator-Bühne, 1928) included articles on Hašek, 'Art and Aesthetics' and 'Humour and Revolution'. Declamatory invective only returned to the programmes in such unsuccessful productions as *The Merchant of Berlin* (second Piscator-Bühne, 1929), and explanations of intention only when a play – for instance *Hoppla, We are Alive!*, – appeared open to attack on doctrinal grounds.

Historical revues: *Despite All!*

Piscator took his experiment with the revue-form a stage further in *Despite All!* Although still a montage of scenes, the mixture of styles was less eclectic, and there was a sequential story instead of a static theme. Repetition was still an important element but this was now simultaneous instead of being protracted, since the scenes were reinforced or elaborated by synchronized film sequences on a screen behind the actors. The effect of immediacy was retained, but tempo was gained from the organization of the subject matter, not from the stylistic device of short, sharp sketches.

The architecture of the Theatre of the Five Thousand influenced the form of the production. Its amphitheatre stage called for free-standing, three-dimensional scenery which had to be of monolithic proportions because of the size of the theatre (which allowed for the use of over two hundred actors), while the short time for preparation – three weeks – enforced simplicity. John Heartfield's stage design was clearly influenced by Jessner, the leading Expressionist director whose famous 'steps' (multiple platforms built over the whole acting area to allow movement in three dimensions) had been used for the last time a year earlier. A construction of platforms, stairs and ramps mounted on a revolve, this was more than a brilliant solution to unusual practical requirements since it gave Piscator opportunities for movement which made it practicable to run scenes into one another, creating a sequential overlap of cause, action and effect.

The demands of the clients were also instrumental in determining the style. The Workers' Educational Confederation had commissioned a 'mammoth revue' from Piscator on the theme of revolution in history for the midsummer festival of 1925. The script prepared by Piscator and Gasbarra, which dealt with revolutionary high-points from the revolt of the Roman slaves under Spartacus to the Spartacist uprising following the November Revolution, was rejected as too radical. A revised version, *Despite All!* was then commissioned by the K.P.D. in its place. This was limited to the period between the outbreak of war and the deaths of Liebknecht and Luxemburg on political as well as practical grounds, because the Party was split by one of its periodic ideological conflicts. In the presidential elections of March and April that year Hindenburg had effectually been given the victory by a split in the left-wing vote, because the K.P.D. had put up their own candidate, even though Moscow had wished support to be given to the combined candidate of the S.P.D. and centre. The result was that there were open differences between the Leninist Group and the Fischer–Maslow faction, and it was felt that on the opening evening of the Party Congress 'the presentation of the revolutionary tradition of the Party in the revue *Despite All!* could bring about the necessary process of clarification in the Party.'[4] The tone was therefore more factual and the approach more detailed than in *The Red Revue*. The concentration on a single subject, the thematic precision demanded by such a specific problem and the political professionalism of the audience prevented the use of sweeping generalizations and simplified satire. True, the finale was still identical to the ending of *Russia's Day* and *The Red Revue*. It was entitled the 'Parade of the Proletariat, Liebknecht Lives!' Fifty 'red shocktroops' marched onto the stage with flags and banners symbolizing the utopian triumph of the revolution, and the audience rose to their feet to join the cast in singing the *International*. This communal singing at the close of a play later became an Agitprop convention equivalent to the Expressionist habit of ending plays with a speech on 'humanity', 'brotherly love' or 'freedom'. Here the *gemeinsamer Schlussgesang* (communal closing song) was advertised in large type at the end of the programme, since the intention was to invoke an apparent demonstration of solidarity with the Party leadership. But apart from this last scene, 'the complete production was a single *montage* of *authentic* speeches, articles, newspaper-extracts, slogans, leaflets, photographs and films of the War and the Revolution, of *historical* persons and scenes.'[5] The film was supplied from the government archives, the speeches were as far as possible quotations and the tone was that of recorded minutes.

Utilitarian theatre

By any standards this type of theatre was closely involved in contemporary events. Present incidents or recent history were its subjects, immediate relevance and practical use were the criteria by which these were chosen, and the intention was both to inform the audience and to exert a direct influence on their actions. Its stylistic qualities were determined by the physical conditions of performance and its themes by political requirements. With *Despite All!* Agitprop matured from a propagation of dogma to a discussion of doctrine, and the increase in objectivity is indicated by the reaction of Communist critics. *The Red Flag* complained that the generals and social-democrat politicians who were presented on stage were 'too human', that Liebknecht was not 'fiery' and Rosa Luxemburg not 'serene' enough[6] – in other words, the portraits of the heroes were not according to Party hagiography and the caricature associated with political commitment was missing. Yet this production had greater impact than any of Piscator's earlier and more obvious work. It generated a mass display of political fervour, participation in the finale was spontaneous and overwhelming, and the play became a public demonstration. The dramatic effects which aroused the audience were not rhetorical devices, but the selection and presentation of fact. The emotional response was due to the clarity with which complex sequences of events were presented, the scale on which a subject of such magnitude was treated, and the compelling impetus of the action – all of which were made possible by Piscator's use of the acting area. To solve the problem of handling the confused and unwieldy material of a World War in theatrical terms Piscator turned the script into a multi-stage, multi-media production. A film sequence of Liebknecht distributing anti-war pamphlets in 1913 merged into a stage scene re-enacting his protest against military preparations in parliament, which was drowned by a sabre-rattling speech by the Kaiser over loudspeakers. This provided a transition to the later vote (which Liebknecht alone opposed) granting the war-credit, accompanied by photographs of mobilization. Synchronized with the raising of hands in parliament, a film of fighting on the Western Front was projected. Then on two separated stage levels the reactions of different sections of society to the opening of hostilities was shown simultaneously in a street-scene and a munitions-factory...Photography, film and stage sequences interacted to build a composite picture of the war years and the activities of the Communist leaders. The approach was still simplistic but this was the result of reducing so large a subject to manageable dimensions. It was no longer, as it had been in the Proletarisches Theater, the involuntary effect of inadequate equipment, incompetent actors and unsophisticated audiences.

Although the emotional effect of Piscator's Agitprop plays had been equally powerful, their makeshift methods were incapable of directing the feelings they aroused. But the two revues revealed that the theatre could be employed as an efficient and precise means of propaganda, and this made it a test case in the Communist approach to art.

Following the 1925 split in the Party ranks, Stalin succeeded in subordinating the German Communist movement to Moscow, and the directness of Russian control on Communist-oriented art is indicated by the attendance of Lunacharsky, the Commissar for Culture, at Piscator's productions during his frequent visits to Berlin, and by the occasional intervention of the Russian Trade Mission in the affairs of the Piscator-Bühne.

In official doctrine the historical materialism of Marx had become linked with the Russian tradition of materialist philosophy. This questioned the intrinsic value of art and judged literature solely by the productivity of its contents. These utilitarian standards were reinforced by the 'class-conscious' antipathy to the culture of privileged groups and by the idealistic attempt to create a proletarian art (which stipulated a lowest common denominator of expression, since it was to be understood and enjoyed by the uneducated). Even Lunacharsky, who protected the best of Russian pre-revolutionary art and was himself an author of traditional historical plays, asked how the Moscow Art Theatre was to be turned from 'this embroidered handkerchief' into 'the banner of our class-struggle'. This was not a passing phase. 'Formalism' is the key condemnation of Communist art critics even today, and the first conference of the International Workers' Theatre Organization in

Moscow in 1930 emphasized that art (for the Communist Party) had no validity except as a means of provoking a hatred for capitalism and proclaiming the aims of Communism.

From 1920 articles had begun to appear entitled 'The Battle for the Theatre' which evaluated drama solely by its practical application and Piscator's attitude then was typical of his time: 'We look on the theatre as nothing more than an instrument to disseminate a specific idea...The idea that we represent is a political one.'[7] As a general statement this is an obvious reaction to the political pressures of twentieth-century life accentuated by the intense commitment that characterized intellectual life in the Weimar Republic, but it became the official Communist line with the supremacy of Stalin, who was not content with 'politically oriented' art but categorically demanded 'propaganda-in-pictures'. This was not inherent in Marxist theory; but the possibilities that the theatre offered for propaganda made its subordination to political purposes inevitable. Music could only be incidentally revolutionary in marching songs or anthems – and even Lunacharsky was forced to such incredible lengths as comparing the effect of symphonies with the conditioning of Pavlov's dogs to justify orchestral compositions as politically valuable.[8] Painting and poetry were of little practical use in mobilizing the masses. Cinema and radio were still in their experimental infancy. Only the theatre – the prototype of the mass media which are now the dominant factor of our modern environment – could reach large numbers of the working-classes. In addition the theatre had had a reputation for revolutionary effectiveness ever since Napoleon had called *The Marriage of Figaro* the prologue to the French Revolution, and it was commonplace for German critics to praise Schiller's plays as 'socio-political acts, historical exploits...equivalent to any national undertaking of primary importance.'[9] This view was accepted alike by Communist politicians, artists and critics who were agreed in principle that the theatre should act as an integral part of the Party organization. As they saw it

> Art is not haze, nor a cultural daze...
> Art is arms![10]

– a sentiment repeated by the manifesto of the English Theatre of Action, 'Theatre is a weapon', and still current in the vocabulary of

Piscator's associates during the Second World War: 'Theatre is a weapon for the liberation of humanity'.[11] But they were vague about the actual nature of the effects that could be achieved and unsure about the exact application of art to the class-struggle. In the *Communist Manifesto* there is no dialectic between interpretation and action, so that revolutionary theory becomes synonymous with revolutionary practice. Carried into artistic terms, this meant that there should be 'no separation between a work of art and its effect',[12] so that a production was judged solely by the immediate influence of the scenario on the audience's actions. This confusion of art with reality produced such curiosities as J. R. Becher's 'Sketch for a Revolutionary Battle-Play', *Workers, Peasants, Soldiers*, at the end of which, directly before an inflammatory 'Red March' speech, the stage directions read: 'Weapons are distributed on the stage and further weapons [in this case machine-guns] are handed down from the stage among the onlookers' – and the actors, having roused and armed the audience, were then supposed to lead them out of the theatre 'to take the police-headquarters by storm'. The logical conclusion to this extension of the Dada desire to create literature 'gun in hand' was the complete rejection of aesthetics. *The Red Flag* declared that art expressed itself in deeds, not words, and therefore street battles were the only true proletarian drama.[13]

The influence of Piscator's revues

The revues were Piscator's nearest approach to this extreme view of art, and their influence on the Communist-oriented theatre was immense. Their success can be demonstrated by the constant recurrence in Agitprop and 'teaching' plays of commentators and discussion-partners – obviously imitated from *The Red Revue* – whose function was to unify a loose scene-structure. On the political level, the impact of *Despite All!* on the delegates to the 1925 Party Congress, who had formed part of its audience, was undoubtedly responsible for their resolution to use the theatre as a means of propaganda.

There were never enough competently written plays with politically acceptable messages to fill Agitprop repertoires – even though such authors as Berta Lask, Béla Balász, Hallup, Leo Lania,

Troppenz and later Friedrich Wolf, all of whom were both approved
and experienced, devoted their talents to turning out 'popular'
plays specifically designed for Agitprop requirements. Aside from
their scarcity, those conventional plays that fulfilled political stipu-
lations were unsatisfactory for practical reasons. They not only
needed longer rehearsals, better costumes and (at least in Lask's
work) larger casts than Agitprop troupes could afford, but were
difficult to alter in order to comment on any particular contemporary incident. Indeed, such plays as were put on were often
completely irrelevant to their audiences. *Free Thälmann* (the K.P.D.
leader, imprisoned for his part in a riot) was translated into English
and formed part of the repertoire of the Theatre of Action – even
though workers in Manchester were unlikely to be interested.

These factors inhibited the growth of the Agitprop movement in
the first half of the decade, but Piscator's experiments provided an
alternative dramatic model. By 1929 there were hardly any Agitprop
groups who still put on plays. Instead there were two predominat-
ing theatrical forms: the 'historical revue' (along the lines of
Despite All!) and the *aktuelle* or 'political revue' which was also
called an 'agitation programme' (modelled on *The Red Revue*).
Their influence spread as far as England. The Rebel Players in
Hackney and the Red Megaphone in Salford were copied directly
from the Berlin Kolonne Links, and when the *Sunday Worker* suggested 'Living Newspaper' techniques, it advocated the revue form
and called for 'satires and sketches acted in the open on barrels,
soapboxes or a couple of planks',[14] which automatically excluded
any conventional plays.

The success of Agitprop revues made them standards by which
the Party judged the value of all theatrical work. Piscator had simply
developed effective structural forms in response to fortuitous circumstances, but in the 1930 conference of the International
Workers' Theatre Organization these were cited as artistic axioms.
The result was that throughout the Agitprop movement lighting,
costumes, make-up and the stage-curtain (all of which most Agitprop troupes lacked in any case, but to which they had formerly
aspired), were condemned as 'obstacles in the way of our reaching
the wide masses'.[15] Similarly, street acting – to which some Agitprop troupes had been forced by police interference – became
the official vehicle for 'true proletarian theatre', on the grounds

that it prevented any element of audience selection and attracted the ignorant and uninterested who would not normally attend a performance. This made stylistic crudity and thematic obviousness appear to be the essence of drama, and forced Piscator to defend his later use of the professional stage against ideological attack.

Piscator's book, *The Political Theatre*, was not just a theoretical work proposing new dramaturgical principles, nor an autobiographical record. It is primarily a defence against the criticism of 'formalism'. It is an apologia that Piscator was forced to make because the bankruptcy of the first Piscator-Bühne in June 1928 had called the validity of a professional Communist theatre into open question, and in some passages the tone is even reminiscent of the confessional self-accusations of the Stalinist purge trials. Ideological justifications therefore tend to be overemphasized as the sole reasons for his experimentation.

The Communist overvaluation of Agitprop theatre as propaganda was – as far as it can be judged – a result of wish-fulfilment rather than actual achievement. *The Red Revue* was specifically designed as election propaganda, but had little influence on the voting figures. There were two elections in 1924; in May when the Stresemann government fell as a consequence of suppressing the radical regimes in Sachsen and Thüringen; and in December after the Centre had failed to form a workable coalition. In May the K.P.D., which had held only four seats in the 1920 parliament, expanded dramatically to a faction of 62 – profiting from the discontent with democratic institutions caused by inflation and the failure of the policy of passive resistance against the French occupation of the Ruhr. In the December elections, for which *The Red Revue* had been produced, a slight stabilization of the economy reduced them from 62 to 45 seats. The enthusiastic response of the audience gave an illusion of effectiveness which was discredited by events. The pattern was demonstrated again and again, until in 1931 Alfred Kerr, a leading critic who three years earlier had demanded propaganda plays as the only means of staving off the right-wing threat to the Republic, commented: 'I really begin to doubt if a political theatre could ever be capable of improving political conditions.'

Piscator spoke in terms of 'direct action' and tended to measure

the artistic value of a production by the decibels from the auditorium. But experience taught him that plays could only act as an
intellectual preparation, and the function of drama was 'preliminary work' leading to decisions, which would then be fought
for in another setting with other weapons: 'Naturally, I never
imagined that art, in my case theatre-art, could replace political
power.'[16] He came to realize that the impressive enthusiasm generated by agitation was not translated into action and, although he
never abandoned his aim – to intervene in current events by influencing the opinions of his audience – his later work concentrated
on presenting evidence for his arguments. This position was neither
uncommon nor unrealistic. All authors try to influence their public,
if only through the selection and manipulation of fact, so that all
art can be said to be political. Sartre even based his definition of
drama on this: 'Drama deals with the effort of a politically minded
individual or group to translate a wish into an accomplishment.'[17]

Theatrical realism: aesthetics v. actuality

Whether it judged a production by direct or secondary effect, this
utilitarian evaluation tied the stage to contemporary reality, since
in order to affect the course of events a play had to draw lessons
from the historical past or offer an interpretation of the actual
present. In times of repression contemporary figures or conditions
are often masked in myth – for example, in the use of the Antigone
legend by Hasenclever and Anouilh to disguise attacks on dictatorship during the First and Second World Wars, or Hauptmann's
symbolic representation of Nazi Germany in the *Atreus Tetralogy* –
but during the Weimar Republic there were no such inhibiting
pressures. Although the police had banned the Proletarisches
Theater for inciting civil violence (ironically basing the refusal to
renew Piscator's licence on a criticism of his work as 'unartistic' in
The Red Flag), the only limit to the representation of reality was the
law of slander, and Piscator was able to portray economic or political crises openly on his stage. This raised the question of the
theatre's relationship to life in a particularly acute form, since the
new technical ability to reproduce reality made it possible to dispense with the 'as if' of all artificial stage conventions that had
previously governed the representation of life. The use of current

events as material, or the performance of a play for an immediate political purpose is as old as the theatre – Xerxes was still alive when Aeschylus wrote *The Persians*, and Essex had Shakespeare's *Richard II* acted to gather support for his revolt against Elizabeth. But such works appeal to the imagination, remaining within the formal framework of stylistic conventions, while modern stage-machinery gave Piscator the potential to make reality the object instead of the subject of drama.

The Naturalists also attempted the direct portrayal of reality. But they had concentrated on achieving complete illusion, which reduced the area of experience that could be depicted on the stage. Naturalism is a convention of expression which is dependent upon subtlety of technique, while Realism denotes a particular approach to the subject of a work and is concerned with penetrating the veneer of appearances on which Naturalism inevitably focuses. In Das Tribunal and the Central-Theater, when Piscator's productions had been naturalistic, the illusionistic conventions which he had used to portray scenes as realistically as possible only made him aware of the 'deep, far too deep chasm' that separated art from life. After his Agitprop experience, however, he began to adopt criteria that lay outside the normal sphere of art: 'Instead of theatre, we demand reality. Reality is always the more important theatre.'[18]

In poetic terms, 'the world's a stage' is an enlightening metaphor, but Piscator's statement is an annotation to his theatrical experiments, not a comment on the nature of life. Behind it lies the total rejection of aesthetics in favour of actuality. Edmund Meisel, who provided the music for Piscator's productions, described his compositions as 'a way of making events audible to the masses in the spirit of the most recent times'.[19] Similarly Traugott Müller, who designed the settings for the Piscator-Bühne, defined his aim as the abolition of stage-scenery.

The style of Piscator's work occasionally approached the grotesque and vicious commonplaces of the *Neue Sachlichkeit* movement in his search for convincing realism – as in the final scene of *The Good Soldier Schweik*, 'Schweik in Heaven', for which a legless beggar and half a dozen real cripples were engaged to parade across the stage, smeared with muck and blood and with their missing limbs hanging out of their rucksacks. Yet horror depicted in detail is both unbearable in the heightened atmosphere of the theatre and pale in comparison to the monstrous realities of industrial exploitation or modern war. Schweik was only shown in heaven once at a closed performance, and the scene then had to be cut from the production because it proved too disgusting for even a picked audience. Conversely, the socially realistic production of *The Lower Depths* was criticized as inverted idealization, while the New York production of *War and Peace* in 1942 was judged to be unmoving in the context of the atrocities reported in newspapers and newsreels. This approach, however, was only a symptom of Piscator's rejection of aesthetics and imagination since he realized that Naturalism could not compete with the scale of modern crises. It was a reaction to the primary question of whether the accepted forms of art – whatever conventions they applied – were capable of handling significant contemporary themes at all.

Both artistic creation and appreciation are connected with the exercise of the imagination, but in the twentieth century imagination is felt to have been outpaced by the overwhelming nature of events. Karl Kraus complained of the impossibility of representing the First World War on the stage because the nature of the catastrophe had invalidated normal concepts. Ordinary standards were inapplicable to 'the unreal, incomprehensible years, inaccessible to memory and only preserved in bloody dreams, when operetta-figures played out the tragedy of mankind'.[20] The same point has been stated more recently by Rolf Hochhuth: 'The most momentous events and discoveries of our time all have one element in common: they place too great a strain upon the human imagination. We lack the imaginative faculties to be able to envision Auschwitz or the destruction of Dresden and Hiroshima.'[21] Habits of thought have admittedly altered considerably over the last decades, but the way we look at the world is still primarily determined by artistic conventions which were designed for different conditions. These are therefore incapable of dealing with the dominant aspects of modern existence, which art either ignores, so distorting our vision, or responds to – like modern painting – by retreating into abstraction. Piscator's aim therefore had to be to free drama from conventional attitudes.

This meant emphasizing content at the expense of form; and one critic of the time, like all who judged the value of imaginative experience by its aesthetic expression, dismissed Piscator's work as being 'without psychology, without eloquence and without dramatic effect'.[22] This was true, but Piscator would have taken the condemnation as a compliment. It was precisely these qualities – the attribution of an illusory importance to the individual, the deceptive beauty of appearances and the artificiality of structuring material around *coups de théâtre* – that made drama irrelevant to the modern context.

Piscator's exclusive focus on reality invalidates his work by the idealistic standards of traditional art which were particularly strong in German culture, whose Parnassus is Romantic. Goethe and Schiller defined art as the aspiration to the Good and the Beautiful, creating a gulf between poetic and public values which academics had deepened by restricting aesthetic recognition to established ways of treating traditional areas of experience; and this dichotomy was particularly obvious in the theatre, where an artificial mode of acting the Classics had become established and dominated other styles of representation. Realistic criteria thus stood contrasted more obviously with accepted ideas of theatrical art than in other countries, and even Piscator's supporters asserted that he was 'no director for works of art. He is the greatest producer of contemporary material that we have in Germany. He needs scenarios which select and handle [concrete] themes. *No fantasies, no fiction, no poetry.*'[23]

It must be noted that plays in which ideas are dominant or the primary aim is the journalistic presentation of actual experience adopt a taut construction where the logic of argument or the selection of fact is the sole organizing principle. This is qualitatively different to the symmetrical patterning of all traditional art-forms, from the sonnet to the picaresque novel. It is the absence of this quality of artificially enclosed design that sets twentieth-century art apart from the work of previous eras – and it justifies the view that new conditions have given rise to a new culture. One definition of art common to all genres is that thought and expression are inseparably fused, for each modifies the other. Form can be defined as an 'elegant solution' (to borrow a mathematical expression) to the structural problems raised by a particular subject, while content is conditioned by its formulation – so that the same battle-scene can be portrayed as a heroic ideal or a degrading ordeal because any variation in vocabulary or word-order alters the meaning of a statement. A new approach to reality in response to a change in environment demands new means of expression which must be developed by trial and error. Piscator's work is in many ways typical of periods of cultural adjustment in his adaptation of techniques; and his attempts to create an appropriate style were not always consistent. Yet the unusual qualities of his experiments are clearly marked by contrast to earlier concepts.

According to his associates, Piscator was no theoretician by choice. As a defence of his practical work against attacks on ideological grounds, his writings contain contradictions, and his statements on artistic theory are confused by his utilitarian view of the stage as a catalyst for social change. But he was well aware of the essential relationship between form and content, and his innovations were always functional solutions to the problems posed by staging particular plays. Instead of approaching the theatre from a doctrinaire standpoint his motto, which was projected onto a screen at the Piscator-Bühne before the start of each performance, was 'we always begin again at the beginning'. Consequently his development led him away from the Agitprop elements which had strengthened the Communist conviction that drama should be used solely for propaganda. Even though he had rejected aesthetic principles, his later work was attacked as 'formalistic' because its qualities did not correspond to the Party line, and he was forced to vindicate his experiments by reversing his earlier standpoint: 'Indeed, it was never *my* plan to produce Agitprop work in the normal sense, which is a job that belongs to others. Instead I lay the greatest value on a permeation of propaganda with artistic qualities (the more artistic, the greater the effect: that is the best propaganda) ...'[24]

Other left-wing directors also found Agitprop theatre insufficient to absorb their experimental energies. Even Meyerhold rejected his famous October Theatre in favour of an intricate burlesque style of production at the end of the twenties, declaring that 'the time for Agitas is past', and Joan Littlewood also progressed to a proscenium stage. Piscator later declared that his goal was 'a political *theatre*, not theatrical *politics* (which apart from anything else were nothing new)',[25] and direct incitement to immediate political action ceased to appear in Piscator's productions after his revues. Instead he concentrated on 'heightening the scenic into the historical'[26] – in other words presenting the universal aspects of particular events, which in itself is one definition of art – and disparaged propaganda as an art work in which the form was not equal to mastering the content. When the Nazi triumph in Germany provided an unmistakably negative answer to arguments for the political efficacy of agitation, Piscator proposed that the Popular Front against Fascism should build up a 'cultural army' who could best act 'in their *artistic* character, through their particular species: *revolutionary* theatre, film, music and dance art-forms'.[27]

This was Piscator's policy statement when he was elected secretary of the International Revolutionary Theatre Association in 1934, and the denial of utilitarian principles was already implicit in his work from 1925. However, it marks a development rather than a reversal, because the art that he advocated had nothing in common with the traditional forms he rejected. It was to be 'revolutionary' in style because it handled new material. The passing phase of 'direct and open propaganda' merely disguised Piscator's constant aim, which was to create a stage capable of dealing with twentieth-century realities. Even his aggressive early declarations about the political function of the theatre were based on 'one fundamental prejudice, namely to speak the truth';[28] a principle that is echoed by his 1942 definition of theatre-artists as 'those who so live in their times that they can re-create them as indestructible reality for our own and future generations',[29] and by his explanation of the reasons for his work in 1954: 'to perceive the situation of our time is simply a necessity for everyone'.[30]

Piscator was able to justify realistic art by the standards of utilitarian propaganda on the ground that to portray the conditions of life truthfully would be enough to condemn the society that had created them without any overt message. His argument was circular. Art as the most effective form of propaganda would revive art which had been corrupted by being classified as 'goods', and out of the conflict of ideas which came from reform 'will awake that art whose purest perfection we recognize in the works of antiquity'.[31] Evolving a new dramaturgy – the first essential for representing modern reality – would make the stage the focus for political consciousness, and a social purpose was the prerequisite for the growth of a modern drama. 'Pure art is not possible in the context of present times. But the art which consciously serves a political cause, as long as it never compromises, will ultimately reveal itself as the only one possible and so as the pure art of our time.'[32] This is the logic behind Piscator's paradoxical statement that his 'political theatre' was 'not founded in order to promote politics, but to free art from politics'.[33]

Political theatre: party politics v. sociology

The statement reveals how far Piscator had moved from the Agit-prop position. Art as the most effective propaganda against social conditions that debased art – art in politics so that art could be liberated from political pressures. The underlying concept is relevance. Piscator had named his new image of the stage 'political theatre' and took this term as a title for the autobiographical record of his theatrical experiments in 1929 because 'quite simply this incongruity [e.g. between ideals and realities] in actual human existence...politicizes every manifestation of life'.[34] He argued that moral or spiritual conflict took place in a corporate context, and that it was not the individual's 'personal relationships...but his relationship to society that is the centre of interest'.[35] Therefore any dramatic conflict could only be seen as the clash of social forces within or against the social organization.

This explanation hardly satisfied the extreme supporters of utilitarian drama, who claimed that 'he oversimplifies or complicates plays and stage-scripts into "productions"'. They accused him of 'bourgeois individualism' and condemned his book as 'a pompous parade of the mistakes he has committed and not a recantation'.[36] Indeed Piscator's style of production, in spite of the political terms in which he evaluated his achievements during the twenties, had little in common with Communist aims.

The word 'political' has a double meaning, and Piscator's use of the expression 'political theatre' is often ambiguous, since his views altered as his style developed. At the outset of his career his productions were clearly intended to be 'party political', being dedicated to the 'conscious emphasizing and propagation of the concept of class-warfare'.[37] But as soon as he gained his own stage in 1927 an objectivity became apparent which belied his most noticeable stage property – the illuminated red star, a permanent fixture above the proscenium. After the Second World War he described his position in terms of the Greek 'polis' and Aristotle's 'zoon politicon' – man (the microcosm) seen as an integral part of his environment (the macrocosm). This confusion between the narrow and the sociological sense of 'political' was accentuated by the fact that Piscator had publicized his new techniques as Marxist and they therefore became identified with Communism. However, he was never a card-carrying member of the Party and throughout his career he intended his stage to be a 'moral institution', acting in the German tradition as the conscience of the public by facing them with their environment – but the situation after the Great War had made morality a synonym for politics and turned politics into ideology. This led him to redefine his terms: 'Earlier I once named the theatre a political theatre, but today I would really rather call it a theatre of affirmation (*Bekenntnistheater*).'[38] The perception that personal conflict was determined by society was not new – even Wagner some thirty years earlier noted that society had destroyed the 'mythos' by enslaving the individual 'so that the art of the poet has become politics; no one can compose without carrying on a political argument'[39] – and the broader definition of political theatre was widely accepted.

'Knowledge – Recognition – Affirmation'[40] became Piscator's formula; and in his last description of his work he summed up his career as a series of attempts to alter the theatre's means of expression so that the stage might be capable of portraying and analysing the complexities of society. Traditional art forms, defined as 'unreal-reconciliatory', had proved to be unusable because they distorted the realities towards which his work was directed: 'We had been degraded to war-material; what wonder that we became materialists! Determined to alter the world by revealing it in exact descriptions.'[41] Even in the twenties he frequently referred to the stage as a laboratory for examining society. Facts were his material, scientific accuracy and detachment were his standards – but the propaganda that Communist dogma demanded made objectivity impossible. It was therefore inevitable that he should distance himself from the Party in order to develop the potential that he saw in his drama. He remained a materialist, but diluted his Marxism.

As the leading Marxist in the German theatre of the time, Piscator became the centre of the ideological controversy about art, and this forced him to over-emphasize the narrow political aspects of his work. However, the pressures from inside the Party had the advantage that they compelled him to clarify his thought and to construct a logical dramaturgy from his *ad hoc* practice. Without this pressure his aims might have been less coherent, while his work would certainly have been less well documented. His theories were always formulated after the event and were not therefore responsible for the form of his experiments, although his career shows a remarkable consistency.

The revue *Despite All!* acts as a focal point. The Agitprop roots of his later work are indicated by his use of the original theme – a history of revolution from Rome to November 1919 – as a film accompaniment to Ehm Welk's *Storm over Gottland*, his final production for the Volksbühne. Yet *Despite All!* also contained the major elements of Piscator's mature work. Even characteristic solutions to particular problems of staging (specifically his distinctive use of stage-constructs and placards) were already present. The emphasis of his direction was placed for the first time on documented fact, while simultaneously the audience was encouraged to participate in the action. The beginnings of 'Documentary Drama' are here in the objective approach to factual material; and the rudiments of 'Total Theatre' appear in the way the optical elements of film, lighting and movement were used at the expense of the text to involve the audience's emotions. These counteracting qualities, inherited from the confusion between 'propaganda' and 'agitation' in the Proletarisches Theater, are here distinct through the development of precision in audience manipulation. At one level Piscator's continual experimentation can be seen as an attempt to resolve this conflict, which was the result of his initial uncertainty about the exact relationship of the stage to reality. If it was to be a mirror, then the documentary aspects had to be developed. On the other hand if it was to be a catalyst, then a more immediate and powerful effect could be gained through the techniques of Total Theatre. In either case, the emphasis on historical and economic forces instead of on personal motivation involved the replacement of nineteenth-century concepts of drama; and because Piscator revolutionized content as well as style in order to realign art with the modern environment his experiments must be approached as new theatre-forms, not merely as *œuvres de mise en scène*.

4 Documentary Drama:
the Material

The director as a creative artist

The position of the director is a recent one. Until the nineteenth century productions were either coordinated by the dramatists themselves or by leading actors, because stock companies and the simplicity of stage-machinery made his function unnecessary. Acting had fixed rules, which were derived from rhetoric, and governed tone and gesture so that there was little variation between the performances of different plays within any period. Although the rules were constantly modified, this tradition lasted into the Romantic age and Kean was able to play major Shakespearean rôles without rehearsal. Only with the introduction of elaborate stage effects and naturalistic underplaying which made careful rehearsals essential – together with the practice of hiring actors for specific performances – did 'the arranger' become an important figure. A director had been engaged for Renaissance court masques or *Commedia del' Arte* improvisations but the first time that his presence is acknowledged on a playbill in England was in 1863 for the première of Byron's dramatic poem, *Manfred*, which needs considerable adaptation for the stage. In other words his services were only required when a play needed extensive revision and the author was unavailable, when the actors were amateurs and the machinery architecturally complex, or in a tradition without set speeches where various conventional elements needed coordination and expansion.

It is significant that Gordon Craig argued the case for an autocratic, continental type of artist-director as 'the ideal stage manager', and that the Duke of Saxe-Meiningen derived his practice from the influence of settings on the actors. As the conditions of performance become more complex, the interaction of lighting and machinery increasingly determines movement and speech – until with such concepts as Wagner's *Gesamtkunstwerk* or Appia's *'l'œuvre d'art vivant'* the control of the technical director becomes absolute. Synaesthetic theories diminish the importance of the

66

linguistic and literary aspects of drama and the director supplants the playwright as the creative artist. There have always been two distinct definitions of the relationship between the performing artist and the author, that of Eleanora Duse – who saw herself as the interpreter of a poet's creation – and that of Sarah Bernhardt – who claimed that actors are 'dramatists of genius'. Similarly Jouvet believed that with attentive perception a play creates its own production, while Terence Gray sees the director as 'an independent artist, using other artists and coordinating their arts into a whole which is the composite art-of-the-theatre'. This claim to creative autonomy is based on the view that a play is no more than the scenario for a production, since drama only reaches its fullest expression in performance. This is an accurate evaluation, although it has been discredited by its extreme canvassers, such as Craig, whose position is clearly untenable: 'I believe in the time when we shall be able to create works of art in the theatre without the use of the written play, without the use of actors.'

Normally, as Hugo von Hofmannsthal realized, a delicate balance is struck between the director and the dramatist: 'In order that a play can achieve its final, complete effect the poet must allow the director free play, the director the actor, indeed the actor the audience – in whose emotions alone the interplay of influences should first be completed.' But Piscator was in the position of a director without a play. His difficulty was not only finding competently written plays with political subjects which were ideologically correct – a difficulty also shared by later Marxist producers such as Joan Littlewood and Roger Planchon – but was also due to the continuing influence of outmoded conventions which made play scripts unsuitable material for transforming the theatre. It was a common complaint in the Weimar Republic that contemporary plays were derivative instead of drawn from life. As one critic remarked sourly, 'elsewhere plays are constructed, in Germany they are poetically inspired',[1] and Piscator himself never denied that his 'complete style of production is solely the result of an absence of dramatic output. Certainly it would never have created such an overwhelming impression if I had found an adequate dramatic output in existence'.[2] He looked on his productions as practical examples, encouraging authors to deal with contemporary problems in an appropriate manner by demonstrating the new possibilities open to the stage: 'The literature that we need is only now coming into existence. We hope that our theatre will give it a powerful stimulus.'³ Seeing himself as the 'servant and exponent of his time' instead of 'the servant of an art-work',⁴ Piscator showed an autocratic disregard for authors' rights, while at the same time encouraging unknown writers. Out of the thirty-nine productions that Piscator staged between the opening of his Proletarisches Theater and his exile in 1931, no less than twenty-six were either first productions or German premières and only four were in any sense 'accepted' plays – two by Maxim Gorki, one by Strindberg and one by Schiller. Established authors were frequently unable to comprehend his aims and uncooperative when asked to revise their work (Gorki refused to generalize *The Lower Depths* at Piscator's personal request, while Max Brod clung to the letter of the law on his copyright and *The Good Soldier Schweik* had to be rewritten without his consent), so Piscator wrote his own scripts with the help of his dramaturge or, when possible, worked in close association with a dramatist instead of accepting finished plays. At other times he revised speeches, altered plots and changed meanings in such a high-handed way that he was discharged from the Volks-bühne after Ehm Welk had accused him of travestying his play, *Storm over Gottland*, and became notorious when he rewrote Schiller's masterpiece, *The Robbers*, as a modern revolutionary manifesto. The radical extent to which he was capable of changing a play is shown by his treatment of *Rasputin* where, aided by Gasbarra, he added nineteen scenes to Alexei Tolstoy's original eight. Above all he expanded the themes of the plays that he produced by applying new stage machinery and by exploiting the visual elements of scenery, lighting and movement which were directly under his control. In the New York Dramatic Workshop he trained authors as well as actors, and his reply to criticism that his productions violated authors' rights was always 'Write better plays!'⁵

Piscator's claim that the leading directors have influenced and altered the modern stage as much as great poets changed theatrical traditions in the past is reasonable. Where he can be distinguished from his contemporaries in Germany – Max Reinhardt, Leopold Jessner, Karlheinz Martin, Jürgen Fehling or even Bertolt Brecht – is that while they created individual styles on the basis of their personal interpretations of plays, Piscator tried to create a dramaturgy which would be universally valid. It was intended to be both representative of contemporary conditions and appropriate for dealing with twentieth-century experience, and he realized that new areas of subject matter 'not only burst the form of the stage, but also the form of the drama'.[6] Like the work of any creative artist, his productions must therefore be evaluated in their own terms instead of as secondary interpretations.

At the Volksbühne he evolved stage techniques which emphasized the economic and political background of the action at the expense of characterization. It was this that caused his summary dismissal in 1927 when Ehm Welk protested 'against a style of production which has become politically and artistically an end-in-itself', the disproportionate importance of optical effects, including film, and the cutting of 'everything...that was in any way designed to heighten the personality of the characters';[7] and drew the management's attention to the fact that their stage was being used for Marxist propaganda. But as soon as he transferred his work to a theatre of his own, the Piscator-Bühne, which he opened in September following the furore of his dismissal, he was able to explore these possibilities for opening the stage to fresh material.

During the next two years Piscator staged plays written specifically for the distinctive style that he was developing. These, as Brecht remarked, attempted to handle the intricate complexities of contemporary subject matter in a direct manner and formed a nucleus of concrete achievements that provided a working basis for the 'New Drama' when it eventually appeared.[8] He also founded a studio to train actors for the novel stage-conditions associated with the new type of play – as he was later to do again with resounding success in New York. His work was judged to be valuable in proportion to its distance from the subject matter, approach and style of the normal theatre, and had a wide influence. It even affected Jessner, and when Karlheinz Martin staged J. R. Bloch's *The Last Kaiser* as a guest producer at the Piscator-Bühne in 1928, the use of stage-machinery, the treatment of the script and the effect were indistinguishable from Piscator's own productions.

The experimental nature of Piscator's work

Piscator's productions were experiments in a double sense. Each was an exploration of the technical resources of the stage in order to adapt outdated dramatic conventions to modern conditions, and at the same time each was a reappraisal of the theatre's social function: 'Experimental does not mean "unfinished" for us, but the search for the basic artistic, philosophical, social and political principles for human thought and action in our age.'[9] However, the theories that Piscator put forward in his book and in his polemic newspaper campaigns were to a large extent rationalizations drawn from observing the results of his experiments, and the most productive aspect of his work was the process of searching rather than the principles. Picasso's description of his own approach, 'when I paint, I show what I have found, not what I have searched for. Intentions are not enough in art', is illuminating as a general comment on the techniques of experimental artists, and applies aptly to Piscator, whose style was formed through trial and error. An excellent description of his method of operation has been given by Hans Reimann, who brings the creative chaos of the Piscator-Bühne vividly to life in his account of the productions of *Schweik* and *Rasputin*, both of which went into rehearsal at the same time:

As soon as the performance was over one group of stage hands swarmed onto the set and dismantled the complicated scaffolding and arches [of *Hoppla!*]. Piscator threw all customary scenery to the winds. As soon as everything had been removed a second group rushed on and set up the heavy machinery that was needed for *Schweik*. From 10 a.m. *Schweik* could be rehearsed, until the hour approached for the treadmills and other gewgaws to be taken away and replaced by the sort of global ball that was the setting for *Rasputin*...The order that exists anywhere else had no place here. One had to be ready for the unexpected, and if the theatre had been afflicted by a tornado, Piscator would have attempted to make it serve his purposes.[10]

Piscator never thought of his achievements as final and, however important, any innovation was 'nothing more than a means that tomorrow can be replaced by a better one'[11] – although he refined and consolidated his advances by repeating techniques that had proved successful. Almost every major production used the stage in some strikingly new way, but each radical novelty became the established basis for subsequent experiments. The treadmill (*laufendes Band*),[12] introduced in *Schweik*, reappeared in both *The Merchant of Berlin* and *What Price Glory?* in 1928 and Piscator deprecated its lack in the Studio Theatre programme to his 1942 production of *War and Peace*. Similarly, the technique of throwing a gigantic human shadow onto a screen to act as a symbol of fate recurred, and the spherical stage-construct of *Rasputin* was employed again in *The Officers' Uprising* as late as 1966.

The experimental nature of Piscator's work, which was marked by energy and a productive discontent, aroused an ambivalent attitude in the drama critics. Hoping for the regeneration of the theatre through his originality, Kerr, Jhering and Diebold, the leading critics of the time, all supported his productions at first – which was unusual, since Alfred Kerr and Herbert Jhering were rivals and tended to disagree with each other on principle. But their enthusiasm vanished as his productions grew in complexity. On the one hand they condemned those productions which were technically successful since no major innovations had been made:

All the performances of the Piscator-Bühne up to now were experiments, which offered advances into a new dramatic world of form and material, without pretending to be final solutions. This [*The Last Kaiser*] is indeed superficially successful, but completely false, suspect and dangerous in its smoothness and perfection.[13]

On the other hand they complained that premières came to resemble dress-rehearsals because, with continual experimentation, the stage-machinery suffered from overextension. Certainly at times this was embarrassingly obvious. When *Hoppla!* opened, the final film sequence was still being run through as the audience entered the auditorium, while in *The Merchant of Berlin* the complex machinery malfunctioned during the first scene, when the chorus who stood on steps leading down to the stalls (the steps were supposed to sink into the pit after the prologue while the stage-floor closed above them and an iron construction was lowered from the flies) were almost crushed when the lift jammed on the first night. This was a mistake that could not be disguised. Frantic cries brought the machinery to a halt, the actors scrambled up into the wings and stage-hands appeared to do repairs.

This production was at once both the apogee of Piscator's mechanization of the stage and proof that machinery alone was not enough to make a performance successful. Piscator attempted to cover the weakness of the play with striking mechanical effects.

The average critical reaction was scathing and ignored Piscator's intentions, concentrating instead on the most blatant elements of the production:

Rolling bands moved backwards and forwards, diagonally and across. Trap-doors here and there...scenery descends from above or rises into view from below, illuminated script and film, a calendar on which the date alters automatically and artillery with light-bulbs to simulate the flashes of bombardment...It is the true old Raimundian magic theatre; with modern aids, of course...The application [of machinery] is taken for objectivity...and has been exaggerated into such a cult that it has been transformed into a romanticization of objectivity.[14]

The difficulty was that the concept was too complex to be realized with the means at Piscator's disposal, so that the machinery malfunctioned; and it was chiefly due to the impression left by this production that almost every interview with Piscator after the Second World War opened with a reference to 'formalism' or 'technical sensationalism', or with the accusation that Piscator's 'only interest in the theatre is technological'.

The actual intention of the machinery was to expand the limits of the stage, to bring the street into the theatre and to link drama with the momentary and real events of the newspaper-world. Its purpose was to reveal the broad patterns of history while documenting the action with details, in order to give an objective correlative to the mechanical complexity and technical refinements of the age while at the same time making the fullest use of spatial movement – and this intention in fact gained its clearest expression in *The Merchant of Berlin*:

The newspaper is the chronicle of the present instant. Complete series of contemporary news headlines are thrown by the film onto the familiar gauze-wall...the historical moments...the incredible sums, marks numbered in billions, flicker like a blizzard over the 'fourth wall'... Rathenau, Erzberger appear like ghosts out of thin air...the antique chorus-form of 'mass man' comes photographically, scientifically, objectively to life in this ghost-film of air and newspaper-clippings...'The Street' was never brought onto the stage like this before. Modern mass drama must, by god, indeed be played out in the streets. We take the town bus through the film canyons of apartment-buildings...Two treadmills run across the revolving-stage which turns round itself in a different direction. On this the tempo-march of the streets unreels with

thousands of paces forwards and backwards, to the right and left...
Space has its own *rôle*: Streets are the place for traffic...[15]

Piscator frequently emphasized that his style was conditioned by
the difficulties of staging new material, which accounts for the
eclectic confusion of his work. As he later commented: 'One must
not determine the form and dramaturgy of plays according to preconceived theories, but instead take plays as the starting-point to
arrive at a dramaturgy...First there was [Gerhart Hauptmann's
play] *Before Sunrise* and then came Naturalism.'[16] But since he
lacked appropriate plays during the twenties he took 'reality as a
starting-point'.[17] This dependence on factual events posed fresh
problems of production in each play so that necessarily he 'always
began again from the beginning'. As a result any duplication of
devices when dealing with different subjects made it appear that the
machinery was being applied independently of the material. The
factors that determined his approach were not the normal considerations of characterization and interpretation – which remain constant since they are questions of aesthetics – but the
grouping and deployment of facts which changed with every play.
The style was therefore expected to vary in each production, and
this had obvious disadvantages. The form was intended to be no
more than a manifestation of the content – but in their nature as
experiments his productions lacked mechanical perfection. This
was accentuated by Piscator's major failing – an unwillingness to
limit himself to what was mechanically practicable, and he later
admitted that 'the undeniably complex apparatus, which I had
simply conceived as a means to achieve the end of greater and more
theatrical simplicity in advancing the action, frequently appeared to
become an end in itself because it failed to function due to some
initial defects'.[18] The same qualities that made Piscator's work
potentially productive therefore ruled out critical approval for his
actual achievements.

Piscator's criteria: objectivity and documentation v. Socialist Realism

The use of fact, however, provided certain common standards –
actuality and immediacy of presentation – which could be applied
as criteria to each production. Piscator had come to see the lack of

realism in his Agitprop work, and in the Piscator-Bühne he stressed the qualities of topicality, truth to fact and clarity in order to gain 'a much closer association with journalism, with the actuality of the day'.[19] His general statement of principle, 'art has only ever been good when it comes directly to grips with life, when it is created out of the raw contrasts from which life is formed',[20] was limited at this point in his development by the qualification that 'the theatre always stood or fell by its "actuality" in all cultural epochs'.[21] 'Actuality' became a key word in evaluating his own work, and he began to use textual improvisation. In *Hoppla!*, for instance, the date of Thomas's release was changed every night to the date of the performance, while reports from each day's newspapers were inserted into Credé's play, § *218*. Such a narrow concept of the relevance of art to life, based on the premise that only the most recent and therefore most obviously relevant facts are capable of holding an audience's interest, is not confined to Piscator. The same desire for immediacy, which in fact emphasizes the transient nature of a production, is found in the Theatre Workshop under Joan Littlewood who trained her actors to improvise before an audience as well as in rehearsal, incorporating the morning's headlines into the evening's performance wherever possible in the belief that 'as soon as a production is fixed it is dead'.

If Piscator's overriding consideration had been topicality alone, this would have brought his productions close to the later theatrical development of the Living Newspaper in the U.S.A., which took the form of documentary sketches solely concerned with current social and political topics. Contemporaneity, however, is only one of the qualities of journalism. Another is (supposedly) truth, and it was on this aspect that Piscator concentrated, since his concern was not 'the mere propagation of a *Weltanschauung* through cliché-phrases and placard-slogans, but...the convincing demonstration that this one alone was valid'.[22] In accepted journalistic practice facts are reported without rhetoric or comment, which is reserved for the editorial. By contrast the theatre presents a world of illusion in which any reconstruction of events is by nature impassioned because the active agents are always the individuals involved. The conventions of drama counteract any effect of impersonality, and the more naturalistically events are portrayed the more the illusion must be self-enclosed, which means that the more the subjective element is hidden the further the action must be distanced from the audience. Piscator's problem therefore lay in gaining objectivity without sacrificing immediacy.

On one level his productions simply accumulated facts to demonstrate a thesis, and so avoided the emotional appeal of rhetoric. Piscator claimed that his theatre was dedicated to a scientific objectivity, and the adjective 'scientific' was echoed by the critics, one of whom called *Rasputin* a clinical demonstration of chaos and destruction and described the production as a blackboard dissection of a murder. Contemporary events or recent history were 're-enacted' instead of being 'acted' while nothing was spoken of on the stage without being demonstrated impersonally in the action, and Piscator spoke of 'this new, mathematical kind of performance'.[23]

On an abstract, theoretical level this resembles Socialist Realism, which was officially defined in a Soviet encyclopedia as 'an artistic method. Its basic principle is the representation of reality in a faithful and concrete manner, in its revolutionary development, and its most important task is the Communist education of the masses.' Indeed, Piscator's ostensible objectivity was a technique of persuasion rather than the sign of an empirical approach, and Karl Radek's general description of Socialist Realism in a speech to the first All-Union Congress of Soviet Writers fits the characteristics of his work perfectly:

We do not photograph life. In the totality of phenomena we seek out the main phenomenon. Giving everything without discrimination is not realism. That would be the most vulgar type of Naturalism. We should select phenomena. Realism means that we make a selection from the point of view of what is essential, from the point of view of guiding principles. And as far as what is essential – the very name of Socialism tells us this. Select all phenomena which show how the system of Capitalism is being smashed, how Socialism is growing.

This bias in selection made it possible for the Piscator-Bühne to be described in the programme to *The Merchant of Berlin* as both 'a theatre of dispassionate analysis' and 'the political battle-theatre... taken to its furthest possible extreme' – a particularly blatant contradiction since the two conflicting descriptions occur in one and the same paragraph.

It seems to be commonly thought that any directly political or proletarian-oriented drama is Socialist Realism. But this art movement, which in fact marked the emergence of an Establishment in Russia, shows distinct similarities to the authoritarian sculpture of the Roman empire. The style chosen as a suitable instrument for public policy and imposed by censorship in the U.S.S.R. after 1925 was the most conventional of nineteenth-century forms since it was designed both as a means of education and a cultural expression of the masses who were assumed to be incapable of appreciating subtlety or originality. Controlled by committees, Socialist Realism developed into a rigidly formal and retrospectively conventional art, while Piscator's achievements were novel and eclectic; and the stylistic difference is the outward sign of a basic divergence in approach. A 'political theatre' comes into existence in opposition, producing revolutionary material in a revolutionary style. But when the revolution becomes reality then criticism and the style associated with it is paradoxically identified with reaction. Piscator's aim was to arouse his audiences to political action, but Socialist Realism, whatever its theoretical justifications, acted as an ersatz 'opium of the people', stilling critical thought by avoiding intellectual demands.

Innovation as such and the attempt to stimulate political criticism made Piscator's work different in kind to Socialist Realism, while his stated determination to discover stage conventions appropriate to modern conditions was an implicit rejection of the techniques approved for 'proletarian art'. He claimed that his political aims were comparable, but even his definition of 'realism' was different and so was his approach to factual material, since his concept of 'actuality' tied his art to social conditions in Berlin – and these were worlds apart from the Russian scene.

In theory both realistic approaches were 'limited...to allowing the naked [but carefully edited] facts to speak for themselves'.[24] This altered the nature of the 'willing suspension of disbelief' which is given to imaginative art. It made the credibility of a play's action dependent on the audience's acceptance of the subject matter. Piscator therefore found it necessary to cite evidence to corroborate facts because the events he selected for dramatic representation were, being contemporary, often those that had already been dealt with by official or right-wing propaganda. This had to be discredited by undeniable documentation before acceptance could be gained for any radical interpretation. In Russia, however, the theatre was integrated with the propaganda of the Soviet news services, and had no need to produce evidence however biased the presentation.

Despite All! handled events which were familiar to every newspaper reader. The subject of *Flags* was the well-known history of the 1886 anarchist uprising in Chicago, and Rudolf Leonard's *Sail Ahoy*, produced at the Volksbühne in 1925, treated an authenticated contemporary incident. The more familiar or controversial such material was, the more carefully Piscator had to substantiate his version with evidence, and when Wilhelm II sued him for defamation of character in *Rasputin*, Piscator's defence was that the ex-Kaiser 'did not have a single sentence to speak that had been invented by us, but solely sentences that were taken from his own marginal comments to the war-documents and from his own orations'.[25] Such claims to factual accuracy, originally a response to libel suits, were soon extended into a general axiom: 'Drama is only important for us insofar as it can be documented by evidence.'[26] It was not enough for a programme to state that the events of a plot could be documented. They had to be demonstrated to be true during the performance.

Documentation and dialogue

Evidence could never be allowed to slow the tempo of performance and Piscator therefore experimented with various means of verification, never restricting the testimony to a single medium, but spreading the load of factual data over all the channels of communication, visual and aural, that could be brought into a production. He used placards and projected texts, pictorial and photographic records, loudspeakers and quoted speeches as well as known historical situations and familiar figures. This detracted from the importance of the dialogue.

The normal dramatic means of presenting a detached view of an action is descriptive speech, but in searching for substitutes Piscator was not simply pursuing novelty. A verbal account of events is always interpretative and subjective since it comes from the mouth of an individual. He therefore introduced the projection screen as a calendar to give dates or as a blackboard to point out essential facts – troop movements in a campaign or fluctuations on the stock market. But effective documentation through this medium was inevitably limited to statistics because more time had to be allowed for reading than it takes to transmit information orally or in pictures. The least time-consuming way of documenting facts is photography, which also has the advantage of recording, or appearing to record actual happenings; so when he wished to expand the documentation from a bare statement Piscator used film (which was in any case physically more impressive than texts or speeches) in conjunction with the stage and the projection screen. Film can compress a time sequence or present a whole scene instantaneously to the eye, while speeches that could achieve an equal precision would be too long and lack impact when applied to such complex, abstract subjects as the economic structure of society or the strategic implications of a military campaign. 'Anything that playwrights cannot encompass in words alone today must find concrete outlines on the up-to-date stage.'[27] Film therefore replaced the 'récit de Théramène' convention to bring scenes and events into a play that could not be represented by the actors.

The new elements appealed almost exclusively to the eye, and the emphasis on visual effects at the expense of the written word can be most obviously seen in the 1927 production of Toller's *Hoppla, We are Alive!*, where the speeches in the final scene were transposed into illuminated letters running along a band (as in the electric teletype in Times Square, Waterloo or Friedrichstrasse) and projected across the acting-structure to represent morse communication between the prisoners. Stage-machinery was substituted for speech, scenery for the actors – and critics frequently complained that 'the excessive supply of the purely visual, of news-reels and contemporary documents makes it hard ... to detect the play'.[28] Ehm Welk's criticism that the staging of *Storm over Gottland* was 'solely optical, independent of the play, indeed destructive of the play'[29] is valid but ignored Piscator's aims.

The realistic style that Piscator evolved focused the attention on fact, consistency and logic, which are theatrical inessentials. This raises certain dramaturgical problems that are peculiar to Documentary Drama – in particular the creation of a theatrically effective structure from facts selected primarily to spell out a political message, and the reduction of an unwieldy volume of evidence to theatrical limits.

The root of these problems was that the conventions of stage dialogue, the primary means of communication in the traditional theatre, are ill-suited to convey information – as the clumsiness of the chorus convention or the falsity of the 'two servants technique' show. In a normal play concerned with the interaction of individuals, dialogue drives the action forward by revealing motives and personal relationships, but where documentary montage acts as both subject and structure the action can only be advanced through a constant stream of factual information, and dialogue diverts the audience's attention from the data to the characters. The production of *Flags* brought this home to Piscator, since the documentary techniques that were applied for the first time in an ordinary theatrical context conflicted with the conventions of the normal play form. The scenes lacked dramatic shape since attention was centred on sequences of events, while the words related primarily to the characters. Speech did not cause action nor did action result in speech; and the juxtaposition of contrasting eye-witness reports, police statements taken from the records of the trial and imaginary speeches by fictitious representatives of the workers caused confusion.

The visual trend of his experimentation itself provided a solution to the acute technical problems of paraphrasing the vast subject matter of such epic works as *Rasputin, Schweik* or *War and Peace*. Optical communication is the clearest and most compressed type of shorthand. Slogans, flags, grotesque puppets or stage-constructs – the whole tone of Piscator's productions was symbolic; not in the inflated Expressionist mode, but because Piscator looked on symbols as being 'condensed reality... a method of stenographically abbreviating material'.[30]

The first step toward this visual symbolism was to replace carefully constructed speeches by functional phrases or, as Ehm Welk complained, by 'banalities, Party-slogans and jargon'. The altered scripts closely resembled 'journalese' – a further indication of the influence of journalism on Piscator's style which reached its fullest expression with the production of *Economic Competition* where the stage was decorated in the format of a newspaper. Frequent slogans are the vocal equivalents of banner headlines, and the more extended speeches, especially those expressing emotion, were infected by the occupational disease of the press by becoming reduced to banal clichés.

From our modern standpoint, this linguistic simplification of ideas through the prefabrication of images and the conveyor-belt production of commonplaces appears typical of the twentieth-century trend to platitudes. Its inherent insensitivity seems linked with Piscator's mechanization of the stage, since it has been our experience that language tends to lose its meaning when phrased for wide circulation and transmitted by technology. Piscator's reduction of language to the lowest common denominator of communication was intended to be a reflection of contemporary conditions. But, like the telegraphic style of the German Expressionists, it was primarily designed to contrast with the conventions of the commercial theatre. Just as Piscator stressed the experimental (and therefore 'unfinished') nature of his work because this in itself demonstrated that accepted artistic criteria were inappropriate, so this simplified and prosaic speech effectively invalidated the aesthetic standards which were normally applied to drama. *Faute de mieux*, facts became the centre of a production because the literary qualities by which drama had been traditionally defined as an art form were absent, and this in turn enforced experimentation.

Piscator disregarded the text, the single permanent element of drama which preserves a play as an artistic work, holding that 'the book is the death of any real [i.e. "realistic", but also with connotations of "immediately effective"] speech'.[31] The improvisation which had been forced on him during his Agitprop period was carried over into even his most intricate professional productions. But here the play itself was extemporized instead of the means and materials (the machinery now at his disposal and his trained actors being precise means of communication). Visual effects aimed at on paper frequently had to be altered in practice, so that the final version of a play could only be created in rehearsal. Scripts were altered constantly, scenes re-ordered or plays completely re-written – sometimes up to and beyond the dress-rehearsal – in order to develop any optical possibilities in the material. This was recognized to be 'a relative catastrophe for the author',[32] but Piscator ignored it on political grounds: 'The question of eternal values in

1 Erwin Piscator at rehearsal, 1953.

2 *All the King's Men*. Multi-level acting area allowing simultaneous scenes, projection screen. Dramatic Workshop, 1948.

3 *Schweik* ('Off to Belgrade!'). Pallenberg as Schweik on outer band, officer-marionette (Grosz) on parallel band. Piscator-Bühne, 1928.

4 *The Fireraisers*. Set design, P. Walter. Placards and screens in auditorium, central and circling stage. Nationaltheater, 1959.

5 *War and Peace*. Pierre as commentator demonstrating the progress of a battle with toy soldiers on the 'Stage of Fate'. Schiller-Theater, 1955.

6 *War and Peace*. Russian battle orders and Napoleon's entrance on the 'Stage of Fate'. Landestheater, Darmstadt, 1955.

art ... should no longer be posed by a Marxist'[33] – a specious excuse, since the devaluation of dialogue had specific practical results which furthered his theatrical aims.

Stage effects and subject matter

Machinery replaced dialogue as a means of expression, since the major techniques of documentation that Piscator developed were non-verbal. At first film and projection were used only as the simplest means of reinforcing the text. In *Flags* photographs of the historical characters were projected during the prologue, background information was shown between the scenes, and the meaning was underlined at crucial moments in the action by captions – similar to the sub-titles in silent films. *Despite All!* included motion pictures as well as stills, but the aim was still the same. The film, a documentary borrowed from the State Archives, was inserted to clarify the factual background of the events and to gain credibility for the action. However, the powerful effect of this production showed Piscator that the compression, the immediacy and the objective impression of film could be used to activate an audience more compellingly than any facts. From then on film became a substitute for acted scenes, and stage-machinery also began to play an increasingly important functional rôle. During 1926 a double revolve appeared in Paul Zech's *The Drunken Ship* and loudspeakers in Paquet's second play, *Tidal Wave*. Radio was added in *Hoppla!*, a rolling stage was constructed for *Schweik*, and *The Merchant of Berlin* was acted on hydraulic lifts and motorized bridges.

The machinery, however, was more than a substitute for verbal expression. Piscator's complex stage technique was intended to represent the technological nature of modern society, and the materials he adapted to the stage were those of mass-culture and the industrial age. Film and the newspaper headline were dominant elements in the audience's everyday life, and even the incidental details of his productions, the car that was driven onto the stage in *Economic Competition* or the radio transmitter in *Hoppla!* – the equivalents of Meyerhold's motorbikes and aeroplanes – epitomized the impact of technology on the conditions of life. However, the major scientific advances of this century are on too large or too microscopic a scale to be of practical value in the theatre, which meant that the basis of Piscator's productions still had to be machinery which was already in common theatrical use, although he drew attention to it by working on the principle that 'everything mechanical should take place spontaneously in front of the onlookers'.[34] Comparisons could be drawn with Meyerhold's anti-illusionistic attitude: 'the actual world exists and is our subject; but this play and this stage are not it' – a point which Meyerhold emphasized by exposing the lighting, showing the stage-hands at work and leaving the rear wall of his theatre uncovered. But Piscator employed the same technique for a totally different effect, suggesting 'the age of the machine' in the abstract by giving even accepted machinery novel functions.

It is significant that the only scientific discoveries Piscator used were those in the field of communications. There was a real need for the new media of film and projection, radio and the public address system, since his aim was to make 'a political world picture visible in its totality',[35] and modern realities could not be represented by traditional techniques which had been developed to reflect differential material conditions. As early as his production of *The Lower Depths* he declared: 'We search for the latest, most sensitive ways of giving expression to this epoch, with the help of the technical and artistic discoveries born of the time, with whatever means come closest to reality.'[36] At times this tended towards mannerism, as in *Schweik* where Meisel exploited equipment that Deutsche Grammophon had just developed for all the incidental music and even some of the dialogue when the speakers were puppets: 'Recording and reproduction were thus accomplished by mechanical means, according to my long hatched plans to mechanize stage acoustics in their entirety.'[37] This type of excess, however, was the exception and the fact that adapting new means of communication for the stage was a practical necessity, not merely stylistic trickery, is supported by Joan Littlewood's later declaration that only by using 'the most recent scientific and technical developments can we create a theatrical form sufficiently flexible to reflect the rapidly changing twentieth-century scene'.[38]

Stage effects reflect the type of experience that directors and dramatists wish to transmit to the audience as well as being solutions to particular problems of presentation, the form of which is determined by the engineering knowledge of the time. The Renaissance, for example, made elaborate use of the mechanical discoveries of their age, providing 'bridges' which could be raised from below the level of the stage to present spectacular tableaux, and turning theatrical entertainment (in the form of the masque) into an allegorical mirror of the Renaissance court. In the nineteenth century technological advances following the Industrial Revolution made it possible to provide startling *coups de théâtre*, while at the same time satisfying a taste for the illusion of reality. This trend reached its height at the end of the First World War, when Reinhardt developed a system of lighting which made it possible to spotlight particular sections of the acting area and enabled actors to use the forestage, avoiding shadows and giving constancy and precision to colour effects – a system which, with only minor modifications, remains standard for all modern theatres and more than any other factor makes illusion possible.

The basic machinery and lighting in Piscator's theatre on Nollendorfplatz had been installed by Otto Brahm, the great Naturalist producer who had owned it at the end of the century, and the appearance of technical novelty in Piscator's productions at this period of his career is deceptive. Even the treadmills of *Schweik*, which appeared so revolutionary to his contemporaries and were counted as his most important innovation, had already been used in 1910 at the Drury Lane production of *The Whip* for a scene in which three racehorses galloped across the stage. As a sensational effect, Schweik's mammoth march was tame in comparison. But Piscator did adapt the existing machines to other ends. He employed them 'in order to give contemporary problems a dramatic shape on the stage',[39] and the novelty of his work can best be measured by contrast to Reinhardt's use of the theatre. This was equally dependent on complex mechanical stage effects but, because it was devoted to the unfolding of a 'kaleidoscopic and so wonderfully superfluous world . . . the magic of the theatre',[40] its glittering *trompe l'oeil* and illusionistic exhibitionism made it essential that his machinery remained invisible. Piscator's technical effects were in no way connected with conjuring showmanship. He extended the meaning of particular events portrayed on the stage by using machines to show universal historical and social trends and, as a symbol of twentieth-century civilization, this machinery was deliberately unconcealed because it identified the action of a play with a general critique of the environment outside the theatre.

The slides and flies, revolves and floats, developed so that cumbersomely representational scenery could be changed without long intervals, and the traps, bridges and lifts for unexpected entrances or sudden exits were now adapted to expand the theatre's scale of reference beyond the temporal limits of a performance and the physical measurements of the stage. Revolving or rolling acting areas, stage-constructs and simultaneous stages widened the imaginative dimensions of the theatre and were used to break out of the 'classical unities' of time, place and action.

The stage is traditionally seen as a microcosm representing the world. Piscator's machinery made the relationship of a scene to the macrocosm explicit. In *The Lower Depths* the roof of the room where the action takes place was raised to reveal streets and factories outside, while the early morning sounds of a city filled the auditorium through loudspeakers. This simple device had the effect of universalizing individual suffering into the typical misery of the contemporary proletariat by opening the 'narrowness' of ten men in a hovel 'to the world' without losing the claustrophobic atmosphere of cramped space, so extending the personal action into the context of the industrial slums. Piscator's aim was to portray life in its 'totality', not to give an illusion of reality: 'Realism may reveal something affecting and true about the individual and the group, but there are times when we find it necessary to relate experiences to the larger realities of the day.'[41] In *Rasputin* a globe was constructed within and around which the actors played their scenes. This doubled as a cinema screen and a symbol for the world, so that the events projected onto it were given historical and general implications beyond their geographic setting in Russia. Swivelling like a tank-turret, it also set the private lives of the characters in the mechanized context of modern warfare.

Communist critics claimed that the aesthetic nature of such experiments detracted from any revolutionary potential. But their assumption that the purpose of a Communist theatre should be short-term propaganda was far from Piscator's transformation of stage conventions to create a modern dramatic art – interpreting 'modern' as Marxist in his own defence. His subject matter, characterized by its global involvement, held the mirror up to the contemporary environment, and his machinery, which made the theatre capable of dealing with such material, reflected modern consciousness.

The use of machinery in *Economic Competition*

The major criticism of Piscator's work was that he abandoned literary communication without creating a sufficient substitute for dialogue from his machinery. Reducing the five-act play to a verbal sketch in order to expand its range of material on a visual level tended to destroy any logical sequence of action, and in Piscator's acting-scripts for more carefully constructed plays such as *Hoppla!* or *The Robbers* inconsistencies are frequent. This can be explained by the unsuitability of the dramas available, and *Economic Competition* is a test of his theories. Usually an apolitical subject had to be transformed into an ideological approach to 'actual' material. But this text, which Leo Lania wrote specifically for the Piscator-Bühne under Piscator's personal supervision, was modelled on his ideas of dramatic structure from the start, instead of having to be adapted from an 'artistic' style. The structure of the play was integrated with the scenery, which marked the progress of the action. During the course of the performance, which began with the bare boards of an empty stage, derricks and the complex machinery of an oilfield were progressively erected by the actors to make 'the material in all its substantiality and repercussions graphically visible through the construction of the set'.[42] 'The decoration' conveyed 'not only atmosphere, but also the content of the drama'.[43]

Economic Competition dealt with a subject of gigantic proportions – the seeds of war and the development of a popular revolutionary movement germinating from international business rivalry. This extrapolation from Communist theory was more abstract than the representation of events in *Rasputin*, and it lacked the Brobdingnagian character of Schweik which had held Hašek's sprawling epic together. It therefore needed a more tangible dramatic construction than any other of the plays Piscator produced. The visual aids had to be more elaborate than a simple symbol or a blackboard to illustrate events because the material was a hypothetical (although 'actual' under Piscator's definition) fiction, not a documented series of incidents. The action itself had to be expressed in the stage-construct in order to gain an adequate optical form for the centre of the incorporeal plot (critical international tension) and the anonymous subject (oil). This plastic form was gained by combining the evolving oil-derricks with a 'newspaper-page'.

The derricks stood for the wider issues of industrialization, as well as representing particular constructions erected in a single field in the backwoods of Albania, while the large-scale effects caused by individuals' actions on stage could be indicated through the publications of a press war between the different countries involved in the competition for oil. The front page format of different national newspapers was projected onto a gauze stretched over the proscenium opening to cover different sections of the acting area, so that the hostility of the prospectors in the wilds was graphically related to crises in the competing metropolitan chancellories. This physical skeleton translated the abstract political thesis into comprehensible and dramatic terms since 'events became graphically illustrated as in a school primer'.[44] As Brecht remarked, Piscator's 'anti-Aristotelian dramaturgy was designed to handle universal social conditions universally'.

Methods of generalization

Adapting machinery to handle a complex and extended series of events might be sufficient 'to break out of spatial limitations, to draw the imagination into the environment and to extend the action'.[45] But the substitution of a wider pattern of factual organization for the Aristotelian 'unity of action' could only be achieved on an imaginative level, because Piscator did not have access to the same resources as Meyerhold, who staged 'the storming of the Winter Palace' for the third anniversary of the October Revolution, using a cast of around 15,000, motor-cavalcades, siege-guns and the battle-ship *Aurora* which was anchored in the harbour. Meyerhold had used complete towns as his showplace taking audience-participation to its furthest extreme by employing the whole population as actors. If distancing and activation of the imagination are essential for aesthetic responses then the October Theatre can hardly be considered art, and even as spectacular re-enactions of history these performances had their limits – Meyerhold's plan to celebrate the Revolution in 1921 with 2,300 infantry, 200 cavalry, complete tank and artillery regiments, aeroplanes and motorbikes as well as orchestras and massed choirs proved to be unrealizable.

There was nothing novel about over-dimensional dramatic productions as such. In Rothenburg, for example, the saving of the town in the Thirty Years War has been acted out in the streets by the citizens every year for over two centuries and Piscator must have been aware of such traditions. *Despite All!* had originally been planned as a twelve-hour production calling for a cast of 2,000 and stage-properties over twenty metres long, but the revue, where his crowd scenes were judged to be one of the most effective aspects of the performance, was the nearest he came to realizing this elephantine dramatic conception. In the only film that he directed, an adaptation of Anna Segher's *The Revolt of the Fishermen*, he employed 12,000 Russian extras, but in the Piscator-Bühne any stretching of the unities of time and place was necessarily suggested rather than actual.

Artistic achievements are dependent on the limits imposed by the conventions of art forms. Design begins when pictures are fitted within a determined frame and, although a single figure in cave art may possess internal design, any more complex pattern must have spatial limitation as a condition of its development. Limited in materials, Piscator's attempts to break out of the physical fetters of the stage were illusory, and his productions therefore remain within the structural bounds that define the theatre as an art form. *Schweik* provides the best example. The double treadmill which ran parallel across the stage gave an artificial impression of the passage of time and a broad and varied spatial area. Scenery was carried across on one while Schweik marched parallel against the direction of the other and thus remained in the audience's view, so that the theatre itself seemed to move through the Bohemian landscape instead of representing arbitrarily limited sections of the characters' environment. At the same time the temporal sequence of the action could be varied by altering the relative speed of the treadmills. Machinery had overcome material limitations and 'a stretch, which can be crossed in ten paces, becomes the course of a whole life'.[46]

Another solution was Piscator's use of acting structures. Built under his direction, these were designed as political images, and their massive simplicity focused the audience's attention. As with the oil-derricks of *Economic Competition*, they expressed the essential content of a play in plastic terms, and ideally their architectural completeness made each 'a unique world in itself'.[47] Like the globe of *Rasputin* they were symbols, but normally more precise. The scenery was substituted for the 'sub-text' of a play, acting as a visual equivalent for the symbolic seagulls and cherry orchards, wild ducks and church-towers of the Naturalists, or as a crude alternative for the pattern of images in poetic drama. Thus the three-tiered stage of *The Merchant of Berlin* stood for the vertical hierachy of the social order, and the four-storied structure of the 'hotel' in *Hoppla!* was designed as a concrete image of the Weimar Republic where in the words of the theme song 'the herd / Of the Proletarians' in the cellar were visibly trampled on by the 'Cream of Society' who were the 'guests' above their heads.

It must be stressed that the visual elements of Piscator's productions were not decorative, but intended to be a concise channel of optical communication. The outline of the structure built for *Sail Ahoy* suggested a ship's decks and bridge, the acting construction for *Hoppla!* gave a physical illustration to Mehring's song, while others were obvious symbols. Yet all were openly canvas, wooden boards and iron scaffolding; and their intention was 'no longer just a decorative stage-picture, but a constructive stage. Purposeful building'.[48] Like all Piscator's experiments, these acting structures were valid in terms of 'theatre' – not only as symbols to hold a play together or as optical fables to explain its action. The structure of interlocking steps and platforms that Traugott Müller built for *Sail Ahoy* provided mobility, gave magnificent possibilities for movement and allowed single actors to dominate the stage easily by distinguishing themselves from groupings – advantages which were gained to a greater or lesser degree by all Piscator's scenery.

But although this visual emphasis had practical advantages, Piscator carried it beyond theatrical or theoretical necessity, and his romanticization of machinery undoubtedly played a part here. It was perfectly possible to gain many of the stage-effects for which Piscator constructed complex and cumbersome machines through traditional (and therefore less eye-catching) techniques. An illusion of movement similar to the treadmills, for instance, could be gained by mounting the cyclorama on vertical rollers, as in one theatrical scene of Prévert's film *Les Enfants du Paradis*, or more simply by stagehands carrying properties across the stage against a non-representational backdrop while the actors run on-the-spot facing in the opposite direction, as in Felsenstein's brilliant production of Offenbach's *Barbe-bleue* for the Berlin Komische Oper. The fluidity of scene change that the treadmills made possible has been gained by Felsenstein in his production of Britten's *Midsummer Night's Dream*, where flats are hung from the grid and can be moved across the stage from above in constantly changing combinations. Even the shift of viewpoint, which Piscator attributed to his introduction of film and placards, can be gained without any destruction of convention, as Anouilh's audience manipulation through contrasting moods in *Ardèle* shows. Right back to Aristophanes there are examples of the awakening of a critical attitude through the traditional means of selection, arrangement and emphasis. Piscator, however, was interested in adapting the theatre to conform to its environment – and both novelty and machinery are emblematic of the twentieth century:

I envisage something like a theatre-machine, as inherently technical as a typewriter, an apparatus which would be equipped with the most modern lighting-systems, with lifts and revolves in vertical and horizontal planes, with a multiplicity of film-projectors, with loud-speaker relays, etc.[49]

The normal machinery of the stage was not the only means of expansion. It was always used in conjunction with film, which was the most striking and therefore the dominating element of Piscator's production, dwarfing the actors who appeared static against the moving scenery of the screen. It attracted disproportionate interest, not only as a novelty in the context of the theatre but also because the audience's attention was constantly directed towards fact – and film acted as immediate and objective documentation. In *Schweik* the effectiveness of the treadmills in extending the imaginative sphere of the stage and the importance given to the projection of grotesque cartoons reduced the film to a naturalistic background, but in earlier productions it was used to give social 'period portraits' and even as 'substitute scenes'.[50] In *Tidal Wave* the film revealed the widespread consequences of actions decided on the stage and showed distant events that had a bearing on the

plot. In the first scene, for instance, after the characters had discussed blowing up a dam to flood the town a film of waterlogged
landscape and flooded streets was projected onto the screen; elsewhere in the play a radio report of revolution in China was accompanied by a film of Chinese mass-demonstrations, and a speech by
Lloyd George over the loudspeaker was synchronized with a film of
Lloyd George addressing voters. In other scenes the screen acted
as an extension of the stage instead of being inserted into the action,
as when the leader of the revolutionaries fled into the wings and a
film sequence showed him galloping away into the forests, or when
a few actors representing a multitude were filled out with a film of
crowds congested onto the screen behind them. This method of en-
larging the apparent spatial area of the stage was paralleled by a
prolongation of the action in *Storm over Gottland*, where the film
gave contemporary relevance to the fifteenth-century plot by
depicting the development of social revolution from the uprising
in the medieval Hansastadt to the Communist movements in
Russia, China and Germany on the date of the performance. The
opposite effect was gained in *Hoppla!*, where the film widened the
scale of reference for a present-day action by drawing historical
parallels. This technique of visual amplification dominated the production of *Rasputin*. For obvious reasons the full title of the play,
*Rasputin, the Romanoffs, the War and the People, who Rose up
against Them*, was never used. But – as it clearly indicates – the plot
contains four distinct centres of interest: a central figure, a family
of individual characters, a spectacular action outside the control of
any individual, and a group of faceless extras cast in the anonymous rôle of a historical force. By splitting the various strands of
action between stage and screen Piscator managed to expand the
material and balance these divergent interests without losing pace
or cohesion. Rasputin was a gigantic shadow of doom projected onto
a gauze, the actors on stage represented the Romanoffs, the German and Austrian Kaisers and any figures important enough to be
mentioned by name in historical records, while the film presented
the realities of war and the revolutionary masses, 'the people who
rose up against them'. In one scene in the Winter Palace, for
example, the Czarina repudiates reports of mutiny and civil violence – simultaneously pictures of the Red troops storming the
palace victoriously a few months later moves across the screen.

The stage portrayed individuals, particular actions and personal illusions; the film showed society, historical events and the world outside the wings.

Generalization remained a constant characteristic of Piscator's style, and can be seen at its simplest in the 1952 production of Lessing's *Nathan the Wise,* where Nathan's lament for his seven sons was illustrated by the projection: '7 – 70 – 700 – 7,000 – 70,000 – 700,000 × 7 – all my sons'. This 'elevation of the scenic into the historical'[51] through his use of machinery and film made it possible for Piscator to handle the 'intricate complexities of contemporary subject matter' on a large scale; and by giving a comprehensive picture of economic and political patterns he was able to portray such sociological abstractions as 'Capitalism' or 'the Class Struggle' comprehensibly.

Claiming to be a 'historical materialist'[52] Piscator did use the commonplaces of Communist theory as a tool to explain social events, but to say that imaginative expansion made his productions 'Marxist stage-works'[53] was an overstatement. He liked to cite the apparent similarity of Meyerhold's style as evidence that political beliefs determined technique, and claimed that his mechanization of the stage depended on a 'commitment to social revolution'.[54] The association of 'intellectual and social revolution' with an 'intellectual revolutionizing' of the theatre is legitimate. Scientific advances alter the relationship of the individual to society at the same time as providing new techniques to present the changed conditions on the stage – so that theatrical innovations and fresh political ideologies ultimately come from the same source. Yet there is no direct relation between stylistic qualities and political theories. In spite of the way that Piscator was accustomed to place artistic styles in political categories, the propaganda experts of both extremes realized that there was nothing specifically Marxist about his techniques. The K.P.D. viewed his work with suspicion, and Goebbels even made Piscator the offer (transmitted to him while he was in Russia by Gordon Craig) of a post under the Nazis, which – needless to say – he refused.

Bronnen's *Rhineland Rebels,* produced in 1925 by Jessner, treated the French occupation of the Ruhr with the same techniques of 'headline' projection and draping the stage with flags at the end of the play that Piscator had used in *Flags* – but the flag here was the black–red–gold of the Republic. Similarly, the play *Schlageter*, first performed after Hitler had taken power, glorified a right-wing terrorist as a martyred hero even while it corresponded to all the formal definitions of Documentary Drama. The 'theatre of involvement' (*Zeittheater*) created by Piscator was taken over by the Fascists, who adopted his supposedly Marxist criteria and 'proletarian' theatrical concepts by substituting 'the intrinsic meaning and the effects resulting from it' for aesthetic factors in a drama where 'the emotions, thoughts, beliefs and hopes of a people [were brought] to the most palpable expression and created the possibility of the most immediate communal experience'.[55] This (apart from the radically different 'beliefs and hopes' fostered by the Nazis and the substitution of 'a people' for 'the people') is almost a précis of Piscator's statements about his Total Theatre – although the vagueness of the Fascist message ('expressive forms of the essence bound by blood and soil – *Blut und Boden*' – etc.) led in practice to emotionalism, romantic pathos and a vicious use of superlatives that Piscator avoided through the 'objectivity' of his style. Yet the fact remains that Piscator's association of a mechanical style of production with the treatment of broad socio-logical questions, like his rejection of aesthetic criteria, can be used to support almost any view of contemporary affairs.

His techniques were tools, political only in the wider, non-party meaning of the word. His theme, like that outlined by the Theatre Workshop, in the 1945 Manifesto, was 'the great events of our time, wars, political upheavals, the frustration of man's social desires'. But the small scale of the ordinary stage turns such im-mense happenings into abstractions, and the theatre demands concrete actions. Piscator's machinery was a means of realizing this global vision, for in a normal play, as his contemporaries were aware, 'war, capitalism and revolution can only be spoken of. Piscator's whole course is a battle for clarity. He wished to portray War and Capitalism themselves. It was therefore a completely logical consequence that he transposed film into the theatre.'[56]

The function of stage machinery

Piscator's machinery also had a more fundamental purpose. Art interprets our environment and gives meaning to our lives by ordering the intensely felt personal present into a comprehensive vision that embraces the past and future. This imaginative configuration of reality is constantly modified by the impression of new experiences which alters artistic conventions. However, when technological advances outpace the artist's capacity to assimilate change then cultural values become fragmented, and the artistic structuring of reality loses its relevance. This can be seen in various periods – notably the Jacobean and Romantic – but the problem has become acute in the twentieth century with the consequence that attention is focused on phenomena, on the process of change itself, instead of attempting to evaluate the results of progress. Piscator was aware of the effect on art: 'The lack of any great literary works, which express the forces and problems of this age in their totality, is no accident but the consequence of the complexity, disruption, incompleteness of the present.'[57]

In expressing this complexity literature has become intricate and dissonant. But this is not possible for the theatre, where the limitations of performance demand structural simplicity and the audience (unlike a reader) cannot pause for reflection or turn back to a previous passage for comparison. So modern playwrights who have felt the need to do more than entertain – to communicate any perception of 'the permanent and universal' – have normally adopted the formal ordering principles of poetry, myth or ritual in order to weave particular facts and individual references into a web of universal relationships. But such stylistic devices falsify reality. Adapted from dead or alien traditions, they are divorced from modern European conditions. Their artificiality is emphasized by Marxist literary criticism, which denies that the 'eternal verities' of the past or the styles that express those values have relevance out of their particular historical context. Piscator therefore used the machinery of his industrial environment to structure his perception of reality. The technology that determined the society he attempted to represent on the stage became the ordering principle of his art as well as a method of representing reality.

This fascination with technology was characteristic of artistic movements in the early 1920s. English Vorticism represented man as a mechanized figure enclosed in a geometrical carapace, the Italian Futurists unequivocally adopted all aspects of applied science as their subjects, and Georges Antheil composed an aeroplane sonata. Enrico Prampolini envisaged an abstract 'theatre of mechanics' – a concept which the Bauhaus put into practice – and Meyerhold replaced scenery with stylized machinery, using cogs and wheels which revolved impressively but were not designed to drive anything, and constructing catwalks and scaffoldings which had no practical function. The progressive attitudes associated with this technology were widely identified with the Russian Revolution, and the Dnieper Dam and the Soviet Electrification Plans were theme-songs for Communist-oriented art (as in Funarov's *Fire Sermon*). Piscator's mechanization, however, went deeper than a reflection of propaganda-themes or a portrayal of the spirit of the age in idealized terms.

Behind his concentration on machinery lies the consciousness that technology determines man's estimate of himself and the intuition that the manner in which information is imparted affects the mentality of the recipient more than any single message which can be communicated. And in this his practice strikingly anticipated the theories of Marshall McLuhan. Piscator's mechanization of the stage was a means of perception, as is clearly shown in a scene that he wrote into *Hoppla!* where a symbol of humanity, defined by a heart-beat, was presented as a machine dependent on machinery:

RADIO-OPERATOR. The first New York–Paris passenger flight is calling...a passenger has had a heart-attack, heart-specialists are requested. They want medical advice. There, now you're listening to the heart-beat of the patient.
FILM. *The Human Machine.*
LOUDSPEAKER. *Heart-beats.*
PROJECTION. *The Airplane Over the Ocean. Pumping Heart* [This was an x-ray picture].
THOMAS. A man's heart-beat above the middle of the ocean!
RADIO-OPERATOR. The cat's whiskers.
THOMAS. How wonderful all this is! And what do men do with it! They behave like sheep a thousand years out of date!

The sound of heart-beats filling the auditorium was reported to be the most striking single stage effect in the production, but the way Piscator employed technology here points to a romanticism of the mechanical which was a constant threat to the integrity of his work. This tendency was emphasized in *Hoppla!* by the cutting of

Toller's scene between a philosopher and the radio-operator, where the destructive capabilities of modern science were discussed.

It is interesting to compare the mechanical nature of Piscator's work in the 1920s with McLuhan's modern sociological theories. McLuhan identifies 'the private fixed point of view' with literary ('sequential') habits of thought calling for critical detachment. His thesis is that modern technology (in particular 'electronic circuitry') has destroyed the perspective of the Renaissance and Augustan *Weltanschauung* which separated the individual from events and gave the single man unique value. Contemporary media have cut across the time-lag imposed by printing, making any reaction to events immediate and fusing men into a global group. Radio and television present a total picture, which is multiple and simultaneous, using all the senses in place of the purely visual and therefore sequential process of reading, which has formed our concept of logical ('linear') methods of thought. This is appropriate to the environment created by modern machinery, which compels commitment and participation, because 'the instantaneous world of electric informational media involves all of us, all at once. No detachment of frame is possible.'[58]

Piscator's emphasis on immediacy, actuality and generalization, audience-involvement, technology and the new mechanical means of communication reduced the rôle of verbal logic. And the visual emphasis of his productions, together with his exploitation of emotion at the expense of the rational intellect, makes his experiments a perfect theatrical correlative to McLuhan's theories about the optical, subliminal kind of communication to which men are susceptible in the modern technological age of 'electronic interdependence'. Apart from the illogicality of McLuhan's style (itself intended as a demonstration of his message), some of Piscator's statements are interchangeable with those of the high-priest of electronic media. Anticipating McLuhen by over thirty years, Piscator was vividly conscious that his audience could contact America on the radio, read about yesterday's events in Bavaria in their newspapers or watch last week's earthquake in Japan on the news-reels:

Technology has made the earth small. But this has brought about a fusion at the same time. No one can hold himself aloof any more or shut his eyes to problems, even when they do not touch him personally. The whole of humanity has gained a quality of instantaneity...[Modern] man carries a picture of the world within him, and not one from last year, but the picture of the world as it is at this minute.[59]

For Piscator, as for McLuhan, the audience had therefore to feel directly involved in the action with all their senses, while teamwork was the essence of artistic creation instead of individual authorship. Piscator normally explained these collectivistic aspects of his work by reference to Marxist theories, but they undoubtedly took on such major importance in his productions because he felt they reflected the true nature of modern life. It is significant that the only basic difference between the standpoints of these two observers, who view society from such apparently opposing political angles, should be one of emphasis. Where McLuhan deals with literature, and therefore stresses the importance of the ear since for him man has been trained by the printing-press to think in purely visual terms, Piscator lays emphasis on the eye because in the German theatre the importance given to the Classics and traditional productions had over-emphasized the literary quality of drama – which on the stage is speech.

5 Epic Theatre: the Actor and the Structure

The medium is more important than the message in the sense that statements are conditioned by their formulation since meaning exists only in terms of its expression; and the use of machinery as an objective correlative for the technological complexity of the age is of less potential value to the modern theatre than its functional possibilities. To take contemporary conditions or incidents from the immediate past for subjects is no innovation. The basis of Documentary Drama is not the material but the objective manner, the ability to reveal the vital issues beneath events. Since historical circumstances are transient, facts – however interesting – only have lasting value as evidence to document the laws governing social phenomena.

Abstraction and precision

Piscator's drama was oriented towards fact, and this inevitably emphasized superficial appearances. But his aim was to depict 'historical forces'[1] and a major part of his experimental energies was directed to solving the problem of gaining a universal scale of reference.

Generalization entailed substituting 'the most comprehensive possible unrolling of the epoch from its roots to its final consequences' for 'the internal curve of a [conventional] dramatic plot'[2] – and this substitution tended to fragment a comprehensive picture into episodic incidents and posed the problem of imposing balance and unity on the decentralized action. The Expressionists had faced the same difficulty in their *Stationen* plays where the action was divided into self-contained scenes on the analogy to the stations of the cross. But their solution of replacing the traditional framework of cause and effect with a psychological pattern of subconscious relationships was unsuited to dealing with large-scale events since it focused exclusively on the individual. In addition it had proved too static to be theatrically successful.

Instead of intellectual organization, Piscator created physical images to hold together the amorphous and extensive collections of facts that formed the subjects of his documentary dramas. He centred his productions around the acting-structures, forming each into a 'concept' (*die Idee*) which was external to the action and unconnected with the characters, while film and loudspeakers extended the range of subject matter that could be directly represented on the stage. But these solutions tended to separate the elements of drama into discrete entities, like pieces of a jigsaw that have no representational identity. Theoretically Documentary Drama should be a collection of existing objects akin to the art of Duchamps or Rauschenberg, whose pictures incorporated clocks or a working wireless-set, or presented a pissoir to the public's attention. In practice, however, it was nearer to the assemblage of existing clichés employed by modern Pop artists, who take nudes from photographs in *Playboy* and copy battle-scenes from comic-strips. The use of mass media in this way drains the apparently real of power to communicate reality, and this side effect was reinforced by the 'factual' simplicity of speech that Piscator had imposed and by his 'objective' acting-technique. In addition, the image on which the production centred was not particularized, since the stage-constructs were used for different scenes and so could only suggest general location. They were primarily three-dimensional shapes, and even the functional machines visible on stage were designed to give an impression of mechanization in the abstract. Thus the extension of the scale itself, while intended to show sociological cause and effect, bringing 'history' out of the background to make it the centre of interest as 'political reality', in fact threatened to remove all significance from actual events re-enacted on the stage.

Piscator was conscious of the dangers of abstraction, and set a 'factual' manner of representation against the vagueness and imprecision that was implicit in his monumental subject matter, carrying over the simplicity, directness and lack of sentiment from his earlier Agitprop work. This was also a reason for the dominant rôle of his stage-machinery: 'The attempt to apply technological means is none other than the search for the clearest form of expression by finding the shortest way to communicate.'[3] The alteration of texts to correspond to the language of journalism by stripping any 'inessential' words that did not directly advance the action was an aspect of this objective plainness which however reinforced the impression of abstraction. Speeches became generalized as 'slogan or cry'[4] while the characters were stereotyped by cutting all psychologically revealing or lyrical speeches. This removed the appeal to any but the simplest of emotions. Simplicity thus led, sometimes deliberately, to simplification: 'from the outset, from the first sentence on I aim at comprehension, analysis, clarity, simplicity and, when necessary in order to reach understanding, at simplification'.[5] In the 1926 production of *The Robbers*, for instance, the excision of 'all humorous and rascally arabesques'[6] reduced Karl and Spiegelberg to the standardized silhouettes of the 'emotional revolutionary' and the 'intellectual revolutionary'. Exactly the same generalization recurred in the main characters of *Storm over Gottland*.

To offset this abstraction Piscator emphasized factual minutiae. The more universal the subject, the more detailed the documentation became – and the greater the volume of evidence, the more machinery had to be used for communication. Film, of course, was the primary means of compressing information: extending the action of *Storm over Gottland* by six centuries in as many minutes, or summarizing the events of eight years as a prologue for *Hoppla!*. A list of over 400 political, cultural, economic, social and sporting events was compiled for this film overture, which presented scenes and photographs to illustrate all of them within a bare seven minutes. Dealing with centuries, global movements and a cast of millions in approximately two hours and some one hundred and thirty square yards demanded a high level of precision in text, acting and production. His deployment of facts on an epic scale caused unusual problems of organization. A shorthand technique equivalent to that of film had to be developed for the stage, and the first essential was a unifying structural principle. Only then could every aspect of a production be sufficiently controlled 'to create a theatre which is a flexible enough instrument to give expression to our *Weltanschauung*'.[7]

Dramatic structure: simultaneous stages

As a symbol the stage-construct of the hotel for *Hoppla!* was considered to be a stronger protest against contemporary social conditions than Toller's text. Yet its primary function as a central image was to replace the logical continuum of the traditional plot with a series of visual connections. Providing Piscator with a multiple simultaneous stage, it could be used to order sequences in temporal and spatial terms instead of relying on dialogue to move the action. In place of a series of distinct scenes acted consecutively, where characters can only speak to each other and must react directly to the words and actions of all the others present, groups and individuals in their separate acting areas (enclosed in this case to form various 'rooms') acted in isolation. They were related only by a spotlight moving from the radio-operator's attic to the banker's suite, to the servant's cellar, returning to the radio-operator and back to the banker. Relationships could thus be shown that were not explicit in the text and of which the characters were unaware. The 'Chorus of Inhabitants' (like the heads in Beckett's *Play*) could be fitted into a wider pattern than their immediate motives, since they acted as marionettes who depended on beams of light instead of strings for their ability to move and speak. In such circumstances the actors play parts determined by a *deus ex machina*, the director or author, who is free to alter the order of scenes because the connections between them are external to the actions of individuals. This reduction of the characters to automata was taken to its logical conclusion when Piscator substituted animated puppets for part of the cast in *Schweik*. With this external control, montage (as in film) dictates the direction and progress of the action[8] – and this made it possible for the individuals and events portrayed on the stage to be 'subordinated to the concept, which presides over and relates everything'.[9] The treadmills in *Schweik* acted in a similar way, linking events by physical movement rather than dramatic necessity. Piscator could substitute a central image for the Aristotelian unities, which he considered outdated since they were 'technically' determined by the limitations of the Greek theatre and these had been overcome by progress, allowing new methods of organization.

Positioning on the stage can structure actions by visual means alone, and the same function was served by turning the normal time sequence of performance into the perpetual dramatic present. Cause and effect could be connected simultaneously by overlaying the actions of the characters with the results portrayed on the screen. Scenes which were remote in time or distant in space could be acted out together on a divided stage area. The technique was similar to that of the early miracle plays where the action could encompass Heaven and Hell and range from Genesis to the Last Judgement. Even for Credé's play, § *218*, produced during the depths of Piscator's bankruptcy, rehearsed in a rented room and performed on tour in 1930, a stage-within-a-stage was constructed in order to divide the acting area into two – the minimum requirement for the physical comparison or visual contrast of different scenes. Piscator's productions in the Volksbühne and during the two years of the Piscator-Bühne were more elaborate and needed a correspondingly intricate visual organization. As early as 1926 Piscator used such complex devices as a double revolve in *The Drunken Ship*, where a *prisma* of projection screens was erected on a small revolving stage, which rotated counter to a larger one beneath it – and the actors, who used both areas, were swung into the audience's range of vision already playing their scenes. The *Hoppla!* construct was the most complicated. It provided eight separate spaces for film or action as well as the stage area outside it, and the front was covered by a gauze while the backcloth acted as a screen so that both could be used for projection, and photographs could overlay or reinforce the composite scene or any particular facet of it. Distinctive social backgrounds could be provided for the different social groups, while the relationships between conflicting political factions could be indicated. Causal and temporal relationships could be discarded, and positioning used to integrate scenes where Piscator had altered their meaning or their place in the original plot.

This effect of the simultaneous stage was reinforced by Piscator's use of film to modify the relative position of object and observer through close-up or movement. The screen illuminated characters and their actions from standpoints independent of the play. It was used to illustrate the factual contradiction between the personal illusions of the characters and the true nature of the events in which they were involved, and showed either the historical panorama surrounding the stage action or revealed details passed over in the speeches. In *Hoppla!* for instance, films of processions and parades of earlier potentates formed an oblique criticism of

Kilmann's ministerial attitudes. Alternatively in *Rasputin* Foch and Haig bickered over their battle-plans against a film background of the slaughter on the Somme, or the Czar gave a bird's-eye survey of the Eastern Front while the screen showed pictures of dead soldiers in shell-holes, in the trenches, on the barbed wire. By combining film and stage Piscator could also arbitrarily juxtapose events which were separated historically and geographically, or draw relationships between single men and social forces, in order to find 'a harmony...where everything re-echoes, and art, life, politics become identical'.[10] This reciprocal action of film and stage was attacked by the left-wing press as a split between content and form.[11] At the time Piscator claimed it to be the visible sign of dialectical thought processes, but freed from political pressure he later quoted sociologists to support its universal nature:

Everything that is immediate, contemporary, integrated with the present moment possesses a particular meaning and value for the people of today...their mental world is atuned to actuality and simultaneity, as that of the Middle Ages was to eternity and that of the Enlightenment to the future. They experience [their world]...in the juxtaposition, in the unity and interconnection of objects and actions.[12]

Techniques of commentary: the development of Epic Theatre

A significant aspect of Piscator's experimentation was his practice of adapting novels to produce 'episodes of the age' (*Stücke der Zeit*) instead of formal plays. *Schweik* (1928) and the adaptation of Plievier's *The Kaiser's Coolies* (1930) were followed by *War and Peace* (1942) and by stage versions of Dreiser's *American Tragedy* (1943), Robert Penn Warren's *All The King's Men* (1948), Sartre's *Iron in the Soul* (1953) and Romain Rolland's *Robespierre* (1963). This plot-poaching from non-theatrical works was not simply due to a shortage of suitable dramatic material. The novel already possessed many of the qualities Piscator looked for in the theatre: in particular the ability to alter the perspective or give an independent viewpoint at will and so to control the reader's judgement – which made a satisfactory treatment of sweeping vistas of fact possible. Piscator designated this quality as 'epic' and defined it as an approach which 'not only portrays the dramatic action, but also describes what social and political conditions determine modern fate'.[13] Modern critics tend to emphasize the formal elements that are the equivalent of such techniques as projection and film, the development of the simultaneous stage and the use of choruses and commentators, when describing epic drama. It is distinguished from traditional plays by the autonomy of independent scenes, and Büchner's *Woyzeck* is commonly given as the 'classical' example of 'Open Theatre'. But in Piscator's work the epic forms are clearly conditional and the approach is the determining factor, since his techniques were no more than experimental responses to a general concept of theatre and a critique of society. Epic forms are merely practical theatrical solutions to the problems of production raised by plays which 'correspond to the sociological situation in their content as in their style'.[14] These discussed the subjects and examined the actions of traditional drama. Man-in-action therefore became an object-on-stage instead of a subject, and interest was centred on the economic and social basis of events instead of the personal motives and the effects on individuals. This is a natural extension of Aristotle's definition of 'epic' as a narrative form describing 'a number of simultaneous incidents'. Audience manipulation through the juxtaposition of contrasting impressions is essential for communicating such a complex vision, and this can be compared to Empson's fourth type of ambiguity where two or more discongruous meanings are combined to clarify a higher or more complicated truth. 'Alienation effects' are a development of rhetoric – according to T. S. Eliot's definition: 'where a character in a play sees himself in a dramatic light' – and the destruction of naturalistic illusion is the outward sign of the introduction of irony to the stage.

Döblin announced the transformation of the theatre into 'the intermediate area of Drama-Novel' as early as 1924 in his criticism of *Flags* (which Paquet had hopefully subtitled 'an epic play') on the ground that the material of drama was traditionally human figures, while here – as in the novel – the focus was on facts. This was premature. Paquet's plot was melodramatic rather than objective, and the only form of commentary that Piscator was able to introduce at that stage of his career were 'headlines' projected over each scene. These captions were simplistic exclamations and could only be employed in two ways; to underline – as in the trial-scene where a caption announced CONDEMNED TO DEATH! – or to explain – as when a caption claimed that THE POLICE THREW THE BOMBS THEMSELVES, although the previous scene had shown the anarchists manufacturing the explosives.

Piscator's concept of an 'epic' treatment of events remained unrealizable until he introduced the simultaneous stage and exploited the potential of film to comment on the stage action as well as to extend its dimensions. In the Piscator-Bühne film could be shown on a backdrop, on the surfaces of the stage-construct or on an additional screen hung above the proscenium. Smaller screens were also set on either side of the stage and could be lowered from the flies for the projection of stills, statistics, captions or quotations, thus creating various poles within a production which could be played off against one another. This made it possible for Piscator to comment on the play through the film, or on the film through the projection – or on any facet of the production through different combinations of the three elements. The placard and the written word could, for example, present a different level of reality to both the celluloid and the acted scene, although normally texts were projected onto the small screen to reinforce the effect of the film. Where the film was dramatic, functioning as a 'substitute scene' instead of being documentary, the projection-screens either replaced the stage as the artificial pole of the production or could comment objectively on the film. In the Foch–Haig scene of *Rasputin*, where the film depicted the murderous results of the generals' grandiose strategy, a text emphasized their incompetence by underlining the futility and waste of the slaughter on the Somme with statistics: 'Loss – half a million dead: Gain – 120 square miles.'[15] Above a photograph of Russian corpses, on the other hand, the text represented the Czar's viewpoint and quoted from a letter to the Czarina as a contrast to the picture: 'The life that I lead at the head of my army is healthy and has an invigorating effect.'

The simultaneous stage, originally developed like film as a means of expansion, was also turned into a technique for interpretation. By the simple method of designating the various acting areas as different strata of existence the characters could play their rôles both as historical figures and private individuals. Stepping onto the 'stage of fate' (*Schicksalsbühne*)[16] that was always set apart by level or by distinctive lighting, they became agents of historical forces. When they returned to sections of the stage where drawing-room chairs, a lamp-post, cell-bars or a throne indicated normal surroundings they reverted to their everyday, limited consciousness and re-covered their personal characteristics. The multiple possibilities of the stage-construct for *Rasputin* proved particularly suitable for this purpose, and Piscator used the same scenic form in *The Officers' Uprising* because

the 'global stage' allowed me to show the World War in its internal and external relationship to men, for example, while simultaneously demonstrating its political and economic effect on society. Thus the sequence of vital and fundamental situations appeared on the main stage level, while the personal, sexual, anecdotal stories, which in the main provide the reason why people go to the theatre, played on the side stages or in the [opening] segments [of the globe].[17]

On the 'stage of fate' events could be given a different scale or figures could step out of their rôles to comment on the wider implications of their actions – like Pierre in *War and Peace*, who both took part in the battles and demonstrated tactics with toy soldiers, or acted as a lecturer ('I must tell you about it, the whole story of War and Peace'). Alternatively, like Napoleon who revealed himself as an agent of destiny in speaking about his dreams of conquest, this device allowed an actor to demonstrate the historical significance of a character's actions in a context where conventional soliloquies would have seemed jarringly artificial. With this type of framework any plot could be given specific relevance, and the miniature world of the stage could show the global significance of political events without sacrificing personal interest. So the figure of the story-teller, the compère, reappeared in Piscator's work, integrated in the complex machinery. In § *218*, Dreiser's *American Tragedy* and *War and Peace*, the commentator was also a character, and his rôle alternated between involvement in the plot and direct addresses to the public. As an intermediary between the stage action and the world of the audience his position was the same as that of the 'Bourgeois' and 'Prole' figures in *The Red Revue*. Not content with this, however, Piscator also experimented with a formal prologue in *Flags*, in which the play was declared to be a 'puppet-show'. Alternatively, for his production of *The Kaiser's Coolies* when he had to make do with minimal machinery, he introduced a 'Master of Ceremonies' who drew diagrams of the action on a blackboard, and in a later production of *War and Peace* he replaced Pierre's rôle as a commentator by a proper ' "Narrator" in the middle of the stage'. Throughout his career Piscator experimented with a wide variety of mouth pieces, and by different permutations of these techniques he developed the ability to alter the tone at will which allowed a subtle presentation of complex material.

Theoretically, this introduction of interpretation and commentary should have an anti-illusionistic effect equivalent to Brecht's theatrical alienation (the notorious *Verfremdungseffekt*) because it breaks stage conventions. Drama is traditionally viewed as an art form which, like the visual arts, cannot comment openly on its material except by using techniques that destroy any suggestion of reality since they are dissociated from the central work. Piscator and Brecht shared much the same definition of Epic Theatre, and Piscator acknowledged that 'Brecht was correct when he demanded that we should be confronted with the action and not involved in it through empathy'.[18] In Piscator's productions when actors stepped out of their rôles to speak directly to the audience or projections were used to explain the action, this was very close to 'alienation' in Brecht's sense, although Piscator rejected his concept on the grounds that 'Brecht's "alienation" rests on the Classical Oriental theatre, which romanticizes the concept'.[18a] But Piscator never took the decisive step of making his cast consciously demonstrate an action instead of enacting it. His rejection of the concept of personality did shift the centre of a play to the portrayal of its factual subject, and the screen did criticize the characters and their actions from standards independent of the drama – but the commentary never intruded within the action or influenced its outcome. Just as the sailors in *The Kaiser's Coolies* disregarded the figure of the narrator who pointed out the course of the Battle of the Skagerrak on his blackboard, so the Czarina in *Rasputin* remained ostensibly unaware of her future fate at the hands of the successful revolutionaries, as shown on the screen above her head. That at least was Piscator's intention, even if he occasionally underestimated the effect of film. Tilla Durieux, who played the Czarina, recalls that at this point in the production the impression of the juxtaposition of her words with the later reality was so overwhelming that it forced her out of character: 'I petrified in my rôle.' However, apart from such involuntary effects the story-telling techniques were kept out-

side the conventions of the stage even though the narrators and
cinema-screens shared the same visual area, so that Piscator gained
the advantages of Epic Theatre without sacrificing dramatic illusion.
The world of the actors remained formally enclosed, but the representation was no longer limited spatially, temporally or in action to
a single unit. Sequences were replaced with a synchronous action
giving the material an optical shape instead of a logical development, and this affected the rôle of the actor since the techniques of
commentary blurred the distinction between illusion and reality.

Film and stage: realism and illusion

The introduction of film into a stage performance was Piscator's
decisive innovation, and it distinguishes his work from both the
earlier 'epic' drama of Büchner and such previous 'documentary'
works as Emil Ludwig's play about Bismarck. Only one of Piscator's productions after 1925, *What Price Glory?*, was performed
without the aid of a cinema or projection-screen – and in this case
a full film version of the play had already been shown in Germany.
Piscator extended his use of film from background to 'substitute
scenes'. Film sequences expanded the action, documented it, commented on it and even regulated the tempo – instead of remaining a
subordinate part of his production they determined its effect. Not
only were figures on the screen normally larger than the actors on
the stage but the novelty of film in the context of the theatre made it
immediately striking, while the actors appeared static and artificial
in contrast to the definition and constant movement of the camera.

Film is a separate medium with its own artistic laws, as was early
realized in Germany, where it was commonly distinguished from
theatre as an 'extensive' rather than 'intensive' re-creation of
reality, denotative rather than connotative. There are two major
schools of thought about the relative reality and illusion of film and
stage. Allardyce Nicoll, like the German critics of the 1920s, defines
film as a primarily realistic medium, forcing the stage into a deliberately anti-illusionistic avoidance of actuality. Eric Bentley, on
the other hand, comes to the conclusion that film is suitable for
poetic fantasy, while naturalistic representation is the true field of
the stage, because the theatre is three-dimensional and real,
although limited in time and space, while the cinema is only two-

dimensional and an image, but can range freely. In the Weimar Republic, however, when moving pictures were still a novelty and the harsh lighting needed for primitive photographic equipment demanded absolute verisimilitude, the dominant impression was one of accuracy, and the primary value of the camera as far as Piscator was concerned was that it presented art with a new relationship to reality – a characteristic which was emphasized when film was used in conjunction with the artificial conventions of the stage. Diebold compared Piscator's technique of splicing film into the texture of a play with the conventions of Greek drama – noting that film as 'the *modern* chorus' defined the wider associations of the action in an overtly objective manner. But where the classical chorus was heavily stylized and the contrast with the main actors made the characters appear more true to life, Piscator's film (being the realistic element) emphasized the artificiality of stage acting.

It was natural for the Germans to consider film and stage as contrasting media, since their theatrical tradition emphasized artifice. Reinhardt's aim was to create an imaginary world which should be completely illusory, Jessner specialized in symbolism, and various theoreticians demanded ritualistic conventions – Indian puppets, Greek masks or the *Noh* style. In the aftermath of military defeat, political upheaval and economic depression, the theatre provided a temporary escape from 'the flatness of reality'. In this, as in other aspects of the Weimar era, things were taken to extremes – a potentially creative attitude since it cleared away compromises; and in this case it spotlit the premises of dramatic art.

Unreality is always present on the traditional stage, although Naturalism (the dominant theatrical form from Ibsen on) has done its best to disguise this fact. Scenery is always representational; the action – set in an environment outside the theatre building – can never do more than re-enact events, particularly if it is historical or imaginary; and the actor's art, however naturalistic, is based on shared pretence, constantly recognizing the presence of spectators and using their co-operation. Even when the audience have been persuaded into 'a willing suspension of disbelief', they remain subconsciously aware that the burning orphanage in *Ghosts* is an effect of stage lighting, just as they know that Mozart's avenging statue is a singer not a supernatural apparition. No one telephones for the fire-brigade, or calls for bell, book and candle. They distinguish automatically between an actor and the character he represents, gaining indirect pleasure from the actor's imitative skills and from the aesthetic patterning of a complete action, conscious that those who are 'killed' on stage will be on their feet to take their curtain-calls. As Stoppard points out in *Rosencrantz and Guildenstern are Dead*, it is precisely the theatricality of a performance that makes it convincing. It is no accident that a dramatic work is called a 'play'. Restricting illusion to the suggestion of reality demands the exercise, or play, of the imagination which Shakespeare appeals to in the Prologue to *Henry V*; and Melchinger has based his theatrical theories on the perception that drama's powers of suggestion lie specifically 'in the tension between being and appearance'.

Film, on the other hand, uses real materials for its background or sets built to correspond to reality in all visible particulars. The dockside of *On the Waterfront* was constructed of bricks and mortar and complete in every detail – not suggested to the imagination by paint on a backdrop. The *Potemkin* was the actual battleship – not, as in Piscator's production of *Sail Ahoy*, a rostrum surrounded by steps and platforms and decorated with hanging ropes symbolizing a ship's decks and bridge. House-fronts may be two-dimensional façades, the desert outside a town may in fact lie half a continent away; but the machinery of illusion in film-making is kept beyond the range of the cameras, cut out, or concealed by trick photography. There is no appeal to suspend incredulity since it is presumed that the camera can never lie. The actions and motives of the personae tend to command a readier belief because they are associated with concrete surroundings. The camera, acting as a recording eye, is independent of its audience, and because (unlike the stage) it is not chained to the present time and place of performance the spectators have no touchstone to separate reality from appearance.

This cinematic effect of actuality was emphasized in Piscator's productions, since most of the film he used at first was known to be official documentary. The photographs of the Flanders trenches projected in *Despite All!* were records of reality and the soldiers were in no sense 'playing'. Then when Piscator set up a complete section in his theatre workshop under the direction of Hübler-Kahla to shoot film specially for productions, sequences were closely modelled on documentaries in order to retain the advantages of historicity and objectivity. Not until *Rasputin* did Piscator borrow from commercial films, and even in his later productions he went to unusual lengths to gain authenticity, sending a camera-crew to Prague for *Schweik* and requesting a documentary from Moscow for *Tai Yang Awakes*.

Piscator had no intention of presenting 'the elevated tragedy of some hero or other, but the political document of an epoch'[19] – and because it was the function of the film, with its apparent objectivity, to demonstrate the wider context of the dramatic action, the play itself became reduced to the status of a sub-plot. Film was seen as 'the keystone. This war-film...determined the atmosphere, it was the immediate element.'[20] Piscator's stage therefore became a three-dimensional extension of the screen, whose impression of actuality was transmitted to it. Owing to the documentation, stage deaths (such as the re-enaction of the murder of Rosa Luxemburg in *Despite All!*) or stage horrors (such as the march of corpses and cripples in *Schweik*) aroused the same reactions as if they were real, while any portrayal of the promised proletarian triumph had the effect of auto-suggestion because it appeared to be an actual event. But this was only when the film dominated the stage completely. At other times it simply emphasized the artificiality of the performance, and the constant shift in the level of illusion caused peculiar difficulties for the actors.

The integration of screen and stage

Piscator was conscious of the contrast between the two media, and on one level his productions were a series of attempts to find a successful means of integrating film. It must be mentioned that the film was of course silent, even though limited sound effects could be supplied through loudspeakers. Piscator's technique, however, was in sharp contrast to the operatic gesticulation we associate with the silent films of the period.

In *Tidal Wave* the screen had been limited to an extension of the scene, but even then the critics had concentrated almost exclusively on the effect of the film and the problems caused by juxtaposing the two media. Piscator was more successful when he tried to create a synthesis by placing the screen on the same visual plane as the stage. The original stage-design for *Hoppla!* had been a single white screen with 'doors' that opened in the middle of the film to reveal the actors in various rooms. Similarly in *Rasputin*, film was projected onto a backdrop, onto a gauze stretched across the proscenium and onto the curved surface of the globe inside whose opening segments the play was acted. However this method of harmonizing stage and screen in fact heightened the visual impact of the film by using the actors themselves and their surroundings as a screen and overlaying them with photography:

One of our experiments was as follows: film was projected onto a screen, then two gauzes were lowered while the screen was flown, so that the film was transferred onto the gauzes and fell through onto the stage. The gauzes too were flown and the whole was turned into a projection. In this way the film was transformed into the movements of the actors and the actions on the stage.[21]

When a particular scene had been played, then the whole process was gone through again in reverse, merging the actors back into the film. This was synthesis through total assimilation.

The traditional conventions of the theatre, swallowed in the extreme realism of film, seemed out of place and fantastical, and the new style of acting that appeared in Piscator's productions – 'hard, straightforward, unsentimental'[22] – was a direct reaction to the dominance of the screen. Indeed in one production, *Rasputin*, Piscator turned to advantage his failure to integrate the different conventions by stressing the contrast between the media in order to illustrate the difference between personal illusion and realities. Here the camera's impression of veracity was exploited so that the film became both the judge of the characters and the interpreter of those events dealt with on an individual level. The reality of the film extended to the personae, who were presented in deliberately 'factual' terms since their speeches were quotations and their appearance was modelled on the historical personages shown in the photographs. Yet it contrasted starkly with the artificiality of the aristocratic society portrayed by the actors; a tinsel society whose vanity was underlined by the obvious artificiality of stage conventions. This made it possible to distinguish between the individuals and the class they represented. The characters remained credible in stage terms, but the film demonstrated that they were out of touch with reality and that their world with its attitudes and customs was anachronistic in the context of their photographic environment.

In 1931 a more satisfactory solution was found. In *Tai Yang Awakes*, Piscator's last production in Germany before his exile, film was projected onto blank placards that were carried by an unceasing line of demonstrators who marched along the rear of the stage, so that the 'screen' was formed out of the theatrical elements of the action instead of overlaying them. This film was projected as a direct reply to an actor in the audience, who called out that the 'terror' portrayed on the stage was invented, and so the device reinforced the action instead of creating the stylistic tension which threatened to fragment Piscator's earlier productions.

Tai Yang Awakes was an exception. In the Piscator-Bühne productions dramatic conventions were adjusted rather than adapting the new medium of film to suit the conditions of the stage. From the early projection of 'credits' at the beginning of *Flags* and of 'sub-titles' during the play's action, Piscator's experiments attempted to force the stage to correspond to the camera. In *The Last Kaiser* the proscenium arch was even altered to resemble a camera lens, so that the stage opening could be dilated to show mass scenes or contracted to gain the effect of a photographic 'close-up'. In effect plays were turned into film scripts: sketches of action to be filled out with optical details by the director, where the primary emphasis is on the efficient transmission of information or material not on the aesthetic form. The reason for this artistic iconoclasm of Piscator's is not hard to find: 'The theatre had become uninteresting. The shabbiest film contained more topical interest, more of the exciting realities of our day than the stage.'[23]

Acting conventions and abstraction

Such a transformation of drama made it imperative to redefine the actor's task in terms of the conditions under which he was expected to work, because Piscator was not simply interested in obtaining unusual theatrical effects but in providing the practical basis for a new type of play. Professional acting styles, whether in Hollywood or Stratford, have been developed to present set characters. They share a certain quality of over-playing which encourages 'star' personalities and produces a double image in performance of the off-stage individual and the character he represents. In documentary films, however, there is no contrast between the public and private faces of the figures, and the most successful film and television actors are those who give an impression of improvisation. The mechanical nature of their medium forces them to underplay, and for this reason the techniques of stage acting used in the early silent films strike a modern audience as inflated.

Piscator's intended effect of actuality would have made normal theatrical gestures and delivery seem equally out of place, but in fact the mechanical nature of his stage and the dominance of the screen made any traditional style of acting impossible. His actors had to compete in a literal way with the machinery, which was never as silent on the boards of the stage as on the drawing-board and occasionally threatened to drown their voices completely. Even with the liberal application of graphite, oil and felt-padding, the treadmills in *Schweik*, which seldom stopped moving throughout the action, were so noisy that the cast had to shout at the top of their voices if their lines were to be heard at all. The fact that this cut out all vocal subtleties seems to have appeared unimportant to Piscator, for he used the same device again in *The Merchant of Berlin* and constructed a circular treadmill, which had an equally deafening effect, for his 1946 production of *Twelfth Night* at the Dramatic Workshop. Although he later called such mechanical defects as 'growing pains', this was entirely in line with his development. In the Piscator-Bühne productions human figures were so obviously peripheral that Hans Reimann purposely tested the attention they attracted during a performance of *Rasputin*:

So, just as I was with a leather beret on my head and my hands in my coat-pockets, I sauntered over the forestage. Right in the middle of a scene. In full lighting. Glancing neither right nor left, imperturbable, without haste. The astonishing thing was that the actors took just as little notice of me as the audience...[24]

This was deliberate. Piscator rejected traditional acting conventions on the grounds that they led audiences to approach his work according to the familiar and outdated standards of normal theatre. They emphasized surface illusion, which distracted attention from the pattern and meaning beneath events. The collective aspect of

Piscator's work, the anti-literary bias of his productions and his determination to use every means of communication at his disposal to the full necessitated the complete integration of the actor into an overall pattern of sound, colour and movement. This meant removing the normal pre-eminence of the actor who, as the only source of movement among static stage properties and settings, was accustomed to being the focus of attention on a conventional stage. Piscator therefore set him within a context of movement, so that he had to compete for the attention of the audience with kaleidoscopic lighting, changing scenery and even with his acting area, which revolved, rose, rolled, opened out, changed its shape or sank from sight. He was also threatened by competition from loud-speakers and music – apart from the unintentional noise of heavy machinery – while his importance as an instrument of communication had already been severely reduced by the cutting of his speeches to a dramatic and linguistic minimum and by the substitution of the written word on placards and projection-screens.

Art, and in particular theatrical art, traditionally deals with men as individuals, but modern politics defines a population by statistics. Since the complexity and vastness of the historical material that Piscator considered suitable for his 'political theatre' dealt with masses whose numbers made them faceless, it could only be expressed in an abstract and simplified form. This demanded the depersonalization of the actor, who had to portray types that were distinguished by their social function instead of by personal characteristics. The actor's physical importance had not only been diminished by the cinema-screen and the loudspeaker, with their immediate impact because of their size and volume, but he was no longer required to bring out the personality of the character whom he represented since human relationships had been replaced on Piscator's stage by the abstract web of economic or political connections.

Piscator's desire to represent the historical forces that were thought to impel mass movement elevated 'the *subject matter* to the principle hero in every play'.[25] Working on the premise that the heroic element for any play of the 'Marxist age' could only be 'the epoch' and 'the fate of the masses', he claimed that the aim of the actor should be 'to portray the human element so to speak in chemically pure form and as *Ding-an-sich*'.[26] The universalized figures, who were subject to historical and economic predestination according to Marxist theory and were therefore denied free will, could only be realized on the stage in terms of 'mechanical materialism' – which meant presenting them as scientifically observable phenomena.

In practice, as the production of *Schweik* revealed, this attempt to portray a Kantian *pour-soi* abstraction (the *Ding-an-sich*) led to representation by means of puppets; but these were, as conceptual abstractions shown in terms of material objects, nearer to the Existentialist *en-soi*. Puppets and masks would have suggested themselves naturally to Piscator and Grosz, with their Dada background, as effective methods of social caricature – but Piscator's first idea was to dispense with all human figures apart from Schweik himself and to represent every antagonist by an animated cartoon or a marionette. That would have resulted in monologue, which itself is abstraction in theatrical terms, and this plan was modified in rehearsal. Although most of the figures were either cartoons or dummies, those who were directly involved in the action were re-presented by actors in grotesque masks that accentuated the characteristics peculiar to their social function. Bretschneider's mask, for example, was reduced to a single huge eye and monstrous ear, thus effectively removing any personal idiosyncrasies and defining his figure simply as a police spy. Similarly the prison warders were given gigantic fists. This exaggerated 'symbolism of clowning'[27] certainly supported the humour of the text – but it was the effect of surrounding Pallenberg, the great comedian who played the part of Schweik, with inanimate objects that underscored Hašek's comedy, since the root of the grotesque is the perception of the animation of the inorganic. The actor, the human individual, was dehumanized by this distortion which transformed him into an abstract element; limited, simplified, typified and unchanging. Even the stage properties were disproportioned. There could be no interplay of character since Schweik was completely enclosed by symbols. The dialectic of drama had been replaced by mechanical processes.

The rôle of the actor: the acting-collective

Believing that social forces, which he described as 'an anonymous

fate', had taken the place of personalities in politics, Piscator removed the focus of his productions from the individual, and the
actor was in danger of appearing a decorative concession to dramatic
conventions rather than being a theatrical essential. In order to
redefine the actor's position by creating an appropriate style of
acting for his conception of drama, Piscator formed an acting
'collective' for his theatre on Nollendorfplatz in 1928, as Brecht
was later to do in the Theater am Schiffbauerdamm. This was
essential for his artistic plans, making his work fully independent of
the traditional theatre, since he no longer needed to employ actors
who had grown accustomed to conventional stage conditions.

The 'montage' of facts and the heterogeneous media needed a
unified tone of presentation (as they required the central image of
the stage-construct) to form an artistic whole out of the discordant
elements in performance. Through his collective Piscator was able
to develop an unsentimental, impersonal, mathematical style of
acting which harmonized with the machinery. This required self-
effacement and self-control if the actor was to operate as a precise
means of communication, since only understated impressions were
effective when working with film.

Piscator worked on the premise that a theatre dealing with
complex factual subjects 'needs naive, direct, uncomplicated,
unpsychological effects'.[28] He therefore insisted on rigorous gymnastic training for his acting troupe to gain exact physical control –
'accurate, clear movements, for which sport is the only training',[29]
and when asked to describe his own acting style in 1930 he compared it with Meyerhold's 'Biomechanics'. The practice developed
in the studio of the Piscator-Bühne was equivalent to the basics of
'Biomechanics' – training the actor as an acrobat since 'he must be
aware that his natural element is space, and must master this
spatial art'. But Piscator rejected the theoretical framework of
'Biomechanics', which Meyerhold defined in similar terms to the
Bauhaus choreography as 'the creation of an order based upon
mechanical laws...the geometrization of movement based upon
deep study of the human body and the laws of movement and
space', comparing this theory of movement to the rigid conventions of the *Noh* theatre: 'The business of the theatre [cannot] be
to photograph real life – for on the stage there can be no reproduction of reality...The theatre is conventional by nature.'[30] In

Piscator's view Meyerhold's emphasis on rhythmic and geometric movement formed an aesthetic principle, while for him acting was no more than one facet of a production: 'as for what I aim at in my work, it can just about be summed up in one word: effectiveness. I apply every possible means – or none...Aesthetic standpoints are never decisive.'[31]

The development of an 'epic' acting style

Whatever Piscator's denials, aesthetics undoubtedly had an in-direct influence on his acting style. During the Weimar Republic various Japanese and Chinese troupes made guest appearances in Berlin, and their popularity can be measured by a theatrical maga-zine of 1926. Out of a total of 70 photographs covering all the season's major productions 16 showed Japanese and Chinese masks, scenes from plays produced in Peking and Tokyo, and Javanese dancers. The ritualized emotion of the masks, the geometric make-up and movement of the actors, the symbolic gestures of the dancers, and the formalized nature of the scenes are similar to the conventionalized precision of acting that made Piscator's collec-tive capable of demonstrating the mechanical laws operating in society and the technological nature of the environment, while re-enacting a series of particular events or a story.

In 1930 the *Kabuki* Theatre appeared in Berlin with a pro-gramme of mimed scenes. The popular basis of *Kabuki* art, the lack of separation between stage and auditorium, and the com-paratively wide use of scenery and stage-machinery made it the nearest Eastern equivalent to European theatre. Its conventions were obviously of more use to Piscator than those of the more aesthetic and aristocratic *Noh* tradition borrowed by Brecht, and its stylized movement and simplicity of gesture aroused wide admiration. When they returned a year later after their influence had had time to sink in, Jhering spoke of their 'gesticular passion', and in the same month Piscator produced *Tai Yang Awakes*, which was judged by many critics to be his maturest production because of the skill of his actors: 'No revolutionary director yet has given such a plastic scenic form to the materialistic dialect of history.'[32] Jean Weidt, the 'Red Dancer',[33] who studied Japanese theatre for his balletic performances, had been engaged as a choreographer for

Tai Yang Awakes, and the strength of the production was judged to be the rhythmic movements of the weaving-women, the mime of execution, and the march of demonstrators with placards which culminated in a symbolic dance. Here the actor, given a new function which was not concerned with interpreting the emotional states of individuals, regained his position as the primary means of theatrical expression in Piscator's productions.

It must be said that Piscator himself implicitly denied that the Japanese theatre had any important influence on his work when he differentiated Brecht's 'alienation effect' from his own 'epic' acting. He claimed that Brecht's style romanticized the concepts of the classical oriental theatre, while his acting style, which he called 'objective', was developed in direct response to his mechanization of the stage, and he defined it as the concentration on communicating 'facts' instead of depicting characters. The example of the *Kabuki* performances at the time, however, are too much of a coincidence to be overlooked. Absolute physical control was essential if the actor was to be capable of indicating external motives for action in figures affected by political or economic forces instead of impersonating individuals – and the Japanese conventions were a striking demonstration of how this might be achieved.

This was the opposite of Stanislavski's 'Method': 'It is not true that your [the actor's] centre of attention lies in the middle of the stage. When you play before a public, the public must be the centre of your attention.'[34] The basis of Piscator's depersonalized acting style was this contact with the audience, and he experimented with various techniques to achieve it. As early as May 1926 in Zech's *The Drunken Ship* the actors had walked into view while the stage-hands were still changing the setting, taken their position as actors, and then altered their style of gesture to portray their rôles.

In *Tai Yang Awakes* he added a prologue in which the actors entered, changed into their costumes and put on their make-up on stage while discussing the political situation in China and comparing it to conditions in Germany. This set the tone of the play and led directly into the first scene without interruption while the final words, spoken directly to the audience, varied a technique that Piscator had used previously. Dressed in his everyday street attire, the actor who played the revolutionary leader came from between the costumed groups of Chinese military and demonstrators to speak lines which directly recalled the discussion in the prologue: 'So run the battle-fronts through China today. And the same battle lines divide Germany – Right or left – You must commit yourselves!' Alternatively Piscator associated 'objectivity' with acting a rôle from a political standpoint – stating that characterization should be a graphic expression of political conviction, so that the personality of a bourgeois would be acted to correspond to the 'proletarian consciousness' – and he advocated political indoctrination as the basis of an actor's training. His grounds for this were that Marxist doctrine alone could teach an actor the true significance of his part in a socially oriented play, while only by identifying himself with the proletariat would he be able to understand his (theoretically working-class) audience and speak effectively to them. The basic principles however remain the same. Distanced from his rôle by concentrating on his audience, the actor's function was to be 'the bearer of world-wide historical concepts' instead of an 'embodiment of individualities'.[35]

A 'collective' as such also had political overtones, being the Communist ideal of a classless society in miniature applied to a particular field – here the theatre, which as a corporate art form is particularly suited to the application of such ideas – but its primary importance for Piscator lay in its discipline, through which he evolved the necessary precision of movement and representation. The collective survived Piscator's bankruptcy as an 'Emergency Relief Association for the Actors of the Piscator-Bühne', touring the major cities of Germany, and since Piscator no longer had the opportunity to apply complex machinery he was forced to gain equivalent effects through actors alone.

This was not a regression to his early Agitprop work, but a development which built on the Piscator-Bühne experiments. The simultaneous stage remained, reduced to its bare essentials of two rooms divided by a wall running down the centre of the stage in § *218*. Film and projection also remained, even if largely replaced by placards, and the techniques both for involving the audience and for breaking illusion were brought to a fine art. It was simplicity through a disciplined control of theatrical media instead of crudity through clumsy methods of representation, and the critics labelled it 'primitive naivety' and 'the true republican simplicity'.[36] Jhering contrasted the absence of machinery – 'no apparatus, no bombast' – with Piscator's earlier work: 'previously Piscator worked for similar goals: for recognition and elucidation, but with the exaggerated means of the illusionistic stage',[37] and praised the style of the ensemble as 'direction which draws its most powerful effect precisely from the unpretentiousness of the means...a success for the Piscator-Bühne under the worst material conditions'.[38]

Acting is organic to the theatre and, without the distracting novelty and disproportionate power of technological effects, Piscator's productions reached a new level of achievement. The earlier mechanical solutions to staging the new material of 'political drama' had obvious faults, but Piscator was able to claim with a certain amount of justice that 'all the new scenic discoveries that I used brought new dimensions for the actor with them'.[39] The machinery that threatened to swamp the actor also gave him new opportunities for movement, which could be turned to advantage by the new style of acting, but a period of adaptation when Piscator's productions appeared unbalanced was inevitable: 'What criticism often calls an insufficient standard of acting in my productions is in actual fact the discrepancy between the schooling of the contemporary generation of actors and the novel, unaccustomed stage architecture in which I set the actor.'[40] The rhetorical delivery of the early nineteenth century had been appropriate when all accessories, apart from two or three standard chairs, were painted onto the flat backcloth. The introduction of the three-dimensional box set with practical doors and real stage properties, however, had banished that grandiose style of acting. In the same way Piscator's new machinery superseded naturalistic representation. Just as the Duke of Saxe-Meiningen in pioneering Naturalism had only been able to turn his theories about the controlling influence of the setting to practical use through his ensemble, so Piscator's collective made it possible for him to retrain his actors, and its discipline helped to gain that precision in movement and character-representation which was essential both for portraying the subject matter of Documentary Drama and for manipulating the emotions of the audience to the extent demanded in Total Theatre.

The style of acting developed to suit the unusual stage conditions eventually made it possible to dispense with the heavier and more unwieldy machines.

The problem of the dramatic hero in the modern age

Together with the development of new functions for the actor came a redefinition of the hero-figure. Based on the concept of individuality, the centre of interest in traditional drama is always an unusual or complex personality. Characters have only been deliberately presented as generalized social types in the satire of Molière, in Jonson's 'Comedy of Humours', or in the highly stylized improvisation of the *Commedia del'Arte*. Even Büchner's Woyzeck, although identified with a group – 'we poor people' – was merely an inversion of the hero pattern, being as far below the norm as previous dramatic heroes had been above it, and the 'antiheroes' of Arthur Miller or Arnold Wesker are no less individual than Woyzeck. The basis of traditional characterization is a moral concept, which can be traced back to Aristotle's *Poetics*: 'Diversities of human character are nearly always derivative from this primary distinction...the line between virtue and vice is one dividing the whole of mankind' – and it was this concept of the individual as a moral being, which had already been weakened by advances in psychology, that Piscator rejected in dissociating his work from 'Aristotelean drama'. From his own experience in the war and his observation of inflation Piscator concluded that 'man as an individual being, independent...of social bonds, focusing egocentrically on the concept of his self, rests in reality beneath the marble plaque of the "Unknown Soldier"'.[41]

The traditional cult of the individual has little relevance to an age characterized by mass-movements and mass-graves, and the problem facing modern creative artists has been admirably outlined by Erich Heller:

In bygone days it was the business of the imagination to create within the world of the senses the image and symbol capable of expressing the wealth of inner experience. It was in art that man, dissatisfied with the triviality of everyday existence, found a reality more adequate to what he felt to be the truth of his life. Today it is different: our task – and difficulty – is to find within ourselves something big enough to be charged with the responsibility for the monstrous dimensions of our external reality...[42]

A theatre which takes documentary material from contemporary history as its subject matter comes up against this difficulty in a particularly acute form – as Karl Kraus found. The personal stature of the participants was so incongruous to the political effects of their actions that it was 'characters from an operetta' who 'played out the tragedy of mankind'.[43] The suppression of the heroic ideal was common to all the literature of the First World War, and 'the poetic general of the past...on a sunlit heath' was quickly recognized to be extinct in the context of the modern battlefield with 'its unaesthetic character that grows ever less beautiful'.[44] Euripides had presented the plague in Thebes as a divine punishment for Oedipus' crime; but the World War (an equivalent catastrophe in modern terms) could only be interpreted as the impersonal result of social forces. Piscator, for example, laid no blame upon the Kaiser as a man, but censured the social order of which he was the representative.

The problem of creating an appropriate dramatic hero for the industrial age was neither initially raised by the Marxist critique of society nor peculiar to the twentieth century. De Tocqueville had already noted on his visit to America in 1836 that 'the language, the dress and the daily actions of man in democracies are repugnant to ideal conceptions'. In a society where rhetoric is suspect, rhapsodies embarrass and political leaders imitate the common man, the statuesque dimensions and postures of fictional heroes seem false and stilted. One solution is the cynical or pathetic 'anti-hero' of the fifties, another the tramp or clown figures of the more recent Absurd drama; but this kind of response was too negative for Marxists, who necessarily believe in progress. The Communists, feeling the need of a hero figure for propaganda, attempted to bridge the dichotomy between the ideal and the real by presenting typified embodiments of 'the aspirations of the people' in realistic revolutionary contexts – the equivalent of the Existentialist 'limit situation', combining the extremes of physical hardship and emotional euphoria. But this solution, though it satisfied ideological requirements, was of little use as a formula for dealing with general social issues.

The Communist hero: mass-man on the stage

Basically there were only three possibilities open to committed German authors after the failure of the November Revolution. Cynicism and nihilism, withdrawal from *théâtre engagé* (amusement was business), or a narrow involvement in politics through the newly formed K.P.D. For Piscator, who labelled himself a 'historical materialist', and defined the standpoint of his theatre as 'an *absolute* historical-philosophical recognition – that of the *Marxist doctrine*',[45] social classes were super-individuals, motivated by economic determination and historical forces. The proletariat, for instance, was seen as a 'mighty I',[46] while the individual lacked personal freedom of decision, being 'inseparably integrated with the great political and economic factors of his age'.[47] Drama based on the clash of character seemed trivial where conflict was between classes or nations and when the impersonal hostilities of modern war or social revolution were designated as the 'fundamental problems of our time'. Since the theatre had been assigned an educational function by the Communists, man had to be presented on stage as a 'political being', and because the concept of individuality had been invalidated by the denial of personal responsibility, 'wherever he enters, his *class* or rank enters with him at the same time'.[48] The difficulty, however, was to find a practical method of representing this sociological abstraction.

Other socialist playwrights and directors had already experimented with various techniques for creating a politically acceptable dramatic hero before Piscator. Hauptmann had to some extent succeeded in articulating a whole class on the stage through isolating representative groups or individuals within the mass, using choral songs and chants to depict the intensification of communal emotion in *The Weavers*. Wachtangov had envisaged a new type of drama without individual rôles, where the masses would enter as a corporate body, triumphing, burying their dead and singing the international song of freedom – in other words, the spirit of 'the People' was to be shown symbolically repeating a ritualized pattern of revolution. Meyerhold's re-enactment of the storming of the Winter Palace came nearest to realizing this vague concept, but he replaced idealized representatives and symbolic figures with sheer numbers, which was impracticable in the existing theatre. The problem was not new, nor were attempts to present mass-man on the stage limited to Communism. It had been outlined as early as 1901:

In our day,...when the dependency of the individual on 'economics' is so obvious, any belief in human liberty or freedom from historical determinism has died...The belief in the supremacy of the individual is dead and the fact that history is a battle between classes has sunk deep into modern consciousness...with the result that the historical stage-heroes of today seem strange and false and theatrical.[49]

– and Jessner had complained of a trend in German theatre which he called 'Americanism': 'This contemporary phenomenon, which began in Berlin and flooded the Reich, was epitomized in the substitution of masses for personalities, of machines for individuals.'[50] Marxism replaced single men by the multitude, psychology by the pathos of history – but the architectural form of the proscenium theatre was unsuitable for staging gigantic crowd scenes. Above all, however, the literary techniques of drama were incapable of dealing with inarticulacy, and 'these masses cannot fully describe what motivates them, what they are dependent on, or which their true destiny is. Multi-figured, a powerful background, they are turned into paper dolls if they express themselves in dialogue. They mouth literature which at best is Party propaganda.'[51]

Quite apart from the impracticability of putting multitudes on the stage, crowds are intrinsically less interesting than individuals because their members can only be explored superficially, and even the Communists showed considerable doubt about the theatrical value of such impersonal generalizations. Gorki called for 'heroic theatre' to present archetypal personifications of revolutionary ideals with whom the working-classes could identify since they would epitomize the 'proletarian virtues'. The first sign of this muscular hero appeared in graphic art, since propaganda posters lent themselves to monumental treatment, and this rapidly developed into Socialist Realism. By the 1930s the 'abstract dogmatism' of Meyerhold's principle that the corporate identity of the masses could only be represented by an equivalent mass of supernumeraries was officially condemned as a 'pseudomarxist, vulgarly socialist concept: the fallacy that the personality is nothing, the mass, the collective is all'.[52] The emphasis on an individual embodiment of the masses, which even led to the rejection of the previously praised *Prolet-Kult*, was undoubtedly due to Stalin's emergence as a hero-dictator figure. But the argument had occupied Communist dramatists, directors and critics since the Revolution, and is still unsettled in Communist circles. Traditional figures which accentuate the cunning, adaptability or endurance of the

common man are rejected as degrading the revolutionary proletariat: 'Eulenspiel and Lazarillo, Caraguez and Stranitzky,
Schweik and Chaplin's Charlie [sic!]...Socialism has thrown all
these onto the rubbish-heap.'[53] Encouraging ideals of heroic
physique or saintly self-sacrifice take their place. As early as 1919,
Bertrand Russell had noted that 'the attitude of uncompromising
heroism' which 'appeals especially to the dramatic instinct' was
responsible for the Communist insistence on violent revolution;[54]
and Lukács, the doyen of Marxist literary theoreticians, limited the
definition of 'epic' works to those that portrayed the 'heroic age' of
world revolution.

Even Piscator identified 'the new drama' with 'heroic elements'
– 'the age and the destiny of the masses'.[55] But, being limited to
what could be achieved in the commercial theatre, he either defined
the masses by their environment or compromised by using film
scenes of crowds in conjunction with the single actors on the stage.
At best individual figures could only be made to stand for 'a type,
the representative of a particular social and economic outlook'.[56]
To fuse them into a social and historical frame of reference film
had to be used, while it was the impersonal symbolism of the stage-
constructs which universalized the dramatic conflict. As a result
Piscator's experiments inevitably tended to withdraw the hero
altogether from the stage; and in *Rasputin* it was on film that the
masses fulfilled their rôle as a historical force, while the stage was
reserved for the 'villains' who as individuals were helpless even to
determine their own actions.

A major difficulty in any documentary approach to drama is that
fact does not mix easily with fiction. In the Foreword to *Tidal
Wave* Paquet had defined his intentions in terms which sounded
appropriate to Piscator's aims: 'It was not a matter of copying
reality, but of epitomizing the driving forces of our time in a few
figures, which would stir our emotions through their vividness, in
the same way that reality stirs them.' But in practice imaginary
characters of this sort detracted from the impression of documentary realism while the factual nature of the subject matter spotlit the falsity of the symbolic heroes.

Piscator tried various ways of overcoming the dichotomy – nameless, undifferentiated figures; rôle-changing; masks of historical
people to disguise the artificiality of acting. But only in *Schweik* did

he manage to present an imaginary character of heroic dimensions whose actions were realistic and representative enough to embody the experience of the working-classes as a whole. The Good Soldier was the most impressive projection of the proletarian image on Piscator's stage, but the K.P.D. reaction to the production was ambivalent. The *Red Flag* criticized the play as 'negative', remarking that the overt expression of 'hate for a corrupt system' was external to his figure and only came out clearly in the Grosz drawings,[57] and Leo Lania attempted to give the play a narrow political interpretation in the programme on the dubious ideological grounds that the Austro–Hungarian Empire represented feudalism which according to Marx had to be destroyed by the bourgeoisie before the proletarian revolution could take place, and that therefore the correct rôle of the proletariat in this particular situation was passive resistance, symbolized by Schweik, while a stage direction written by Piscator noted that Schweik 'played revolutionary songs on the harmonium'. But Schweik as a 'conformist' was out of character, and Piscator's original criticism of the Brod/Reimann version applied equally to his own adaptation:

The play was not biased enough for them [Piscator, Brecht, Lania and Gasbarra]...In view of the political commitment of the Piscator-Bühne they claimed that the play was unstageable in its present shape [the Brod/Reimann version], since it deviated from the Party line and stood in sharp contradiction to the resolutions of the Third International.[58]

Schweik, however effective as theatre, hardly corresponded to propaganda requirements, and even Czechoslovakia has found it necessary to modify and 'interpret' Hašek's work. As Piscator himself realized, 'Schweik remains anti-social man, the demolition charge, the saboteur of *every* social organization',[59] and he felt it necessary to defend comedy against attack as counter-revolutionary in another article in the programme, 'Humour and Revolution' by Erich Mühsam, which argued the questionable premise that 're-volution is a cheerful matter'.

Historical figures, who had already become established as symbols in Communist hagiography and therefore possessed an aura of emotive associations, were an alternative method of presenting a politically acceptable proletarian hero: Liebknecht and Luxemburg in *Despite All!* and Lenin in *Rasputin*. These, however, were tied to particular historical incidents. They were therefore of limited use as the foundation of the new drama for which Piscator intended his productions to provide outlines – even though the figure of Lenin, as the visual embodiment of the spirit 'of the politically aware proletariat, consciously working toward the Revolution',[60] was used out of context as a general symbol both in *The Robbers*, where Granach who acted Spiegelberg was made up to look like Lenin, and in the preliminary film for *Storm over Gottland*, where Lenin reappeared as the eternal revolutionary, martyred and resurrected in succeeding ages.

Attempting to create an embodiment of the proletariat that could be used in more general contexts, Piscator returned to the direct portrayal of the masses in *Tai Yang Awakes*. But instead of being presented as social types the various figures were differentiated by individual characteristics and formed a multiple hero, related by dress and make-up and coalesced into a single unit by choreography. This solution, avoiding dominant rôles, has been claimed as the first realistic representation of a proletarian hero on the stage,[61] and the way in which it was gradually worked out can be traced in earlier productions. In *Tidal Wave* Piscator had broadened the rôles of the working-class characters, which Paquet had left completely without characterization, by introducing generalized behavioural details. In *Hoppla!* he had used typical figures, speaking from the crowd as spokesmen of the masses. Here, in *Tai Yang Awakes*, 'no character has a private face, but only a generalized one', but the choreography 'allowed the main character of each episode to become the dominant figure the moment he stepped forwards, even though he always remained associated with the dim crowd in the background'.[62]

The generalization of the hero figure in *Hoppla!*

Hoppla, We are Alive! can be taken as a typical example of the process that plays went through in Piscator's productions in order to evolve this kind of hero figure. Toller wrote it as the (semi-autobiographical) tragedy of an individual; the subject is 'Karl Thomas', and the action is concerned with the psychological destruction of a single person. Thomas' mental deterioration is caused by contact with his environment, and it is the contrast between his political idealism and the degrading realities which leads him to suicide. Social criticism is the basis of the play since Thomas, like Woyzeck, acts as a touchstone by which his world is judged – but it remains a personal statement, and Piscator rewrote speeches extensively. He reduced the importance of Thomas' individual characteristics and turned him into a proletarian figure. He expanded the rôle of the working-class characters, emphasizing their environment and associating the society portrayed on the stage with the contemporary world outside the theatre by his use of film. Finally, he changed the ending, making the language impersonal and generalizing Toller's criticism of society. The lyrical expressions of Thomas' personal agony were cut, so that what remained was a stereotyped set of attitudes. His last speech, for instance, was pared down to:

THOMAS. Are you all here again? All here again – is it like that? Once more waiting, [waiting, waiting] – I cannot [wait again] – Can't you see then? – [Can't you hear then?] – Defend yourselves! – No one hears, No one sees, no one... [63]

while his more personal thoughts were spelt out simultaneously in the 'illuminated lettering' which represented morse communication between the prisoners. These were also cut to a simple expression of basic emotion and reinforce the monosyllabic monotone of his direct utterance, being removed from the personal sphere, in spite of the use of the first person singular, because the sentences are written instead of spoken and therefore objectivized:

THOMAS (*illuminated script*). I cannot wait until you understand. O madness, madness of the world. What is to be done? What to be done? I cannot wait, I cannot wait till you can wait no longer.

This repetitious simplicity is characteristic and was deliberately designed to aid the impression of impersonality, contrasting with Toller's Expressionistic pathos. But the language loses its connotative reverberations. Here the 'madness of the world', which in Toller's original ending gained additional meaning because he had set the last scene back in the mental institution, is reduced to a simple statement by Piscator's prison-setting where all the main revolutionary characters could be gathered – a change which removed the effect of individual tragedy.

Piscator emphasized Thomas' function as a yardstick for society by the introductory film of 'Scenes from the years 1919 to 1927'. The screen was made an extension of Karl's padded cell by his appearance in a straitjacket 'at intervals...wandering backwards and forwards' and the theme of this film – that 'men are running mad' in their daily actions – stated the paradox implicit in Toller's play in unmistakable terms. Thomas, whose position seems as detached as that of the Martian in one sketch of the earlier *Red Revue*, is depersonalized since he has been cut off from humanity and condemned as mad by the lunatic standards of normality. His presence alone acts as a condemnation of contemporary society, and therefore his comments, couched in impersonal language, seem to be objective. For this reason his suicide was not lamented as the unnecessary death of an individual, but could be presented as the symptom of a diseased community:

EVA. He was broken by everyday life.
MELLER. Damned world! It must be altered.

Hoppla! marks an intermediate stage in Piscator's development towards abstraction which culminated in the marionettes and masks surrounding Schweik. Thomas, who is both separated from society by his unfamiliarity with its recent technological developments and divorced from humanity through his sanity, was transformed into a type – the Outsider. The minor characters were also generalized and lacked individual differentiation, but their social functions were not exaggerated into unnatural caricature and they were distinguished by formal means – tenor, baritone and bass for the election-candidates, for example – while the workers' speeches were replaced by a 'soft monotone', and their confusion and resentment was summarized by an old woman who acted as their mouthpiece. Indeed there was a certain superficial emphasis on individuals because Piscator wished to create the impression of numbers. The line of voters was formed of single figures picked out by clear contrasts in clothing so that they could change their hats and coats, re-enter and vote again, thus giving the impression of large bodies of men. They were not, however, given personalized actions or individual speeches, and the true emphasis of the production was on the mass, as in the final prison scene where the empty cells were 'occupied by supernumeraries'. This creation of an illusion of numbers through using a few universalized figures defined by external characteristics points forward to the technique evolved for *Tai Yang Awakes*, where a file of actors marched in a circle around the stage and individuals stepped out of the circle of marchers to reveal themselves as particular figures and returned to anonymity after speaking their lines.

In spite of the use of film to overshadow the sufferings of the hero with a sociological cross-section of the epoch, and in spite of the textual alterations to typify his personal characteristics, the production of *Hoppla!* was criticized as being 'still too personal to obtain a true political effect'.[64] The play was condemned as 'defeatist' and 'pacifist' and Thomas' character was described as 'bourgeois' and 'intellectual' – the worst kind of insult to a Communist – in spite of his working-class accent. In theory the proletarian personality was a compendium of the characteristics of his class, but Toller's hero remained an individual figure, projected onto a social background. The true importance of the production, however, lay in its dramaturgy not in its message, and the critics were complimentary about its artistic worth, in contrast to their comments on its politics. Piscator's inability to turn Toller's individualistic hero into a valid representative of modern society outlines the problems in such a metamorphosis of the theatre. As far as the characterization was concerned, this production fell between two stools, but it was an essential stepping-stone in Piscator's development towards the creation of a new drama.

6 Total Theatre: the Audience

The basis of Documentary Drama is evidence and actuality, calling for epic techniques to handle and interpret the factual material. But any narrow political approach distorts the criteria. Relevance is defined by persuasion rather than objectivity – and this, together with the necessity for using all the resources of the stage to communicate and comment, meant that in developing epic and documentary elements Piscator was also working towards an antithetical type of production that has since come to be known as 'Total Theatre'.

The example of the Piscator-Bühne had made 'Topical Theatre' (*Zeittheater*) fashionable overnight: news reports and even dramatizations of the criminal code became the staple of German *avant-garde* stages. Bruckner's *Criminals* in 1928 was followed by Wolf's *Cyanide*, Duschinsky's *The Unemployed*, Horvath's *Sladek*, Graff's *The Endless Street* and Kraus's *The Unconquered* in 1929, until even left-wing critics complained of superficial and badly written plays, while Kerr commented sourly that the 'agonizing drama' (*Elendsdrama*) of the 1880s had returned. Piscator himself was dissatisfied, and although he continued to call for a 'theatre of actuality' his practice began to diverge from his theories, explanations and comments. The conventions of Documentary Drama were – like the stark architectural forms of the *Neue Sachlichkeit* movement – functional, yet the techniques of documentation and commentary attracted a disproportionate interest. The new style of performance was intended to focus attention solely on the pattern of meaning beneath events. But simply because it contrasted with the recognizably artificial conventions of the traditional theatre, it was taken as a rejection of all aesthetic values. A glance at the cartoons and headlines of Berlin newspapers following any of Piscator's major premières indicates what aspect of his productions aroused the strongest feelings: DOWN WITH ART! THE RAPE OF ART! PISCATOR TRAMPLES ON OUR CULTURAL LIFE!.

This concentration on stylistic details at the expense of the subject was paralleled by the reaction to detailed factual material. Statistics and quotations were meant to be no more than evidence for general sociological theories, and stress was to be laid on the interpretation of events, not on the particular incidents through which the theories were demonstrated. Thus Piscator judged the reading of the legal injunction won by the ex-Kaiser to be a satisfactory substitute for the censored scene of *Rasputin* in which the three emperors appeared. But the impact of the techniques in fact spotlit the documents they communicated. The style emphasized historical situations which had been selected solely as examples, with the result that the apparent subjects of Documentary Drama came to resemble Tolstoy's description of history as a clutter of unnecessary dates and unimportant names. This was accentuated when the material was contemporary. Even such perceptive and sympathetic critics as Diebold supported 'Topical Theatre' primarily on the grounds that 'we desperately need works about housing problems, the breadlines...syphilis, the police...The realities lie on the streets.'[1] Such comments ignored any issues of universal significance and encouraged audiences to concentrate on specifics. So the insistence on detail which was intended to counterbalance the tendency to abstraction actually obscured general outlines and pandered to the psuedo-scientific fallacy that truth is determined by a simple accumulation of facts. These disadvantages led Piscator to reject the accepted concept of Documentary Drama: 'It was never my intention to create journalistic theatre, and it was only with reluctance that I watched the concept of a "Topical Theatre" replace the "Political Theatre". Those truths which are revealed by a really political theatre should outlast topicalities.'[2]

The unintentional emphasis on superficialities, together with the eye-catching impact of particular techniques also tended to scatter the audience's attention. Piscator was therefore forced to use all the means at his disposal 'in order to concentrate the imagination of the onlookers and to avoid any opportunity for distraction, such as is caused by scene-changing intervals'.[3] The extensive subject matter and multiplicity of scenes made it essential for the stage-forms to become versatile and elastic in order to relate the parts to the whole, while swiftness of communication and the speed of scene-changes came to be a dominant consideration in order to portray a complete picture within the time available. The settings had to vary and the action had to unfold without a break, and as early as 1926 his guiding principles were already fixed:

As far as I am concerned there can only be a continuous action, which must not be interrupted by any curtain. There can only be a cohesion, a continual interlocking of scene with scene through the most flexible use of the stage machinery...through impelling and forward-driving music, through accentuation of the atmospheric environment.[4]

In *Tidal Wave* film had been used as 'an optical kind of musical interlude'[5] to hold the attention of the audience. But in developing techniques to break out of the representational limits of the stage, Piscator gained the ability to run one series of actions into another, which dispensed with the need for such stop-gap scenes to cover pauses. The machinery automatically accelerated the tempo of a performance, carrying the audience irresistibly along and making a compelling impression on the imagination by intensifying the expression – a stylistic emphasis which was required by the global significance of the themes. Traditional theatrical conventions were inadequate to portray the inhuman proportions of the Great War or the dehumanizing misery of the Depression, and Piscator later implied that this was one of the main reasons for his use of modern media: 'I admit that I am still always overwhelmed by the age. In comparison to it no means seem great enough, deep enough, power-ful enough. Poetry, words, forms, art sink back helpless before it.'[6] A film of the Somme was more powerful than any way in which a handful of actors could indicate the horrors of trench warfare on the stage. Loudspeakers made a greater impression on the eardrums than any orator. Continuous movement assaulted the senses more than a structure of distinct and separated scenes.

Fluidity and force of expression remained Piscator's object even when he was concerned with the normal rôle of a director, interpret-ing plays, instead of attempting to create a new type of drama. His concern with imaginative impact and dynamic tempo becomes understandable in the light of his conviction that 'due to lack of imagination the majority of men are incapable of experiencing even their own lives, let alone their world. Otherwise the reading of a single page of any newspaper would suffice to set mankind in an uproar.'[7] Factual statements were not enough, and Piscator spoke of his productions in terms of a ' "symphonic" synaesthetic artwork on the broadest dramaturgical basis...in which all possible means [of expression] were to be brought into play'.[8] The escalators, revolves, treadmills and film sequences, which were essential for representing the picaresque type of material that spanned centuries and continents, were also used to shatter the complacency of the audience by drawing them into the action.

Objectivity v. involvement: the use of tempo in production

A crescendo of action became directly portrayed in a furioso of movement formed from every part of the stage, scenery as well as actors, which naturally involved the audience on an emotional level: 'It is precisely the technical machinery which must make it possible to generate a compelling tempo...[producing] the unity of actor and spectator and drawing the latter into the dramatic proceedings'.[9] Yet this contrasted with the principles of Documentary Drama since in theory the same techniques were intended 'to keep the onlooker in a cool and critical mental state and to bring him to the recognition that the world revealed on the stage could not be allowed to remain as he saw it exposed'.[10] Like the 'alienating' acting conventions of Brecht's Epic Theatre, which attempted to suppress the audience's natural identification with the characters, Piscator's style of production was intended to distance them from the dramatic events. But at the same time as requiring critical thought it was demanded that the audience should come to the 'correct' conclusion, and to achieve this they had to be forced to take sides in the action. Piscator's comments on this point are (understandably) confused. Involvement could enlist support for the mass-movements represented by the actors, as well as imprinting the interpretation of society forcefully on the memory; and Piscator worked to achieve that desired 'direct action' upon the public which is still the official Communist justification for drama. Yet if the identification with the stage action produced an unwanted effect – as when, instead of a pacifist reaction, military enthusiasm was aroused by the final scene of *What Price Glory?* where the exhausted soldiers marched back to the slaughter singing, which was meant to demonstrate the waste and futility of war – then Piscator still demanded a critical distance from the performance.

The whole question about the relative value of involving an audience's emotions or exercising its rational faculties was complicated still further by ideological considerations – as usual in Piscator's case. When seen from 'the correct viewpoint' the Marxist critique of social history was supposed to be obvious, convincing and logical, while distancing was considered essential for a comprehensive perspective. Yet the Marxist interpretation of the commonplace that no man is an island called for the total involvement of the onlookers as supporting players in any revolutionary subject matter. An objective style was therefore fused with inflammatory techniques – and the amalgamation of these two mutually exclusive qualities was defended by Piscator with superb illogicality on the ground that, since truth is inevitably convincing and rational conviction is shown by emotional excitement, a production which arouses an audience has proved the objective truth of its thesis. Following this line of argument, the programme for *Rasputin* attributed the effect of tempo to euphoria aroused by 'the awareness of the purpose and fruitfulness of the revolutionary struggle'. In fact the techniques for accelerating the action had little to do with any political message. It was widely realized in the Agitprop movement that the excitement aroused by tempo increased the effectiveness of indoctrination. But the involvement of the audience frequently appeared to be an end in itself for Piscator. The same programme also contained a reply by Meisel to the left-wing condemnation of his music for *Hoppla!* as 'hideous'. Meisel never wrote descriptive programme-music. His compositions were always intended to reinforce the tempo of a production, and he openly declared that the sole aim of his work was 'to stimulate all the senses of the audience at any cost'. Similarly, Piscator tended to equate 'psychological turmoil' with response to art. Tempo was valuable whatever its political justification. As a 'collective hypnotizer', it immersed the individual in the group and suspended any disbelief in the action or criticism of technical defects, so that although both the democrat Kurt Pinthus and the critic of *The Red Flag* agreed that § 218 was a bad play, both found this immaterial since the production provided 'the most lively and enlivening evening of this type of theatre'. Tempo gave an impression of vitality that could outweigh both political and artistic considerations. *Hoppla!* was criticized from all sides on ideological and aesthetic grounds, but as one perceptive evaluation of the production, quoted with approval in the programme of *Rasputin*, pointed out: 'The ideological message is incidental. It is the tempo, the quality of life, the continuity, that gives this theatre its significance.' Piscator, however, was bedevilled by trying to engage the audience on an intellectual as well as emotional level, even though each discredited the other – echoing again the distinction between 'agitation' and 'propaganda' – and it was only later that he acknowledged the paradox contained in his work: 'The public should not be over-taxed or made to exert themselves [emotionally] when one expects them to meditate as well.'[11]

The emotional involvement of the audience

Emotional participation occurs, of course, to a greater or lesser extent in all plays, and the French still use the word *assister* to describe attendance at a play, although in the context of the picture-frame stage and the passive demand for entertainment this denotes no more than imaginative receptivity. The actor concentrates his attention on the public, and the public enter into a 'play relation-ship' with the actors in which the performance comes alive through 'a willing suspension of disbelief'. For this reason rehearsals, lack-ing audiences, always seem incomplete since it is the reciprocal animation of actor and onlooker which creates the atmosphere of a performance: 'It is the aim of the theatre to draw the spectator into the action, and the history of the theatre is simply a record of the major or minor success of the illusion that the public have taken part in the play.'[12]

It seems to be widely agreed that the dramatic impulse is pri-marily emotional; that those ideas which are natural to the theatre are so fundamental, being accepted by all, as to be 'almost feelings'; and that intellectual intentions are 'inimical to the very being of the stage'.[13] Piscator was even able to cite Aristotle's comment that the Eleusian mysteries taught by experience (emotional participation rather than rational elucidation) in order to defend his practice of involving the audience in the action.

All this assumes that the public is a corporate body sharing basic thoughts and feelings. But the modern theatre has been deprived of a homogeneous audience if it operates at any but the lowest level of entertainment since the lack of a common cultural ethos has fragmented society. As a complex and expensive institution it cannot rely on a small clique for financial support, yet a performance must evoke a unanimous reaction to be successful. To withdraw specialized material from the stage, as Yeats did with his *Plays for Dancers* which were performed in drawing-rooms and are now only read as poetry, is no solution. It implies that drama is no longer a viable art form.

As usual when dealing with problems that other theatre-artists try to avoid, Piscator accentuated this. He consciously set out to attract a proletarian public while knowing that his theatre depended on bourgeois backing; and this awareness explains the extremes to which he went to gain a uniform response by drawing the onlookers into a stage action. In the performance as a whole the public was to play a part equal to the actor, machinery and music. Actor and audience always react upon one another through mutual appreciation, but Piscator expected audience emotion to play a positive rôle in a dramatic action. His earlier revues, in which the entrance of the 'Bourgeois' and 'Prole' figures had awakened instant recognition in the audience 'who at once intervened in the argument', had demonstrated the effectiveness of audience-involvement: 'The audience participates. Hurrah! How they whistle at that, cry, storm, shout encouragement, fling their arms up and help us in our thoughts.'[14] It was this sort of reaction which convinced Piscator that the 'fourth wall' which traditionally separated the stage from the auditorium should be eliminated in order to communicate revolutionary material as a directly felt experience. Rather than demonstrating a series of facts a performance was to be a political discussion, the outcome of which would be decided by the audience – an effect which was actually achieved in the production of § *218*, where

the public participated through speeches and shouts...until finally this [involvement] reached its culmination with a real vote that swept the public into an almost unanimous rejection of section 218 of the criminal code by a show of hands, through which for the first time the ending of a play corresponded to a public meeting.[15]

The tempo generated by the machinery was not enough to gain such intense involvement, and in some of his work Piscator placed actors among the audience – a technique that was particularly successful in § *218*. Credé's play is written in a dull naturalistic form, and Piscator altered it by the simple means of scattering those characters who were not directly involved in the main action among the public. From their seats in the auditorium these actors (apparently) interrupted the action by speaking their lines, so that a continual two-way discussion seemed to replace normal dialogue. The critics, educated by Piscator's previous experiments, were impressed:

Piscator turns the production of this message-play [previously condemned as 'the most inept of all topical plays'] into a democratic assembly. Representatives of religion, theology, medicine – and of the monied classes, who are exempt from the cogs of the murderous law – seated in the stalls, discuss and intervene as active agents in the story of the play...The events of the play become a conclusive demonstration. The argument is brought to an even higher pitch through allowing space to reports given by specialists. Added to this are the spontaneous interruptions from the gallery which cannot be regulated. The personal fate of a proletarian that is shown on the stage becomes a public concern. It is only appropriate when the evening in the theatre is brought to a close by a vote on the paragraph.[16]

The paragraph referred to was the civil law concerning abortion. Considerable suffering was caused by its harsh application during the hardship of the Depression, and the production of § *218* caused riots in the streets protesting against this section of the legal code. The involvement of the audience in a play thus had the reciprocal effect of involving the play, which had taken an actual incident as its subject, in the contemporary situation outside the stage. Since the theatre was literally transformed into a debating hall (with predetermined arguments) performances became public demonstrations.

It is on the basis of this quality in Piscator's work that a recent Communist evaluation has claimed his 'political theatre' as 'an example of how the theatre could intervene in the class-struggle with the means at its disposal in an immediate, concrete and flexible way'.[17] But in Piscator's eyes there was no necessary connection between involvement and bringing public pressure to bear on acute political problems. In the America of McCarthy, fearing repression on the grounds of his previous Communist association, Piscator carefully avoided specific political issues. Yet his productions for the New York Dramatic Workshop aimed at audience participation in an equally aggressive manner: 'instantly you were catapulted into the midst of a crackling theatre world; actors leaping out of seats, men shouting from the aisles, loudspeakers blaring from the rear, scenery shifting on stage before your very eyes'.[18]

Though he never directly admitted it, Piscator clearly came to identify the significance of any dramatic material with the effectiveness of the techniques that communicated it. This can be seen in the plan for a 'Total Theatre' that Piscator commissioned from Walter Gropius in 1927. The architectural design allowed the fullest possible use of the area enclosed within its walls, as was to be expected from the director of the Bauhaus whose members concentrated on the problems of 'vision in action' and the relationship of man to space. There were to be multiple stages, one of which could be revolved into the centre of the auditorium – during the course of a performance, if the director so wished, thus instantaneously altering the relationship of the audience to the action. Additional space was allowed for scenes to be acted out around the walls, on platforms lowered from the roof above the seats, or in the aisles. The design also made it possible for film to be projected onto all the walls and the whole expanse of the ceiling. Enclosed by the unbroken ovoid shape of the building, the spectator would have been completely encircled by the action, while the events represented on stage could be placed in the middle of the public. No less important, the audience were to be collected into a single group instead of being divided into the customary segments of stalls, boxes and balconies – and although Piscator gave political reasons for this organization of the public, the emotional effect of seating spectators in a unified crowd would have had a direct practical value. It would also have simplified the task of the actors by allowing them to work on the audience as a whole instead of having to 'play to the gallery' or to the pit.

In the use envisaged for this theatre Lenin, for instance, could have been presented calling for revolution on the stage. The public surrounding him, architecturally impressed into a single crowd, would have been forced into responding by the example of actors behind them, among them or in the aisles, and by films of revolutionary masses projected around them on the walls – a single vast political demonstration.

The aim of this theatre is...not the material accumulation of refined technical equipment and tricks; on the contrary, all of these are no more than tools and expedients to ensure that the spectator will be drawn into the middle of the scenic events, that he belongs spatially to the stage and cannot withdraw from it behind the curtain.[19]

It was the architecture, however, which determined the function of this machinery and spearheaded the assault on the personal reserve of the onlooker. The capacity for individual judgement would have been submerged beneath the emotional unity of the mass, insofar as the physical positioning made it impossible for a member of the audience to distance himself from either the action of the play or the reaction of the people around him.

Piscator never possessed the capital to build a Gropius-Theater, but he adapted what means he could to achieve a comparable effect. In *Tai Yang Awakes* he turned the whole theatre into a representation of the workers' meeting hall in China, where the play was set, by combining the various sections of the building into a single architectural unit. Platform stages were built in the stalls, and the stage decoration extended through the auditorium into the foyer. Flags and placards hung from the walls, and actors were dispersed among the audience as in § *218* to draw them into the action and to act as 'cheer-leaders'. Even in makeshift form these means of involving the audience proved so effective that Piscator was still using them as late as his 1959 production of *The Fireraisers*.

This kind of participation formed the basis of an idealistic concept of Marxist drama described by Béla Balázs as early as 1919.[20] In expressing the political aspirations of the proletariat this would return to the theatre of ancient Greece, which Balázs saw as 'a creation of the mass-soul, a mass which is not formed from the isolated atoms of heaped up individuals, but a mass which in its Dionysian enthusiasm really achieves a 'unified consciousness'. Reinhardt's Theatre of the Five Thousand acted as a model of what was possible in the contemporary theatre. Here simply the number of onlookers submerged the individual in the mass, and this mass was made conscious of its corporate identity by the arena stage which, surrounded by the public, forced one half of the audience to observe the other in the overspill of stage-lighting on the further side of the acting area. Individuals were indistinguishable in the semi-darkness, and each member of the audience was therefore made aware of the reactions of those around him as a crowd. 'The crowd is the soul and the significance of stage plays', Balázs declared, and he envisaged a theatre where 'the monumental might take the place of intimacy, symbolic reality the place of illusionism'. Balázs worked with Piscator as one of the 'dramaturigical collective' which he formed in 1926, and the influence of this concept of 'the theatre of Communist culture' on Piscator's practice is obvious. It was the theoretical justification for the gradual development of Total Theatre within the analytic and rational framework of Documentary Drama.

There were also political reasons for this involvement of the audience. Communist social historians viewed 'the individual' as a concept created by the bourgeoisie which was no longer relevant after middle-class forms of civilization had been fragmented by the First World War. The masses were thought to dominate the new (Marxist) age because each single person was demonstrably dependent for his existence on the actions of the sum of all others. If it could be said – as Brecht did – that a coolie involved himself in global politics by earning his daily bread, then it was no less true that European proletarians could influence the outcome of the Chinese revolution, and this was the theme of *Tai Yang Awakes*, which could not be more explicit than in the final words: 'So run the battle-lines through China today. And the same battle-front divides Germany.' International pretensions were so widely accepted that the K.P.D. even lost the Prussian elections in 1932 by ignoring local issues in favour of slogans condemning Japanese aggression in China – and the corollary to internationalism was an attempt to suppress any qualities, such as self-consciousness or intellectual awareness, which distinguished personal identity from the mass.

An essay in the programme to *Rasputin* underlined these aspects of audience participation. The film for this play was supposed to demonstrate that the common soldiers had been 'not simply spectators, but protagonists' in the 'dramatic' history of the war and the Czarist state's collapse. But Piscator wished to drive home the extension of this lesson – that the spectators in the stalls had also participated, even if they had been munitions workers or medically unfit for military service – and he therefore sought to involve them in the action. 'They [or men exactly like them] were also there in the slit-trenches along the Stochod and in the

Carpathians', and even those who remained at home had influenced and been affected by the outcome of the conflict. Dovetailing stage and film could bring the global environment into the theatre, but in order to give 'a graphic illustration' of this political world picture Piscator had to prove that no individual was neutral or could stand independent. Since the audience were a part of the historical period dealt with in the play this could only be treated as 'a comprehensive entity' by fusing the individual spectators into a single emotional unit and drawing this collective into the action.

It must be noted that such involvement is the opposite of the modern vogue for provoking the public. This provocation, which we have become familiar with in the work of such producers as Peter Brook, attacks the audience as individuals or as the representatives of particular sections of society, instead of drawing them into a crowd. It has reached its fullest extension in Peter Handke's *Abuse of the Audience* (*Publikumsbeschimpfung*) and is given its clearest expression in the acting edition of *Look Back in Anger*, where Osborne noted that his play could be judged as successful if the audience was provoked to walk out of the auditorium during the performance.

Political theatre, however, needed the active engagement of the onlookers on simple dramatic grounds – quite apart from its usefulness as a tool for propaganda. The tension of drama comes from conflict. But in a play that illustrates Communist dogma the conflict is decided and the end inevitable before the action begins. When in addition it deals with recent history the plot is known to the audience and there can be no real element of surprise. In classical tragedy, which is also characterized by inevitability and where the story was equally well known to the public, this tension is provided by the unities which (as T. S. Eliot pointed out) 'do make for intensity' by giving a formal element of concentration. But in dialectic dramas the mosaic of an episodic structure sets one scene against another and breaks the time-continuum of a play's action, so that involvement becomes essential to give dramatic excitement to the demonstration of an argument – a need that was accentuated by Piscator's mechanistic style. It is accepted that radio and the cinema, being mass media, are quantitatively different to more traditional means of transmitting information. But they are also different in kind from the printed word or the spoken description, being marked by a completeness of data and a sharpness of definition which creates a different relationship with their audiences. Advertisers therefore call these media aggressive and designate them as 'cold' since the recipient remains passive. The stage, on the other hand, although it too can reach a large number of people at the same time, always requires an active imaginative effort because only the outline of the data can be provided and the technical quality of definition is poor. The extent to which a performance communicates is therefore determined by participation. Indeed, it is primarily this that distinguishes the theatre from dramatic entertainment on radio, television or film, where there can be no feed-back from the audience to the performer. Piscator therefore offset the effect of his machinery by using all the means at his disposal to prevent the natural and self-protective disengagement of the spectator in order to create 'a partnership, in which the public plays as large a rôle as the stage'.[21]

The audience and the crowd

At this point it becomes necessary to examine the distinction between an audience and a crowd. In the Shakespearean 'wooden O' or in the court theatres of Molière or Goethe the audience were conscious of each other because daylight or the same chandeliers lit both stage and auditorium. But the relatively small seating capacity and the presence of an aristocracy, who came to be seen rather than to see the play, distinguished individuals from one another. Even the modern proscenium theatre, darkened, compartmentalized and focusing the audiences' eyes exclusively on the scenes separated from them by a picture-frame and an orchestra pit, preserves each member's consciousness of personal identity. Theatre-in-the-round, however, has the opposite effect since the semi-darkness and serried ranks give an impression of featureless masses and the individual, aware of being part of a unified group, has the reactions of that section of the audience which faces him across the stage forced on his attention. This was the seating arrangement in the Theatre of the Five Thousand where Piscator had produced *Despite All!*, and its advantages for involving onlookers as a group are clear.

In normal productions, although an audience reacts primarily on an emotional level and can be affected by mass-suggestion, there is the element of distancing that is common to all artistic appreciation, without which subtleties of feeling would be lost. There is also at all times the consciousness of unreality due to artificial conventions. For this reason plays seldom affect the opinions of an audience or issue in any 'direct action'. The imaginative world of the stage remains isolated from real life outside the theatre – and Piscator had to change the nature of the audience in order to alter its relationship to the stage.

As Somerset Maugham has observed, the 'mental capacity [of an audience is]...less than that of its most intelligent members... When the intelligent look for thought in a playhouse, they show less intelligence than one would have expected of them. Thought is a private thing.'[22] But an audience remains an aggregate of individuals, and that instinctive protection of individuality, 'the giggle', is a constant possibility that every director has to guard against. A crowd, on the other hand, reacts as an entity. Personal differentiation disappears and is replaced by an openness to suggestion and an emotional blanketing of the intellect: 'We think as a crowd only in platitudes, propaganda, visual dogma and symbol...'[23] The more primitive the emotional stimuli, the deeper and more immediate the effect on a mob, and – more relevant as far as the relationship of crowd-psychology to the theatre is concerned – 'the unreal has almost as much influence on them as the real. They have an evident tendency not to distinguish between the two.'[24] When undirected, the mass hysteria latent in the negation of the self results in the wanton destruction of football crowds, but it can lead to the storming of a Bastille if controlled. Piscator's aim was obviously to turn his audience into a crowd – and this cannot have appeared as extraordinary to his contemporaries as it now does to a world that has experienced the stage managed mobs of May Day parades and Nuremberg rallies. This was theatrical policy under Stalin, but before that left-wing intellectuals like Balázs had justified it by reference to their idealized picture of the classical actor/audience relationship. Even democratic critics stated that the aim of the actor in every European culture had always been 'to repress all the intellectually differentiating elements [of the onlookers' consciousness] and to allow everything that is emotionally integrating to expand mightily'.[25]

In the 1920s Piscator was able to use at least the proletarian part of his audiences as a positive element in his productions because they were already politically committed, and therefore, although they were unrehearsed, he could allow accurately for their actions. A slogan, a symbolic gesture or a familiar tune was enough to provoke a known and invariable reaction from the seats alloted to the Subscribers' Club, which was composed of members of the General Workers' Union, the Syndicalists and the Communist Youth – at least at a simple level, as when the *International* was sung 'spontaneously' at performances of *Hoppla!* or *Rasputin*. Later, prospective audiences were encouraged to read the play beforehand and to attend rehearsals so that they might 'come to understand every nuance' – the aim, of course, being to get 'the playgoer to collaborate closely in the performance' on a more complex level.[26] Apart from its impracticability, however, this would have been counter-productive. Attending rehearsals lessens the impact of surprise in a performance and reveals the machinery behind a stage illusion, whereas involvement demands 'an intensification of the powers of illusion'.[27] Thorough knowledge of a script encourages a critical attitude to the director's interpretation, and this works against the audience's total acceptance of a play. By arousing intellectual appreciation it effectually emphasizes the individual and so negates any mechanical techniques of involvement that might be applied during a performance. This was a miscalculation, not a reversal of his opinions, and Piscator's approach to an audience remained basically anti-individualistic.

The Gropius-Theater and the emotional elements of drama

The design that Piscator commissioned from Walter Gropius as a physical formulation of his novel theatrical concepts was intended to be an architectural embodiment of modern conditions. Without the class distinctions implied by boxes or galleries, the seating demonstrated the mass nature of contemporary society while machinery dominated, and sophisticated communications media were to be incorporated as a basic feature of the building, instead of being tacked onto a traditional edifice as the need arose. More important, these political and technological aspects of the architecture would have created specific conditions for performance –

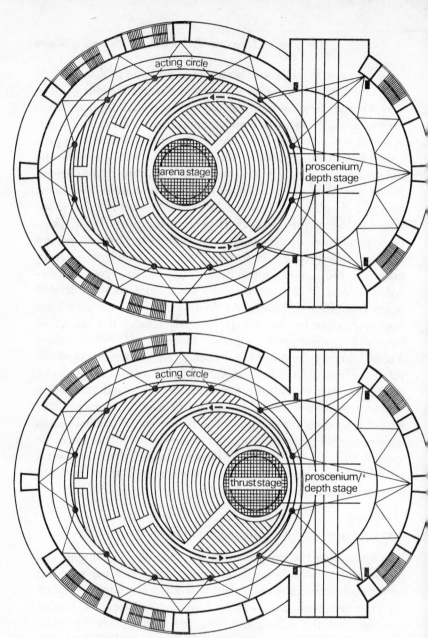

Despite All! Stage designs, John Heartfield, 1925.

accentuating the element of emotional identification, participation, 'direct action' – and this in turn would dictate what sort of material was staged.

146

Although the Gropius-Theater never got off the drawing-board, the design indicates the actual qualities of Piscator's experimentation in a diagrammatic form, freed from his confused rationalizations and polemical comments. It underlines the profoundly anti-literary nature of this type of theatre and demonstrates the basic distinction that Piscator and (in a more extreme way) the Bauhaus drew between printed plays and performance by underlining the optical elements of drama. The blueprint extended the mechanisms which Piscator had developed to gain visual effects, with the result that the technical direction would have had more influence in interpreting the text than the speaking actors. Language would in no sense have been the primary means of communication.

To a certain extent this is a rationalization of an existing state of affairs. Literature conveys meaning primarily through syntactical connections and verbal definitions that can be checked in a dictionary. The writer has to rely for imaginative reconstruction on the visual fantasy of his individual readers – unknown quantities, whose reactions cannot be more than approximately anticipated – and his only optical means of organization is typographical. This can reinforce or counterpoint the logical linguistic structure, but cannot replace it entirely, even though James Joyce, Gertrude Stein and the 'stream of consciousness' school have adapted the poetic technique of the visual and aural deployment of words to prose. The legitimate media of drama, on the other hand, are physical movement and grouping, lighting and sound, vocal and bodily expression, as well as language. In the theatre a speech communicates as much by tone, gestures and facial expressions as by the grammatic sense of the text, and meaning ranges from the subtleties of accent or the instinctive effect of posture to the ostentation of waving a flag. The tone of a production can be altered to allow for the differing moods of every audience, while a novel or poem is transfixed in print and limited to the single medium of the word. The stage exerts more control over the spectators than the isolated author can over his reader, because there is direct contact between the actor and his audience (as there is between a matador and his bull). Yet because the production of a play is transient, changing in its details nightly and in its interpretation from one revival to another, and because the audio-visual elements of a production are seldom recorded, a play survives only through its script.

The methods of notating ballet-choreography have seldom been employed in the theatre, and few productions have been filmed. Only in the classical oriental theatre, where productions are unchanging since gesture and tone have been ritualized, in the New Moscow Art Theatre, where it is still possible to see Stanislavski's original stagings of Chekov's plays, and in the *Modellbücher* which document every movement in the Berliner Ensemble productions of Brecht's major plays, are the audio-visual elements of bygone productions in any sense preserved. The text of a play therefore assumes a disproportionate importance.

Several eminent twentieth-century dramatists have attempted to reform theatrical technique in order to emphasize the literary qualities of their work – W. B. Yeats wished to restore 'the ancient sovereignty of words' by rehearsing actors in barrels to prevent movement, a limitation of physical expression that Beckett has since enforced in *Play*. The aim of many prominent directors on the other hand has been to reduce the literary element in their productions. Moholy-Nagy, a leading exponent of the Bauhaus who was responsible for the stage design and film direction in Piscator's production of *The Merchant of Berlin*, was expressing a common view when he stated in the programme that 'when the optical, acoustical and kinetic elements are given as much space as the literary ones, we draw nearer to the essence of "theatre"'. In this statement (surprisingly moderate considering Moholy-Nagy's extreme views) the qualities listed are those added to a script by the players. The assumption that drama is the sum of all the parts of a production was taken a step further by Piscator, who emphasized the mechanical aspects of direction at the expense of the actor. Concentrating on the 'total effect' he levelled all the various elements of the theatre and defined the relative importance of the actor, the only channel for communicating the words, as 'simply having a function to fulfill, exactly like light, colour, music, structure, text'.[28]

Dissatisfied with the plays that were available and primarily interested in the immediate effect of a performance, Piscator emphasized the ephemeral aspects of drama in his stage experiments. Reducing literary scripts to 'slogan or cry', he replaced the syntactical connections of language with visual relationships – and this substituted emotive association for rational communication. Dramatic necessity can be defined as a pattern of cause and consequence that is logical in its own terms, but the physical montage by which Piscator organized the material of his productions was by nature outside the sphere of logic.

The proposed architectural involvement of the audience was an ideal which Piscator had already partially realized by other means. The anti-literary bias of his productions was one basic aspect of his attack on intellect. The montage structure was another. All Piscator's machinery, whether it was used to gain continuity or to connect and cross-reference facts, to clarify and compress material or to extend the relevance of a message, appealed directly to the senses. Stage effects engulfed the onlookers, inducing emotional participation which automatically suppressed their ability to view a play objectively. Even the neutral element of documentation integrated an audience in the action since 'the boundary between play and reality is blurred'.[29]

In his personal copies of play-scripts, annotated for production, Piscator notes the tempo, the lighting, the sound effects and the positions of acting-structures in detail, while the individual movements of actors are only broadly indicated and speeches are cut (with the result that logical inconsistencies often appear in the text). Those elements which transmit and heighten feeling – atmosphere, tone and symbolism – were emphasized, and Karl Kraus complained correctly that Piscator's work was 'Dionysian' in its effect. Béla Balázs, on the other hand, commented that the justification for a politically committed theatre was precisely this 'Dionysian contact between stage and auditorium' since total involvement was only possible when an audience had a common identity. The mingling of reality and illusion and the blurring of distinctions between the various theatrical media gained a similar effect to the emotional prostitution of Wagner's work – and Piscator himself approved of the comparison, quoting a comment by Grosz to illustrate his aims: 'A piece of the old Wagner-desire lives in him [Piscator] too, and so we see him continually on the thorny quest for the great synaesthetic art-work which embraces all the arts.'[30]

'Total Theatre': variations and definitions

Synaesthesia is at the other extreme to documentary or epic criteria, but it was implicit in the techniques that Piscator found essential for dealing comprehensively with contemporary realities, so that in developing Documentary Drama his experiments automatically transcended the limitations of the 'topical' plays he came to reject. His lack of certainty about the exact nature of his achievement, however, led to confusion concerning 'Total Theatre', and the name has since been applied to three distinct types of production.

The term was originally used by Gropius to describe his architectural design which gave a director the choice of setting a play on an arena stage, an amphitheatre, behind a conventional proscenium arch or on any combination of them all. He called this 'the total theatre' because it was completely flexible, 'as systematized as a typewriter, which could do justice to all demands from Aeschylus and Shakespeare up to Chekov and Brecht or the new documentary plays'.[31] Piscator adapted this meaning, identifying the opportunity to play all types of drama with the ability to represent the drama of life as a whole.

But because the most striking characteristic of this ideal theatre was the new relationship that it produced between actor and audience, making the auditorium itself the scene of action, he associated Total Theatre primarily with the absolute integration of the onlooker in the play. This could only be achieved by the fullest use of all the various media – film and loudspeaker, placard and music, scenery and mime, as well as and at the expense of the speaking actor – so that the second definition gave rise to the third: 'The theatre is no longer satisfied with mastering reality in *excerpts*, it wants *total* coverage. Yet in order to set the *totality* of the world on the stage, it needs new means of expression...'[32]

Piscator himself described this use of all the media at his disposal as the '*total mechanization* of the stage', which returned full circle to the original architectural concept of the theatre as a flexible machine. But others never saw further than the stylistic *pot-pourri*, and the formal aspects of Piscator's productions came to dominate discussions about Total Theatre. Some critics confused it with the revue-form, judging it unworthy of serious attention, and Diebold found it necessary to defend Piscator's mixture of techniques by stressing that the theatre was not and never had been a 'pure' art. The Greeks, he argued, had exploited the contrast between naturalistic actors and a stylized chorus. Shakespeare had alternated prose clowns and down-to-earth peasants with poetic kings and the magic of the imagination. Opera counterpointed spoken recitative with *bel canto* arias. Therefore Piscator's synthesis of song and naturalistic film scenes, stylized stage acting and actual photographs, declamation and statistics was a development in the mainstream of theatrical tradition. It is this aspect that has come to dominate definitions of Total Theatre, which John Russell Taylor lists in his *Dictionary of the Theatre* as that 'concept of theatre as above all a director's medium, using the text only as one relatively minor part of an overall theatrical experience of lights, music, movement of all sorts, sets and costumes'.

Jean-Louis Barrault is the most famous exponent of this type of theatrical eclecticism, and his production of Claudel's *Christophe Colombe* in 1953 and again in 1962 has acted as a model both for dramatic critics and his followers. Claudel's play was first written as an opera and then reworked in conjunction with Barrault. Film sequences were introduced, and the text was redesigned for a simultaneous stage. Acted scenes and chorales alternate with dance and pantomime, and side by side with techniques for involving the audience are 'epic', anti-illusionistic effects. The action is interrupted by the criticism of the chorus who both represent the audience and question them, the orchestra is visible on the stage, the rôle of the hero is played by two different actors, and there is a 'speaker' who introduces the scenes. Claudel intended the performance to be 'like a Mass in which the public takes part'; but the projections were all symbolic – for instance a dove hovering above a globe – and the juxtaposition of different effects was organized ritualistically, so that the production was a grand 'spectacle' and the participation was a passive, congregational kind.

This kind of production was superficially so similar to Piscator's work that Piscator found it necessary to distinguish it from his concept in an article differentiating between 'Complete Theatre (*Totaltheater*) and Total Theatre (*Totales Theater*)', which was specifically directed against the Barrault production. *Théâtre complet* he rejected because this 'conglomeration of representational forms of expression' was created for purely aesthetic reasons, while in his concept of Total Theatre the medley of techniques was functional. The justification for the mixture of styles was the representation of a total sociological picture and the total involvement of the audience in the action which (in theory) fused theatrical experience with the totality of world events.

7 New Drama: the Author

Documentary, Epic or Total Theatre – the confusion can be explained by the provisional nature of Piscator's experiments. Although they were designed to create appropriate stage-conditions for the modern context, he never thought of his productions as ends in themselves but as a means of encouraging authors to write plays in a new style by demonstrating the effectiveness of modern media. He expanded the temporal and spatial limits of a performance, made the stage capable of commentary, evolved an acting style that worked with his machinery and gave examples of characterization which were not tied to any outdated concept of individualism. His techniques established a new approach to reality and showed that areas of experience previously considered to be outside the range of the theatre could be handled dramatically and staged successfully. Lacking a body of existing plays which corresponded to the twentieth-century environment or modern needs, he took material from recent history and current events, adapted classical works, altered suitable contemporary scripts and dramatized novels to provide a temporary substitute. He had not only educated his actors. He also brought authors into direct contact with the new theatrical conditions which he had developed (as he was later to do again in the New York Dramatic Workshop) by forming a dramaturgical collective and by working with Gasbarra and Lania, Toller and Wolf, forcing them to revise their plays during rehearsals which acted as practical instruction in the standards required by his stage. But in spite of his efforts it was many years before his productions bore fruit in the shape of a new drama.

The influence of Piscator's experiments

Apart from the superficial level of scandals, law-suits and critical argument which publicized his techniques, Piscator's earlier experiments did have a measurable effect during the Weimar Republic.

By the close of the decade every workers' organization, whatever its ideology, sponsored Agitprop performances based on his revues, which became the established form of politically involved drama; while the 'Topical Theatre' that imitated his documentary work swept the professional stage, making 'objective' treatments of factual material standard practice. But Piscator, who had progressed beyond the narrow application of simplistic propaganda or superficial contemporaneity outdated by every turn of events, rejected these movements which he had fathered. His influence in the Agitprop line affected stage-craft, but not authors, whose services were dispensed with by this theatrical genre; and the dramatists who turned to 'topical' plays had assimilated none of his developments after *Flags*.

Even the best of them, Erich Mühsam's *Reasons of State*, a memorial for Sacco and Vanzetti which was 'written for the first anniversary of their death, 23 August 1928', or Rehfisch and Herzog's *The Dreyfus Affair*, produced in 1929 and judged by Jhering to be 'the high-point of journalistic theatre', although topical successes, have no interest today. They never rise above particulars to examine the general issues which made the situations significant, and the objectivity of Mühsam's approach is undermined by the intrusion of sentimentality, while the flat speech of Rehfisch's characters falls into another pitfall of this type of drama. Determinedly untheatrical, it is also undramatic and appears still duller in contrast to the long and much livelier passages of Zola that are included in the text. Even though the courtroom setting of these plays lends itself to conflict and in-depth explanation, their bare re-enactment of facts relied too much on relevance and overestimated the intrinsic interest of their subjects. *Reasons of State* was on the boards before the reverberations had vanished from the newspapers, and *The Dreyfus Affair* appeared when anti-semitism and partial justice were beginning to be serious problems in the disintegrating Weimar Republic, but these plays are too tied to their period to hold attention today. The scenes have been given precise dates and places, the characters repeated the actions and words of actual persons, and in Mühsam's play news-reports were read out to indicate the world-wide reaction to the trial. This conformed to the surface elements of Documentary Drama, and Mühsam emphasized in a postscript that the internal structure of the play is simply the transference of reality into the theatre...no dramatization in any usual sense was intended. The historical sequence of events has created a drama of such immense effectiveness that practically nothing has been left for the poetic imagination to do.

But pathos and crude political jargon make his style seem juvenile today. The texts of these plays do not reflect the technical advances made by Piscator and the scale and sweep of vision that characterized Piscator's productions is completely lacking.

The sharpening political situation, however, brought the exciting period of theatrical experimentation to a close before dramatists could reasonably be expected to have recognized the implications of Piscator's achievements for their work. Piscator, who had been chiefly responsible for turning the stage into a political instrument, was the first casualty. In 1929 the second Piscator-Bühne opened with *The Merchant of Berlin* – and closed, a victim of inflation and resurgent nationalism. In 1930 the National Socialists won 107 seats in the Reichstag, leaping overnight from an insignificant faction to the second largest party, and disrupted debates by demagoguery and mob-disturbances. This turn in Weimar politics was almost immediately reflected in the theatre, ever the most sensitive seismograph of social attitudes, where technical or aesthetic qualities now took a very subordinate place:

Then arguments were based on standards which had nothing to do with art, standards which were derived from racialism on the one side and the ideology of class-warfare on the other. The theatre became a focus for battle because it had a value as a political platform. The concept of the theatre as a 'moral institution' was now filled with the most varied contents.[1]

From 1930 on there was an increasing exodus of artists from Berlin. Jessner was forced to resign from the Staatstheater, Reinhardt took refuge again in Austria, Piscator was arrested on a trumped-up charge of tax-evasion after the success of § *218*, while at the same time Karl Credé was imprisoned in Stuttgart for allegedly procuring abortions, and in 1931 Jhering noted that 'the theatre of today has stumbled into a void'.

Just as the Communist Party, acting on the principle that every sign of constitutional stability set back the expected World Revolution, had itself helped to prepare the field for Fascism, so Piscator's early use of the stage for open propaganda and subsequent defence of his productions on ideological grounds contributed to the conditions which prevented the growth of a new dramatic tradition. Piscator's condemnation of the political implications of traditional art forms, however, was shown to be justified. The traditional attitude that 'drama is a spiritual experience' and that therefore 'the stage has only one task: to act as a humble servant of the poetic word'[2] led directly to recommendations for an 'official Ministry of Culture for contemporary drama and theatre arts'[3] to encourage positive moral and aesthetic values – which was a short step from burning books of 'negative' value. The atmosphere in the closing years of the Weimar Republic can be measured by the increasing number of plays written about Napoleon, who was looked on as the epitome of dictatorship. The only liberal-oriented stage that continued to exist was the Junge Volksbühne organization and, even before Hitler became Chancellor, theatrical productions fell into two major categories. The left-wing dramatists and directors were forced to revert to crude Agitprop performances, while the professional theatre celebrated a return to the plush and pomp and the naturalistic illusionism of the pre-war period.

In the Third Reich blank verse became the approved mode of expression, and the stage subsisted on a diet of second-rate social comedies, the Classics performed in a rigidly conventional style, and – more harmful – the monumental glorification of the 'heroic' virtues associated with 'warlike man' in the 'blood and soil' pseudo-philosophy. Such plays as Dietrich Eckhart's *Lorenzaccio*, first performed in 1933, or Mussolini's *Hundred Days*, the most extreme of all the glorifications of Napoleon, produced in 1932, are of interest as historical documents but made no attempt to handle contemporary issues or to use a style appropriate to the modern world. Wagner, whose ideas were distorted and emphasized at the expense of his artistic achievements, was seen as the ideal dramatist, 'who wished to draw the dark subconscious of his nation into the sacramental arms of the cross',[4] so that wallowing sentimentality and impoverished mysticism, hollow rhetoric and loud voices became the characteristics of Fascist plays. Any form of technical or literary innovation was labelled 'negative' and therefore out of the question, as were objectivity, irony or (naturally) any form of social criticism, while 'positive' aesthetic standards were defined as 'the expression of the German being and German character, measured by the high value of moral content'.[5] Hitler was sycophantically hailed as the reformer of German drama: 'In all of German life at the present time there is no man with such a fanatical will to art and in particular to theatrical art as Adolf Hitler'.[6] But the theatre stagnated so much under the Nazis that even Goebbels was reported to be bored by the plays produced under his aegis. In such circumstances art, progressive or relevant, could not flourish. It was replaced at worst by empty posturing, at best by mere entertainment, and the Third Reich represents a total break in artistic tradition that first had to be bridged before German artists could again create works of true value.

Total war reinforced the effect of Fascist cultural policies. In 1945, in contrast to the end of the First World War, many of the theatres lay in ruins, and the leading authors and artists who were capable of recreating German drama had been driven into exile, where those who had survived the war remained, waiting for conditions to improve. Brecht came back to Europe in 1947, but had to wait until 1948 in Switzerland before he was allowed to return to Berlin, and Piscator stayed in America until 1951.

Piscator's dramaturgy had demanded intricate and expensive machinery which could not be provided at that period, and as a guest director his productions were mainly limited to the Classics – Lessing, Büchner and Pirandello, Shaw, Schiller and Shakespeare – until he was appointed director of the Freie Volksbühne in 1962. As a result he had little influence on the initial development of post-war drama, so that when the first new German plays of any importance appeared they were, like Borchert's *Heimkehr* play, *The Outsider*, a return in technique to the more conventional dramas of the early 1920s. The lack of significant German dramatic work in this decade and a half (even Brecht had virtually ceased to write new plays) is well illustrated by most critical books on twentieth-century German drama, which devote their consideration of works produced after 1945 almost exclusively to the German-speaking Swiss playwrights. But when Rolf Hochhuth submitted *The Deputy* to Piscator the situation changed.

In the 1920s Piscator had to work with machinery alone, hammering out a script from financial textbooks for *Economic Competition* and filling out Alexei Tolstoy's play with passages from memoirs and state documents, or adapting a novel for the stage in *Schweik*. Inevitably the literary element of drama had suffered in his productions. Hašek's work had been unavoidably reduced to a skeleton in order to compress its material into a performance, and he had come to associate poetry or carefully constructed phrases with undramatic or unrealistic treatment, replacing them with a linguistic medium that he could manage: journalese and short, denotative sentences. Here a dramatist had provided him with a play that treated a relevant subject in an appropriate style, and even though he expanded the dramaturgical form with machinery and cut some of the more lyrical passages and symbolic scenes, as he had done in the Piscator-Bühne, the body of the text was produced as it stood. His production in 1963 acted as a model for other dramatists and directors, and a wave of epic-documentary plays followed, from his production of *In the Matter of J. Robert Oppenheimer*, by Heinar Kipphardt in 1964 and *The Investigation* by Peter Weiss in 1965 to Palitzsch's production of *Toller* by Tancred Dorst in November 1968.

Mechanical difficulties: the delay in the development of the new drama

If we look back over the whole of his career, and with the critical distance of half a century which makes it possible to trace the development of Piscator's experiments, the relevance of his approach to reality can be seen more clearly than it would have appeared to his contemporaries in the 1920s. Other associated factors would have been more immediately obvious – the party-political nature of his theatre, the sensational novelty of his machinery, or the scandals which seemed an inevitable sequel to his productions. Above all, the technical difficulties that arose as a result of his application of new media to the theatre directed attention to the particular means of portrayal and away from the general effects that they were intended to convey. Piscator tended to put this down to 'a deep split between our existence and our desires', claiming this to be 'the unavoidable consequence' of the discrepancy between the Communist orientation of his theatre and the capitalist attitude of his audience.[7]

The true reason, however, was the inefficient nature of Piscator's stage-machinery – and it was this as much as anything else which kept authors away.

Few playwrights were prepared to sacrifice as much independence as Wolf, who later recounted an anecdote to illustrate the control exercised by Piscator: running from the stage after a dispute with Piscator he was recalled by an actor who said, 'Wolf, come back quickly! A whole sentence of yours is just being spoken on the stage.'[8] The first night of *Tai Yang Awakes* was postponed for over two months while Wolf rewrote the play three times, but with this play, performed with minimal machinery, the critics praised the text. From *Storm over Gottland* on, the more usual criticism was that Piscator sacrificed plays to his productions; and the authors, for whom the performances were intended as demonstrations of the material and stylistic possibilities that could be made available, must have viewed his experiments with mistrust. Not only was Piscator notorious for his autocratic alteration of texts, but he constantly overreached himself in his efforts to create contemporary theatrical forms with insufficient materials, and the elements he substituted for the literary qualities of a play were clumsy and frequently malfunctioned. The weight of the acting-structure for *Hoppla!* made it difficult to move around the stage. Even with the lavish application of soap, graphite and lubricating oil the treadmills that he had invented for *Schweik* tended to drown the actors' voices. The global construct for *Rasputin* had fallen apart in one performance, and Piscator admitted the justice of Alfred Kerr's unkind description of it as a 'cumbersomely crawling crustacean of grey canvas'. *The Merchant of Berlin* was in one sense the culmination of his efforts; but looked at in another light it was a technological disaster:

Two retractable bridges rose up and sank down – when they functioned. Two running bands ran – when they functioned. Everything rattled, roared, hummed – with funereal slowness. Nothing went right – waiting or running legs were seen beneath curtains, tableaux stuck half-way as they were lowered out of sight – scene dragged after scene cumbersomely and reluctantly. From 7.30 until 11.45.[9]

As might be expected, dramatists were unwilling to risk their reputations by writing plays for this sort of production and even Brecht, though he worked closely with Piscator, never gave him any of his plays to direct.

Piscator's conceptions ran ahead of the capabilities of his engineers, and his recurring complaint was that 'as ever the technical possibilities, measured against the ideal, were insufficient'.[10] In fact the technical aspect of his productions appeared even more unsatisfactory than it actually was because he was forced to combine new media with outdated machinery. Even if he had been freed from the financial pressure which contributed to the makeshift effect of his work by demanding more premières than he could produce with the resources at his disposal, at that time his ideas could never have been more than partially realized. The apparatus which was intended to create a continuity of action weighed down the individual scenes and tended to retard the flow of events. The film and projection, that should have drawn the audience into the subject and impressed the material upon them, drew attention to themselves. Machinery that was meant to serve dominated by its novelty and became particularly conspicuous when it failed to function. Under these circumstances, and with so few years between the opening of the Piscator-Bühne and Piscator's exile it was hardly surprising that the new drama he awaited did not develop during the Weimar Republic.

In the 1920s Piscator's machinery had seemed too complicated, heavy and specialized to form a permanent addition to the theatre's armoury of expression, although some critics (in particular Bernhard Diebold) had perceived the potential in his experiments. But by the time Piscator returned to Germany in the fifties technology had advanced far enough to make his ideas practicable. What had been startlingly unusual was common enough by then to be accepted, and the new theatres built in the place of those destroyed during the war were largely equipped with modern and efficient machinery.

The mass media, which encourage superficiality and popularize new ideas, accustom the public to extraordinary methods of expression and can turn an original insight into platitude overnight. As a result Piscator's machinery passes unnoticed today – Palitzsch's use of film, trick cartoons in the Grosz style, placards, projections, and a complex acting structure mounted on a revolve for his production of *Toller* hardly raised a mention from the critics – but the accompanying demand for continual novelty undervalues the effect of Piscator's experiments. In 1959 Piscator defined his aim as being to accustom the public, actors and critics to his innovations, so that 'the special techniques of the stage: like the revolve, treadmills, mechanized stairs, motorized bridges, the functional acting-area, lighting from beneath...film and projection... the removal of the barrier between the auditorium and the stage'[11] would become as invisible as normal stage-machinery, which is unnoticed when everything works. This indeed happened, but as a result his production of *The Deputy* was criticized for its conventionality, although the machinery that he used was in fact no less complex than that which had raised such violent reactions in the days of the Piscator-Bühne.

Functionalism v. Formalism: 'living theatre' and the 'light-stage'

Piscator's stage-machinery, however, was not intended to be completely disregarded since it had symbolic importance as a correlative of the contemporary environment. In 1928 he had defended the mechanical nature of his productions by claiming that the 'dictatorship of dead apparatus', of which he had been accused, was a condition of life 'in the factory, in the mines, in prison, in the barracks and in war'[12] so that, as he repeated in 1956, technology was the 'legitimate means of expression for the modern age', and its use was necessary for 'the adaptation of a modern, publicly relevant stage to the present time'.[13] This view, far more than a defensive justification, led to the apparent contradiction that as an image 'the technical means themselves must become a work of art', although at the same time 'technology is in the final instance no more than a means of intellectual expression and must overcome itself'.[14] Even in his early productions, where overcoming practical difficulties had been Piscator's primary concern, his technical means always had a tendency to become ends in themselves, and the condemnation of the staging of *The Last Kaiser* or *The Merchant of Berlin* as 'formalistic' was not without justice. In these plays machinery which had been developed to compress subject matter, explain it and expand its scale of reference, was used for extrinsic effect to cover the weakness of the text with an almost baroque extravagance. But this hardly rules out the intrinsic value of such machinery and, even if it had provided a harmful image in the twenties, attracting the wrong kind of attention because it malfunctioned, when Piscator spoke of making it invisible he only meant that it should work smoothly enough to be unnoticed except on a subconscious level. It was a potential form of expression, but like speech, if tongue and lip movements absorbed too much concentration then the words they laboured to articulate would be ignored. However, realizing after his return from exile that it was now possible to extend his experiments, Piscator began to speak of creating a 'living theatre'. Every element of the theatre building was to be a functional part of a production; architecture was to come alive.

This had been an integral if seldom emphasized aspect of his earlier work. It formed the basis for his conception of Total Theatre, and as early as the *Tidal Wave* production Piscator had pointed out that a projection-screen 'forms the fourth dimension of the theatre as a living wall in its continual transformation'.[15] To get the effect of movement with stills, Piscator had planned to use between six and ten projectors, but this was too clumsy. In the following year he experimented with film, and after *Storm over Gottland* it was possible to speak of 'four-dimensional theatre with a *living* backdrop. The living backdrop is the film'.[16] Piscator was, of course, primarily referring to the capacity of photography to create a 'milieu which would extend far outside the scene in question to form a global frame for it'.[17] But the description also fits the surrealistic world created around the prisoners in *Hoppla!,* where instead of a conventional representation of the usual cell-bars a double film was projected onto a gauze, showing the shadow-figure of a warder walking his beat across the width of the stage, while the figure of a second warder was superimposed on the first, marching in perspective towards and away from the audience and growing to giant size as he approached the footlights. In *Schweik* the floor of the stage and the scenery as well as the screen background were in movement, and instead of a series of pictures being projected the caricatures and cartoons developed and dissolved: a point expanded into a full face; a line grew into a tree, bore hanging men as fruit, and stiffened into the symbol of justice. 'The stage...should become kaleidoscopic as a whole and must be mobile in all its smallest parts.'[18]

The concept of 'living theatre' was not original. The Expressionists had shared similar ideals, and the architects of the Bauhaus had imagined 'a great keyboard for light and space...a flexible building, capable of transforming and refreshing the mind by its spatial impact alone...The playhouse itself, made to dissolve into the shifting, illusionary space of the imagination, would become the scene of action itself'.[19] But the Bauhaus practice was abstract, replacing drama by geometrical equations, while the asymmetrical scenery and wildly unnatural shapes petrified Expressionist productions. Their settings remained a 'dead gesture' which detracted from the 'living gestures' of the actors, while the Bauhaus eventually dispensed with actors altogether. Even a suggestion that constantly changing lights should be substituted for scenery proved impractical, and it was Piscator who developed the machinery which made such ideas working possibilities.

Both scenery and the stage floor were mobile. The proscenium arch had been transformed into a camera lens for *The Last Kaiser*, contracting or expanding according to the scene, and in his last production before leaving the States (*Macbeth*) Piscator substituted for the house-curtain a gauze upon which pictures could be projected and behind which the scenes were lit up, thus integrating even the most recalcitrant architectural features of the theatre into the movement of a performance: 'That this curtain is a gauze serves to let the document shine through history – through history, fate – through fate, character.' This, he claimed, turned an otherwise purely stylistic effect into a practical means of expressing complex subject matter: 'Thus the gauze becomes an essential stage-property, and ought to be used as such. Openly, directly – without...illusion.'[20]

From 1953 on he experimented with a 'light-stage' (*die Licht-bühne*), which carried one step further this process of giving every inanimate part of the acting area a positive dramaturgical function. Here the stage floor was replaced by glass, so that the actors could be lit from beneath. In 1927 Piscator had realized that stage-lighting could be used so that it 'loses all its dependence on space, gains life and transforms the theatre'[21] – with the 'light-stage' he believed that this conception could at last be put into practice.

Although all Piscator's other techniques possessed significance for the theatre on a purely formal level, they had been evolved in response to the difficulties of representing actual subjects on a global scale and were defended as functional (in the strict sense of the word): 'and there "technology" stepped in: as a means of elucidation, as commentary, as documentation, as reportage, as analysis, it was intended to raise the action from the individual to the universally valid, for comparison, for example, for demonstration'.[22] Here, however, the primary effect was stylistic, although Piscator related it to the material of the plays and gave it an interpretative rôle by limiting the area of under-floor lighting to the 'stage of fate' (*die Schicksalsbühne*), so that characters who stepped out of their personal surroundings to play a part in the wider arena of history were sharply differentiated.

Piscator's attitude to stylistic questions had always been ambivalent. In his book he repeatedly denied that stylistic ends were being served by revolutionizing the stage, and in newspaper articles he had argued that the effect of his machinery was limited to transmitting facts clearly and economically and to impressing the audience with the truth of the social critique. But at the same time he made careful stylistic evaluations of his work, and his studio was explicitly founded to form 'the *style* for a new theatre'.[23] *Hoppla!* had been taken to indicate a complete rejection of art, a view which Piscator fostered for political reasons. But this rejection was limited to discarding traditional aesthetic principles, which were no longer relevant to modern conditions, since he saw art as 'without principles and protean, like life itself whose most elementary experiences and achievements appear new every day and are radically changed by the state of scientific knowledge. In spite of this, art is and always was my starting-point.'[24] Later he admitted that in *Hoppla!* he was 'not solely concerned with the technical in the sense of our technocratic civilization or even with scientific analysis, but with the break-through to a new stage-form'[25] and claimed that 'the work of the political theatre has been anything but unartistic'.[26] With the addition of the 'light-stage' to his range of theatrical effects the stylistic nature of his work became too obvious to explain away, and unsympathetic critics attacked this use of lighting as an 'emigration out of the present. A withdrawal from reality. Eschatology'.[27]

The 'light-stage' was indeed qualitatively different from his other machinery, but it had an important side effect which was not merely stylistic. Where Piscator's other innovations had emphasized environment at the expense of the characters, this lighting from beneath focused attention on the human individual, throwing the actor into high relief and separating him from the setting: 'When men can walk on light – they become independent of space. Then there will not only be the "placeless" [unrepresentational] but also the "spaceless" stage...[The actor] becomes man in himself [*en soi*].'[28]

The 'light-stage' and literary drama: Piscator and the Classics

The 'light-stage', Piscator claimed, would 'bring freedom from technology – since in it technology is brought to its last and ultimate, subtlest expression'[29] – the same type of syllogistic argument that he had once used to assert that the aim of political theatre was to free the theatre from politics. But this invention had significant implications for Piscator's work on a completely different level. With the new precision and variation of lighting effects new rhythms of movement could be created on stage because words could control, conduct and concert the interplay of lights – and as a reflex of speech the 'light-stage' made the spoken word a focal point in emphasizing the actor.

Such a radically different use of stage-machinery reflected a change of attitude. Before his emigration it was inconceivable that Piscator could have made the statement that

if I were to put Chekov into rehearsal, of course I would employ Stanislavski's system, which fits Chekov's plays like a glove...Nor is there any need to modernize them either. I am completely against playing Chekov's plays on a stage without luminance, for in doing that one runs the danger of losing the atmosphere and aroma of the production.[30]

This contradiction of his former practice is more apparent than real, since he never did direct any plays of this type after his early Central-Theater productions, which were excessively naturalistic in style, and he qualified his statement by commenting that it would be pointlessly anachronistic today to write a three-act play with a conflict that was resolved on the personal scale. Yet his position had been significantly modified: 'The director's task is to bring a stage script alive, to translate the book into life.'[31] The actual extent of the change can best be seen in his practice, and his two productions of *The Robbers* provide a unique opportunity for direct comparison. The way he staged Schiller's play in 1926 outraged all who looked on drama as art and the author as the creator of a play. By contrast his 1957 production aroused their admiration.

The Classics, which can be defined as plays that retain an immediate appeal over the centuries, are the basis of any theatre's repertoire; but due to accretions of meaning and shifts of viewpoint their effect differs for each generation. Any established style, when the conditions for which it was considered appropriate change, tends to vitiate the material that it clothes; and in Germany academics perpetuated an anachronistic form of playing the Classics. They appeared irrelevant, and Piscator's summary treatment of *The Robbers* under Jessner's aegis in 1926 excised all the attributes of Schiller's play associated with the expected style of its representation.

The question of costume epitomizes the difficulties of producing a well-known play when the director's intention conflicts with the traditional interpretation on which the accepted ideas of the audience are based. There was nothing new in setting a Classic in contemporary dress – either to startle the audience out of their preconceptions or to reveal fresh relevance. In 1921 Erich Ziegel had followed the approach of Garrick – who used to play Macbeth in the dress of a general in George II's army with the occasional addition of a 'period' cloak – by producing *The Robbers* with steel helmets, 98-mm cannon and red flags. Jessner had turned *Hamlet* into an attack on the ex-Kaiser's court and made the grave-digger's speeches a proletarian accusation of society, taking 'Something is rotten in the state of Denmark' as his theme and drawing explicit parallels between Claudius and Kaiser Wilhelm II, and between Polonius and Bethmann-Hollweg – but emphasizing that the text was unchanged. The feeling that the traditional approach was in need of renovation had been gathering support since the turn of the century. As early as 1913 Otto Brahm argued that all plays, whether by Sophocles, Shakespeare or Schiller, should be deliberately aligned to the spirit of the audience by being produced in a naturalistic form (the dominant style of his period) since dramatic art was contemporary and only existed at the time of its performance. Even Reinhardt had rejected the 'patina of pathos and empty declamation in the fossilized tradition of court theatres' and had stated that 'the Classics must be played in a new way; they must be played as if the poets were writing today and their works were the life of today'.[32] But such formal experiments as Hamlet in a steel helmet, Karl Moor in command of artillery, or Oedipus in an apartment-building simply underlined the problem, and Brecht (responding to the furore aroused by Piscator's production of *The Robbers*) was not unjustified when he claimed that 'in truth one could no longer dare to offer [the classical repertoire] in its old form to grown-up news-paper readers'.[33]

Piscator had gone further than merely setting Schiller's words in the trenches or altering their implications. Spielgelberg, masked as Trotsky, became a Bolshevist hero, while Karl Moor's character and motives were altered and his tragic flaw was made an object of ridicule as 'a bourgeois weakness'. The ancestral home became a fortified prison, while Old Moor ('lively, healthy, happy') and Franz were presented as brutal representatives of the ruling classes, so that the breaking-in of Schweizer's band appeared a proletarian equivalent of the storming of the Bastille. The performance ended with a cry of 'Freedom! Freedom!', and the unorthodox approach was underscored by introducing a saxophone for incidental music.

Piscator had taken Otto Brahm's argument to its logical con-clusion. Since theatre is a transient art, dependent upon 'all the elements of the day', a director must 'see himself as the servant and exponent of *his time*' instead of acting as 'the servant of the literary work'[34] – and therefore the script itself must be altered because 'Tasso's complaint wakens no echo from the concrete chambers and steel walls of our century...Hamlet's neurasthenia cannot count on any sympathy from a generation of hand-grenade throwers and record-breakers'.[35] New clothing and hair-cuts were not enough to make a Romantic play relevant to modern audiences. The language was updated in the same way that the characters were given contemporary preoccupations, and the surviving acting-copies show a progressive alteration of the play from Schiller's text to Piscator's final production. Modernizing the phraseology which associated *The Robbers* with the eighteenth century, and deleting any outdated vocabulary was a preliminary step in making the writing correspond to the new content. The first major cuts were in descriptive passages, since the extensive use of film and photography made word-painting superfluous. Images, similies and poetic terms were struck out. Philosophical generalizations (for example: 'to each comes his appointed time at the last, whether on soft cushions of down, or in the harsh hurly-burly of battle, or on the open gallows and wheel...') and ethical meditations (such as Karl's reflections on the explosion in the powder-tower) were removed, transforming the play from a moral conflict into a series of revolutionary actions. Finally any complex sentence structure that remained was replaced by simple statements. Even though some of the speeches were later replaced by new material in type-script, the final text, including additions, was under half the original length. Yet the actual performance-time was comparable to a normal production, and notes of actors' positions and movements show that the lacunae were filled in with extensive physical action.

Taken together, the changes indicate a definite pattern. The textual alterations progressively reduced the verbal logic of Schiller's dialogue, dismantling the intellectual design and psychological structure of the play as a whole, and replaced it with a visual organization of mime, gesture and movement, which depended on the use of a simultaneous stage to relate the disparate and fragmented scenes. The eye dominated. The most important statements, held up to the audience on placards or projected onto a screen, were removed from the context of logic and used to form additional optical associations. A sentence became the equivalent of a flag, waved above the actors, arousing emotion and involving the audience. Little was left of Schiller's play except the main line of its action, its title and the names of its characters. But it could be argued – as Piscator did – that Schiller had originally intended the play to have a politically revolutionary effect, and that this radical interpretation was the only way of gaining the equivalent response in a modern audience. Truth to the spirit of Schiller's work could only be achieved by sacrificing the text, since the specific details which had contemporary relevance for Schiller's public were now outdated, while his characterization of the revolutionaries, lifelike in the Romantic era, no longer corresponded to everyday experience, and the language set over a century as a barrier between the dramatic event and Piscator's audience. Consequently the production, which enraged the majority of the critics, was praised for its 'sharpness and clarity' by Herbert Jhering, who found 'substance...instead of aesthetic finesse' – and from then on performances of the Classics became a subject for public dispute.

Yet from another point of view Piscator was definitely using the play for his own purposes. He was interested in giving an example of how the stage could be made politically effective, no suitable modern scripts being available, rather than in giving a valid interpretation of Schiller's work, and to Jhering it was immaterial that this was not the play Schiller had written. 'Since there is a complete lack of modern revolutionary plays', he considered it justified to produce *The Robbers* 'as if it portrayed an actual revolutionary action. [Piscator] takes the fable from the play and gives it reality.'[36] But the effect of this production was more stylistic than specifically political. After it, the transformation of Classics into contemporary plays became the rule rather than the exception and the stultifying hold of the old rigid style of staging dramatic masterpieces was broken until the Nazis revived it.

Piscator's approach to the Classics after the war was subtly different. In 1940 he had interpreted *King Lear* 'as an indictment of modern dictatorship', which appears to parallel his early production of *The Robbers*. Yet at the same time a claim for tradition was made: 'We are not portraying Lear as a romanticist but as a dictator – which is the way the famous David Garrick played the rôle'[37] – and in comparison the textual changes were minor. Similarly, before his 1957 production of *The Robbers* Piscator disingenuously expressed the intention of staging Schiller's play 'exactly as faithfully and piously...as Herr von Dalberg [the original producer] believed himself to be doing in 1782'. Yet his intention of making the subject matter relevant to modern times remained the same: 'Perhaps not quite such a museum piece, for indeed at that time he [von Dalberg] didn't dare to allow *The Robbers* to play in the "present", as Schiller had intended, but turned the time of the action back by 300 years.'[38] Piscator did in fact cut over a third of the text – but this was in order to bring out Schiller's meaning more clearly, and critics praised the production for its faithfulness to the author's intentions, which rather than textual accuracy is one touchstone of any interpretation of the Classics. As Peter Brook has summed it up: a director 'must be able to discriminate between archaism and the essential living heart of the play – the poet's inner dream – for which it is his job to find theatrical correlatives'.

Piscator's 1962 production of the *Atreus Tetralogy* is the clearest example of his approach. Hauptmann's work is a damning critique of the situation in the Third Reich, but the allusions are disguised because dictatorships discourage a critical approach and Fascism had made free speech impossible. Piscator cut much of the mythical material, seeing it as no more than a smoke-screen. He accentuated passages which had relevance to events in Nazi Germany and added film, recorded speeches and statistics from the Nazi era to make the references clear, claiming that in so doing he was restoring an original conception which circumstances had prevented Hauptmann from carrying out.

The 1926 production of *The Robbers* had been largely conditioned by the overheated atmosphere of the time, and contemporary needs had overridden artistic considerations. Piscator 'saw too clearly that behind his [Karl's] pathetic speeches about freedom the cynical phrases of the up-and-coming Nazis lay hidden', and had therefore given '*The Robbers* the topicality of the revolutionary situation, i.e. *The Robbers* was intended as a call to action for the execution and sustaining of the revolutionary movement'.[39] By 1957 the ideological boundaries had become blurred. Russian Communism could no longer be seen as a universal social panacea – particularly in a divided Germany – and nineteenth-century individualism appeared less of an evil than it had in the aftermath of the Kaiser's war. Since there were no urgent political demands comparable to those of the twenties and no authors of any stature had supported Hitler, the reaction to the Second World War did not arouse the same repudiation of art. The differences are expressed in Piscator's production of *The Robbers*, aided by the 'light-stage'. In the director's copy of 1926 every single monologue and the greater part of the longer or more lyrical speeches had been cut. Here, on the other hand, Piscator declared: 'I wished to stress the monologues. My technical invention of the "scaffolding of light", on which the actor stands, is not just an effect, but a dramaturgical necessity.'[40]

This attitude was more calculated to encourage authors than his previous rejection of the literary qualities of drama as limited to an artificial world of the imagination. His machinery which now functioned efficiently was no longer overwhelmingly conspicuous, his new reliance on light emphasized the individual characters, and the spoken word seemed to have regained its importance in his productions. From Piscator's viewpoint, however, the effect on an audience formed the major criterion for drama so that this about-turn was no more than a choice of alternative means in response to changed circumstances. He was able to use the play in a different way since he felt that the spectators, unlike those of thirty years before, were capable of perceiving the essential relevance of Schiller's theme beneath the historical trappings. Style was relatively unimportant to him – as he repeatedly remarked, he was always prepared to discard any method of expression, however satisfying technically, if a better means became available – and his statements of intent show a remarkable consistency. Before the war he had laid down the principle that 'congruence with the time creates outstanding works of art',[41] and in the last years of his life he defined theatrical achievement in the same terms: 'the most fleeting, transitory art...it is purely present time, or it is nothing. As theatre with a conscious purpose, the political theatre understands this present time as contemporaneity.'[42] Nor, in restoring the place of literature in his productions, did he abandon the visual nature of his stage that had been so important to his work in the Piscator-Bühne. On the contrary, he acted on the principle that 'there has never been a time when the spectator was so pampered optically as today. Film and television prove that. The audience hears and learns more, better and faster through the eye than the ear.'[43]

Drama can be divided into two basic types of play. There is the poetic and imaginative, in which the script provides the essential pleasure, the actors embody the author's images, and the stage devices are the servants of the verbal meaning. This can be clearly distinguished from the spectacular, where rhythms of movement and music, lighting and colour form the main appeal, where the actor or singer, setting and stage effects are the centre of the entertainment, and the text is primarily a pretext for the actors and a cue for technical devices. Piscator's work falls into the latter category, following a theatrical tradition which runs from the Roman mimes to Reinhardt. This remains true even of his later productions, though to a lesser degree, and the new drama gains much of its effect from the visual impact of movement and machinery. It might be objected that many Documentary Dramas, including *The Investigation* and Hochhuth's plays, are written in poetry, normally the most literary of linguistic forms. But the verse used by Weiss and Hochhuth is denotative, avoids metaphors, and relies on rhythm for effect. It has little in common with the poetry of the last century which Piscator had rejected. It is not lyrical and fits the mathematical precision of speech demanded by Piscator's machinery. But although Piscator's concept of drama remained basically the same, he had moved away from one pre-war standpoint that directly affected his working relationship with playwrights. He no longer claimed that an author 'provides – stated bluntly – the material...which only becomes alive through particular theatrical techniques'[44] and he had revoked his decision 'not to accept any more completed plays at all',[45] although he remained convinced that 'far in front of and indeed higher than literary theatre there is a poetic theatre, the poetry of acted expression, of gesture'[46] – a perception also shared by certain playwrights, Cocteau and Tennessee Williams to name but two.

Imagination and evidence: plot v. expression

Reliance on stage-machinery and accentuation of the theatrical *gestus* of movement and mime – the only theatrical elements under his direct control – to make up for the inexperience of the dramatists: these were expedients capable of solving most of the problems in creating theatrical models for a new drama. But one difficulty, primarily literary, lay outside the scope of Piscator's experiments. Apart from the 'light-stage' his innovations emphasized the apparent actuality of the documented events introduced to support the plot, and as early as *Tidal Wave*, when his machinery was still in a rudimentary state, there had been what could be called a 'credibility gap' between the visual dimension, which gave the illusion of reality, and the verbal dimension, where Paquet had deliberately concentrated on ' "poetry" instead of reality, symbol instead of document, emotion instead of knowledge'.[47] This dichotomy also crept into Piscator's use of film, a medium peculiarly suited to communicating imaginary effects in spite of its documentary nature. In *Rasputin* he had combined scenes from feature films (including such highly stylized work as *Ivan the Terrible*) with passages from news-reels. In *Hoppla!* critics had noted a similar confusion, caused by the switch from documentary to symbolic film – as when pictures of Ludendorff and Hindenburg were juxtaposed with a grotesque representation of two psychiatrists.

Such contrasts between an imaginary story and the style of production were not limited to plays Piscator adapted. The credibility gap was also evident in the scripts written under his direct control, and even in *Economic Competition*, Piscator's most factual production, there was a clear break between the first half, which dealt with the discovery and exploitation of an oil-field, and the second half, in which agents of the great powers entered and the growth of global conflict was portrayed. At the beginning of the play the events were suited to documentary treatment but with the entrance of Tilla Durieux (as a romantic heroine who was simply a concession to the box-office) the action appeared invented and the situations seemed contrived clichés: 'not therefore epic drama, but rather a dramatized novel'.[48] Not that this was entirely Piscator's fault. At the dress rehearsal, representatives of the K.P.D., the Soviet Trade Mission and the Soviet Embassy had protested against Tilla Durieux's original rôle. As a Russian spy, she incited a revolution – not with idealistic aims of social justice, but simply as an economic tactic to remove capitalist competition so that the U.S.S.R. could exploit the natural resources of the underdeveloped country. The Communist officials protested that this picture was counterproductive as propaganda – its truth was unquestioned – and forced Piscator to realize that there were 'political limits' to objectivity. The only change possible before the première was the addition of a 'surprise ending', supplied by Brecht straight from melodrama, in which Tilla Durieux revealed that she had only been pretending to act for the Soviets and was in fact employed by the South American states. This aggravated the existing split between the presentation of evidence, compiled from engineering autobiographies and textbooks, and the story which had been abstracted from sociological hypotheses. The first half had dealt with concrete objects. It demonstrated the creation of capitalist values out of mud and manure through a plot of land changing hands, first for a handful of coppers, then for a banknote, and finally for a pompous cheque. With the appearance of legal documents of ownership in the place of the field, however, the focus of the play had been transferred to abstractions – capitalism, imperialism, international competition.

The problem emerges more clearly in Piscator's first version of *War and Peace*, where there was an obvious dichotomy between the love story and the epic treatment of the historical period. A typical criticism was that while Tolstoy had *illustrated* a universal theme through 'the lives and loves of three noble families, . . . Piscator and his associates make the conventional Hollywood approach of telling a love-story against the background of the invasion of Russia'.[49] The production was judged to be 'a valiant attempt. . . to provide something of the huge-scale picture of an entire people at peace and at war. . . but the proper scope is simply impossible to capture'.[50]

In fact the problem was not only one of scale. Film could run through years in as many minutes, expand the dimensions of the stage into continents, or make it possible for the audience to master factual complexities which they could not be expected to hold in their memories. But historical movements and economic processes are only significant in so far as they affect human beings. Plots dealing with personal relationships could not be completely replaced by structures of anonymous evidence – yet any story on an individual level was inappropriate to the impersonality of epic conflicts. To take part in the wider action, characters had to be given symbolic stature – yet as symbols they destroyed any impression of actuality by putting the documents in an imaginary context.

At first Piscator had rejected symbolic figures: 'it was a mistake to drain what is materialistic away from such material [the revolution depicted in *Tidal Wave*], since all that can be achieved is a disembodiment, not a heightening'.[51] His use of film had enlarged the actions of Paquet's poeticized characters out of proportion to the power of their speeches, demonstrating the weakness of normal literary symbolism. But later he returned to Paquet's attempt 'to epitomize the driving forces of our epoch in a few figures', trying various methods of giving characters historic significance. In subsequent productions of *War and Peace* the generals moved ranks of foot-high toy soldiers around the stage, where before Pierre had traced the fortunes of battle on a map – and, by combining the 'stage of fate' with the 'light-stage' Piscator finally succeeded in integrating the actors with the clash of historical forces. At the end of his career he was able to stage wide-reaching contemporary events without sacrificing concrete reality, so fulfilling his pre-war intention to create a drama which 'draws its effect and meaning from embodying the battle of characters representing [conflicting] ideas'.[52]

Piscator's, of course, was only one possible solution. The discussion about appropriate styles for portraying the modern world on the stage continues. Although our environment makes actions anonymous and the concept of personality has been called into question by psychological discoveries, the primary means of theatrical representation is still the actor, as Piscator's experience demonstrates. Contemporary realities are more powerful than fantasy, yet drama must give 'a local habitation and a name' to abstract forces, and this involves the creation of imaginary forms. Technology dominates modern life but can never be the primary means of portraying it, and in effect after experimenting with all ways of communicating through machinery Piscator returned to the symbolism he had previously rejected.

The new drama

Although Piscator's machinery had initially inhibited the development of the new drama it was designed to encourage, it played a positive rôle in providing working demonstrations of new methods of approach. The value of opening areas of experience, previously beyond the capacity of the stage to represent, can best be illustrated by returning to Piscator's treatment of *Schweik* in 1928.

The original Brod/Reimann play had a conventional plot centering on one of Lukasch's love affairs (invented by Brod) with the daughter of a colonel (characterized as a 'war-monger'), who was to be married to a jam manufacturer ('the epitome of the war-profiteer, who supplies mouldy tinned food to the front').[53] The episode began with Lukasch's acquisition of his batman and ended with Schweik blowing up the factory. In this way Hašek's gargantuan novel had been reduced to a contrived and enclosed story which could be competently presented by traditional theatrical means. In spite of copyright difficulties, which were customary where Brod was concerned, Piscator managed to completely rewrite the script with the aid of Brecht and Lania, building speeches around machinery which he invented specifically to keep the episodic, 'epic' form of the original novel. Since the majority of Schweik's speeches were transposed verbatim from the book, an 'epic voice' was essential, and the treadmills that acted as a valid theatrical correlative for the picaresque nature of Hašek's work – giving the same illusion of movement as in a train, where the railway carriage seems still and it is the telegraph poles that appear to move – also acted as the equivalent of Hašek's raconteur who alters the scenery and the cast of each chapter arbitrarily from outside the action. In addition, the contrast between the animated cartoons and moving scenery and the human and stationary Schweik translated the novel's uneasy mixture of brilliant comedy and bitter satire intact to the stage.

Brod, who failed to realize that Piscator had not merely altered but completely replaced the text he had submitted, complained that the production 'fragmented the artistic whole' which he had created while (ignoring the actual success of the Piscator version) 'the success, and also the potential political effect of a self-enclosed play, would have been far greater than that of a collection of anecdotes centred around a star-figure'. But even Brod was forced to acknowledge the effect of the machinery: 'Since those responsible for turning the novel into a play could hardly have conceived of the Piscator-Bühne, nor of the treadmill when they wrote the play, no scenes with rapid or multiple changes of place were transposed from the novel into the stage script'.[54] Conventional stage-machinery was incapable of dealing with such material and, but for Piscator's treadmills, Schweik would have been degraded to a comic servant in the stock tradition of boulevard theatre. Piscator could claim with justice that 'technology opens up new subject matter',[55] and his final innovation – the 'light-stage' – with technological advances which meant that the machinery no longer obtruded, created favourable conditions for the long awaited appearance of dramatists who would provide his theatre with suitable plays.

The Deputy, the first to appear, approximated to the concept that Piscator had noted in his diary when he was first appointed to the Freie Volksbühne: 'I must find plays – the like of which have never existed before – hard, difficult plays, saturated with reality. Back to the style of the twenties.' Hochhuth's theme is of contemporary importance, his material is documentary and his approach is objective. Events are depicted on a global scale and their historical repercussions demonstrated without losing sight of the human details. The dramatization has a clarity which Piscator had associated with the practical intention to exert a direct effect on the audience, yet preserves a high literary standard. Above all, here the 'fate of an individual' was treated 'comprehensively enough to be symbolic, exemplary in the original meaning of that word, "representative" for the generality'.[56] It is indicative that the production appeared comparatively conventional. Previously Piscator had been forced to add all the elements which were not contained in the plays themselves through manipulating the physical properties of the stage; but even by his standards the meaning and effect of this play needed little revision or reinforcement. It is also significant that the play contains no specifically Marxist message. The criteria of human behaviour are Christian rather than Communist, and *The Deputy* is 'political' theatre in the general sense of the word. This vindicated Piscator's belief that a political theatre did not necessarily need to be tied to any particular ideology – a popular confusion which had hindered his work in the 1920s.

Piscator's production of *The Deputy* provoked the German public as no other play had done since the Weimar Republic. It gave such an incentive to German dramatists that the critics noted 'documentary theatre has become the fashion' – as they had in the 1920s after the influence of *Tidal Wave* made itself felt. But here the techniques, the approach and the effects that impressed critics and dramatists were the polished result of a lifetime's experimentation, not the preliminary stage in a process of theatrical exploration. Hochhuth's portrayal of real individuals and public figures, Gerstein and Pope Pius XII, was only a beginning. Between 1965 and 1966 Eichmann, Oppenheimer, Kaduk, Boger and Hitler's general staff appeared on German stages. The figures of Lee Harvey Oswald, Churchill, Brecht, Toller, Mühsam and Levine have followed. The November Revolution, the Third Reich and the Nuremberg trials have become subjects of open discussion in the theatre, and dramatists have shown themselves capable of dealing effectively with large-scale events of direct relevance to their audiences. It was a breakthrough. Not all the plays are good, but compared to their counterparts in the Weimar years they are technically mature. In the postscript to the most recent edition of his book, a postscript to his work as a whole, since it was written immediately before his death, Piscator analysed the characteristics of these plays as being an adaptation of his principles: the use of the actuality of documentation and the discipline of historical analysis to determine the dramatic form, without losing the artistic freedom to create an aesthetic pattern.

Hochhuth's play is a descendent of Schiller's 'drama of ideas', but Schiller's maxim that the playwright can use 'no piece of reality just as he finds it, untransmuted' has been rewritten. This use of undisguised reality has created a new relationship between stage and audience, which is exploited even by such different playwrights as Peter Handke in his *Abuse of the Audience*. The spectator has been forced from his position as a consumer into the rôle of judge, accuser or – more frequently – accused, by the choice and treatment of dramatic material.

But this dependence on actual facts and analytical discipline places Documentary Drama on the periphery of art and has raised doubts as to whether these plays can be evaluated by aesthetic standards at all. The anecdote about the politician who refused to see *Hamlet* because he had already read the play and knew how it ended can be contrasted with the hypothesis that a historian who had studied the original documents of Oppenheimer's trial or was familiar with the facts of Auschwitz might justifiably refuse to see *In the Matter of J. Robert Oppenheimer* or *The Investigation*. Literature is distinguished from *Hansard* or *The Times* not by its style but by its imaginative nature, in which facts are fused into fictional patterns that can strike unexpected truth precisely because they are not, except in the case of allegory, related by causal logic to reality. *Wallenstein* or *Maria Stuart* are historical falsehoods, but they have the authenticity of images and are true as expressions of Schiller's personal vision. In Documentary Drama, however, there is a tendency to substitute verisimilitude for veracity, leaving the facts to speak for themselves. Then the technique alone remains exciting. This is well illustrated by Kipphardt's *Joel Brand*, first produced on television. Here the stylistic tricks which were used to communicate the subject – a series of commentators, montage, photo-mixing and film – lent the material spurious interest. The later stage version was changed to an enclosed, pseudo-naturalistic form. The director, Everding, made no effort to break out of the conservative structure of the play, and the playwright's unimaginative approach to the story was underlined by a sterile setting.

The advantages and dangers of Documentary Drama can be clearly seen in *The Investigation*. In contrast to the work of Hochhuth and Kipphardt, where statistics and documents are used as a physical embodiment for moral themes, the oppressive ruthlessness of facts is the only dynamic in Peter Weiss's play, and the dramatic form is shaped by the simple variation and intensification of historical suffering from the 'Song of the Platform' to the final 'Song of the Fire Ovens'. Limiting the action to a total and static concentration on facts, Weiss deliberately avoided any attempt to reconstruct the reality of Auschwitz, and in the Freie Volksbühne production the photographs and film from the archives with which Piscator had originally intended to substantiate the statements of the witnesses were not used.

There is no dramatic conflict in the normal sense because the accused are confronted with anonymous figures. As the prologue dictates, 'in as much as the witnesses in the play lose their names, they become mere speaking tubes. The nine witnesses sum up what hundreds expressed' – and the bare vocabulary together with the strictly denotative use of language, in which simple grammatical relationships are emphasized by the free verse, deliberately excludes emotion. The effect is undeniably powerful. The magnitude of the events is enough to absorb attention, and the clipped neutrality of style leaves no doubt of the actuality of the crimes described. Even the impersonality of the characterization is valuable because an impression of total objectivity is essential for the portrayal of such a subject, where the slightest touch of sentiment or any empathy would reduce the play to normal standards. But *The Investigation* depicts Auschwitz through court protocol and, because processes of justice concentrate on deeds not thoughts, the real motivations of the characters escape the dramatist. The personal sadism of Kaduk, Boger and Stark is spotlit, but they were minor figures and the system – the paperwork and planning, the 'pure' science and the 'uninvolved' bureaucracy – can only be glimpsed where it was touched on in the evidence. The dramatic speeches are transcribed from the court records, and the words are therefore taken by the audience to represent the truth. But in life –

and particularly in court – language is used to disguise and hide reality. The danger of documentation is superficiality, and since the representation of data in an 'actual' manner makes 'truth to the facts' the primary criterion, any normal standards of criticism outside historical accuracy tend to be disregarded. In such circumstances Documentary Drama comes to be judged as evidence rather than theatre. Thus Bernard Naumann was able to criticize the 'Auschwitz-oratorio' by comparing the play with a tape recording of the trial, and Weiss was accused of factual alterations, of introducing invented material and even of falsifying the evidence by changing commentary into direct speech. The effectiveness of the play on stage was forgotten in arguments over the truth of its message; rebuttals or corroborations of its indictment of German society on the basis of fact alone. To a certain extent the same has happened with all the other documentary plays, as a glance at the paper-war fought over Hochhuth's plays demonstrates,[57] and their success has been in proportion to the inflammatory power of their subjects.

The Investigation, however, is an extreme example, and critics normally allow documentary dramatists more freedom in the creative processes of selection, ordering and formulation of material because the aesthetic qualities of their plays outweigh the mere reproduction of reality. Not only was simplification and commentary essential in order to compress the court report of 3,000 pages into two and a half hours for *In the Matter of J. Robert Oppenheimer*, but Kipphardt was aware of the tendency to superficiality latent in such a concentration on facts, and he made a deliberate attempt 'to replace word-for-word accuracy with fidelity to the spirit of the subject'. A similar focus on inner meaning is characteristic of Hochhuth's work, where the structure is formed from the conflict between moral absolutes that have been abstracted from the historical facts.

Solutions have not yet been found for all the dramaturgical problems peculiar to Documentary Drama, but in the last few years the genre has come to rival the parable type of play created by Brecht as one of the dominant forms in the German theatre, and its influence has spread through England and France to America. Piscator's are not the only valid techniques for a theatre that wishes to deal with contemporary issues or reflect the modern environment, but his work does give a practical example of one way in which this might be accomplished. His achievements proved that it is possible to deal directly and realistically with the global movements of the twentieth century and the mass anonymity of industrial society on the enclosed, individualistic and artificial world of the stage. His earlier imperfect attempts finally issued in a body of internationally acclaimed dramatic works, since he consciously followed through his Weimar experiments in his post-war productions, which provided the opportunity for Hochhuth and the impetus for Kipphardt and Weiss.

Like Documentary Drama, Piscator's concept of Total Theatre has become established after his death, and his continuing influence is indicated by the plans to build the theatre that Gropius designed to his specifications for the 1972 Olympic Games in Munich. His productions should not be dismissed as mere *oeuvres de mise en scène*. His aim was 'the abolition of the bourgeois theatre, ideologically, dramaturgically, spatially, technically. We are fighting for the reformation of the theatre'[58] – and his stage experiments must be evaluated as practical steps in the creation of a new theatrical tradition, 'the adaptation of a modern, topically relevant stage to its time'.[59]

8 Piscator:
Contemporaries and Critics

The influence of Piscator's contemporaries

Some of the techniques that identify Piscator's political theatre are found in the work of his contemporaries and immediate fore-runners. It was not the individual elements of his productions so much as their combination and the way they were applied that was original and revolutionized the theatre.

The Expressionists had made simple use of simultaneous stages and the 'dramaturgy of the spotlight' that went with them. Music and dance had accompanied 'space-staging' in their plays. Their scenery, like Piscator's, was intended to be 'visible architecture' which would be 'cubically-architectonically creative' instead of being 'lyrical' and decorative.[1] They had also introduced a structure similar to montage and the revue in the continuous sequence of fragmentary scenes which they preferred as a dramatic form. The style developed by the Expressionist directors who were Piscator's contemporaries, Jürgen Fehling, Ludwig Bergner, Karlheinz Martin and Leopold Jessner, was comparable to Piscator's in one important point – they gathered all the scenic means of expression and subordinated them to a single vision or *Idee*. Even the New Pathos, that poetically inflated ideal of the early German Expressionists, foreshadowed Piscator's aims in a way since its intention was to create an 'intimate, glowing contact with the masses'; while the dangers of this type of emotionalism were realized to be grandiose posturing and banal language or slogans[2] – faults which were inherent in Piscator's work. The similarities can be indicated by setting Stefan Zweig's rejection of 'l'art pour l'art', 'Technical abilities and values should...no longer be an end in themselves, but only a means for arousing enthusiasm,'[3] beside Piscator's statement, 'The formulation should not become an end in itself. It must always be functional.'[4] The differences lie in their interpretation of 'function'. For Piscator enthusiasm was only a step to arousing the political awareness of the public.

Similarly Reinhardt's aim had been theatre for the masses, creating 'a unity of participating, inspired and inspiring fellow-countrymen' in performance. Reinhardt had realized the importance of architectural forms for welding the audience into a 'community of the people', justifying his innovations by reference to the ancient Greek theatre. There he claimed that the same public/player relationship, where the auditorium divisions and the proscenium arch of the baroque theatre were absent, had made the theatre 'the assembly of a popular community'.[5] In this he had anticipated Piscator. He also forestalled Piscator in his appreciation of the effect of an arena stage in a 'circus' building. The walls appeared to be formed by the steeply raked seats in his Theatre of the Five Thousand, so that only men were visible and the shape therefore automatically formed a 'council meeting and...cathedral'. This was intended to be a theatre for all, 'consciously aspiring to influence the masses' through its gathering of 'stage-space and auditorium, actor and public' up into 'an uninterrupted whole'.[6] As popular theatre, Reinhardt's work inevitably had political connotations. The most detailed aspects of his direction were crowd scenes, and in his production of *Danton's Death* in 1916 he had placed 'the people' on stage as a political entity. Piscator recognized this aspect of Reinhardt's work, acknowledging that 'he was certainly also aware that one must reach the masses', but accusing him of 'inflating appearances'.[7]

Many of Reinhardt's techniques point the way to Piscator, yet the effects that he achieved were at the opposite end of the theatrical spectrum because his aims were very different. He moved toward Piscator's later concept of Total Theatre in three important points – the involvement of the audience and the associated exaggeration of the emotive elements of a production, with a corresponding disregard for the literary aspect of drama: 'Light and colour, which are supplied by the direction, are more important than the play.'[8] In *Danton's Death* Reinhardt's use of lighting had even anticipated the ability to comment on the action through visual juxtaposition that Piscator gained with his use of simultaneous stages:

Only seconds divide scene from scene: blackout, darkness, re-illumination takes less time than one can draw breath...in a private room Danton reclines in the arms of a sentimental Grisette, while at almost the same time the opinions which mean life or death for him burst out wildly one after the other in the Jacobin Club.[9]

But Reinhardt dissolved speech into a pantomimic pattern and drew the public into the action solely in the service of enchantment. Shakespeare's comedies were his favourite material because they gave him the best opportunity to create a 'bewitching, perfect world', and the principle behind his work was that 'the theatre should not bring men to the realization of their situation, but dazzle them'.[10] Reinhardt can be said to have determined the theatrical atmosphere in the first years of the Weimar Republic, and the predominance of 'culinary opera' that Brecht objected to was mainly due to his prestige. Yet in spite of apparent similarities the direct influence of his productions on Piscator was negligible. Reinhardt's style had become atrophied by the time that Piscator reached Berlin, and the efforts of Reinhardt's epigones to rival their master had brought the most striking of his techniques into disrepute.

As with Reinhardt, the connections that have been drawn between Piscator and the Expressionists are superficial. Although one or two techniques are comparable, their effect on an audience was very different because Piscator was absolutely opposed to Expressionist aims: 'The epic theatre arose out of a rejection of the O-Man-drama, the cry of pity, the brotherly love for the "helpless".'[11] An over-emphasis on sentiment, and indeed sentimentality, lay behind the 'O-Man' Expressionist techniques for involving an audience in the action of the play – 'If a whole legion of men could just once be moved to shameless tears by a true poem...we would all of us be saved'[12] – and the lyricism in their theme of 'the Calvary leading to the spirit' was undramatic in nature. This made it imperative for Piscator to avoid their influence. Their model for making the spectator 'a participant and involved sufferer' was a medieval cathedral congregation, as can be clearly seen in Vollmoeller's *Miracle* – the opposite of Piscator's ideal of the active political discussion of a workers' parliament.

The Expressionists who came closest to Piscator were the *Young Germany* movement, a development within Reinhardt's theatre. 'Their artistic aim was: politics. Storm against the oppressors',[13] and during the war they had produced plays of social criticism, including Reinhard Goering's *Naval Encounter*. This production indeed anticipated Piscator's work in the way stage-machinery was applied. A stage-construct which represented a battleship's gun-turret, with flashing lights, alarm signals and exposed machinery, 'fulfilled its purpose in engrossing the eye and at the same time embodied this godless world of devouring machines to perfection'.[14] A functional image and the exploitation of stage-machinery – but in protest against technology. Even the politically committed wing of the Expressionist movement were solely concerned with spiritual regeneration and rejected modern conditions, seeking to educate proletarians up to pre-war aesthetic standards, instead of using the stage as an instrument of propaganda to change society. They believed that 'mass theatre in our time can only be a matter of the cheapest and simplest possible dissemination of good [i.e. "pure"] art, which will take effect in the future'.[15] This confusion of social revolution with spiritual edification gave birth to such ambivalent plays as Kranz's *Freedom*, which had an 'actual' subject and, like the later Agitprop theatre, was performed in beer halls and working men's clubs, but was written in a sentimental, hectoring oratorio style – a type of art that Piscator condemned as politically reactionary. Piscator certainly knew the details of these productions and his experiments may owe something to their techniques. But the difference in intention between the *Young Germany* movement and the Communist theatre, whose aim was to make the proletariat aware of their class rôle in the social struggle, formed essentially different types of drama. One of the Expressionist directors, however, deserves special mention: Leopold Jessner.

In constructing his productions around a central concept (*Idee*) Piscator was following Jessner, who subordinated his techniques to a play's 'thematic motif' and had already created an effective 'anti-Reinhardt' and disillusionistic theatre. He had shaped a style in which 'tempo is all...there is only one criterion: intensity', and where movement was made possible on the stage in three dimensions through the famous 'Jessner stairs'. Above all the symbolism of his scenery was close to that of Piscator's stage-constructs, and the connection is indicated by the position of Caspar Neher who, after working with Jessner, designed the settings for Piscator's productions of *What Price Glory?* in 1929 and *Danton's Death* in 1956. Jessner's work has been described in terms which are equally appropriate to Piscator: 'Leopold Jessner staged the concept instead of the illusion. He created symbols, not a pretence of reality. He articulated space...His style was factual, clear, direct. And abstract...'[16] It is significant that he encouraged Piscator, giving him the opportunity to direct *The Robbers* in the Staatliches Schauspielhaus in 1926, and approved of his work, supporting him against the management of the Volksbühne in the scandal caused by *Storm over Gottland*. But Jessner's techniques lacked both the documentation and the audience-involvement that were characteristic of Piscator's work, and the abstraction and precision of his style was designed to concentrate attention on the poetic qualities of dialogue. The nature of his symbolization was also different. It was typically expressionistic, his identification of costume and lighting with emotion being similar to Marc's theories concerning the intrinsic worth of colours.

It is clear, then, that Piscator's immediate contemporaries and rivals, although working at times along parallel lines and developing similar techniques, used the theatre in essentially different ways. The atmosphere they helped to create undoubtedly encouraged Piscator, but because their aims were opposed to his, Piscator must be treated as an independent innovator. However, the initial motivation for Piscator's attempts to modernize the stage came from the Russian Revolution, and the development of 'political theatre' is commonly associated with theatrical innovations in Moscow: in particular with the work of Vsevolod Meyerhold. Apart from the presumed links between the Soviet and German Agitprop theatres,[17] it has been claimed that the achievements of both Piscator and Brecht would have been 'inconceivable' without Meyerhold's preliminary work.[18]

It is certainly true that there are striking similarities, particularly in Meyerhold's emphasis on machinery – his exciting deployment of lifts and revolves, of motorbikes and trucks driven over bridges through the auditorium. He had experimented with film montage, documentary placards and direct agitation in the theatre (including the communal singing of the *International* at the end of a production) early in the 1920s – before Piscator had developed any but the most rudimentary of his techniques.

Even the details of his work correspond to characteristic qualities of Piscator's style. In his production of Ostrovski's *How the Steel was Tempered* he had replaced music by a 'noise orchestra' –

identical in many ways to Meisel's cacophanous accompaniment –
and ballet by a 'dance of machines' – gaining a comparable effect
to the mechanized, moving, opening stage-construct in *Rasputin.*
Similarly he had built multiple simultaneous stages for Mayakovsky's *Mysterium Buffo* and later described the principles on
which he worked: 'Electioneering slogans, street cries and journalistic jargon were dovetailed into the verses of *Mysterium Buffo.*
The action is the movement of the masses, class conflict, the clash
of ideologies: a miniature of the world, carried into the circus.' The
dominance of slogans, the substitution of emotive catch-phrases for
literary language, the links with journalism, together with ideological themes and plots centred on mass movements: these were the
basic elements in Piscator's work, and a not unjust statement by
Jelagin, Meyerhold's biographer, has been quoted to back up the
contention that Piscator owed the Russian master an unacknowledged debt: 'I can state with a clear conscience that I have seen no
scenic device on the stages of Europe and America, which Meyerhold had not used earlier or put up for discussion at one time or
another.'

But *How the Steel was Tempered* was forbidden and never performed; Meyerhold's other productions – apart from his early
work in the October Theatre – were unknown outside Moscow;
and his troupe first appeared in Berlin in 1930 after Piscator's style
had already reached maturity. Nor was there any second-hand
report of Meyerhold's work. The first mention of Meyerhold's
experiments whatsoever in Germany is an article in 1925, which was
too short and general to be useful as a working description of
Meyerhold's techniques.

The guest appearance of Tairoff's actors in 1924 had given the
Germans a low opinion of Russian theatre, and Jhering's criticism
is representative: 'schematic pathos was the only memorable thing –
limited and rigid as it was...the Russian dramaturgy is passive...
It has nothing to teach our theatre either in action or direction.'[19]
When Meyerhold's productions finally appeared they hardly cor-
rected this unfortunate first impression, since they were judged to
be *passé*: 'superfluous for Germany in this arrangement and
form. Simply because we are dramaturgically ahead.'[20] Not
only had German ensembles already developed more sophisticated acting techniques, but even the plays in Meyerhold's

repertoire had already been translated and successfully produced.

In spite of the apparent similarities in their work, when Meyerhold saw one of Piscator's productions during his visit to Berlin he is reported to have expressed dislike for the documentary style of drama. Conversely Piscator condemned Meyerhold's achievements as a 'purely artistic development of the theatre'.[21]

When accused in 1928 of borrowing wholesale from Meyerhold, Piscator denied that he even had the opportunity for plagiarism ('I cannot judge [the similarities] because I have no knowledge of Meyerhold's work') and offered the explanation that perhaps their experiments shared a common basis since they both viewed their material from a Communist standpoint.[22] After actually seeing Meyerhold's work he commented that the same *Weltanschauung* was indeed capable of producing unrelated styles and forms – 'e.g. the difference between Meyerhold's treatment of themes and my own'.[23] He returned to the point in his postscript to the 1968 edition of *The Political Theatre* with the comment that 'in every period, as a result of the way in which circumstances determine its form, the theatre adapts (and permanently varies) all the means of expression available at any particular time in a natural way which makes any question of authorship irrelevant'. As with other suggested sources, Reinhardt, Jessner and the Expressionists, there is no evidence of direct or conscious influence. Meyerhold may have anticipated later theatrical innovations; but any connection with Piscator's achievements must be put down to the close relationship between the theatre and contemporary conditions. Being exposed to the same social changes, political theories and scientific advances that together made up the intellectual environment of their age, both innovators moved for a time in the same direction.

However, there are other creative artists, outside the sphere of the theatre proper, whose work was definitely adapted by Piscator. Film played an important part in his development – and if he owed anything to Meyerhold, he learnt it indirectly through Eisenstein, who had been trained by Meyerhold. The influence of the cinema is obvious, not only in Piscator's use of film, his adaptation of cinematic techniques to the stage and his adoption of montage as an organizing principle, but also in the direct effect of individual films. The impact of Eisenstein's *Battleship Potemkin* can be traced in

Piscator's staging of *The Robbers, Storm over Gottland* and *Hoppla!*, as it can in the writing of Wolf's *Sailors of Cattaro*, while the 'knock-about' style Piscator experimented with in *The Drunken Ship* and *Schweik* was clearly modelled on Chaplin's early films, which made a sensational impression in Berlin at the time. Even details were important. Piscator copied Chaplin's bowler hat and cane for 'timeless costumes'.

There was one further source of influence, seldom mentioned in this context. The Bauhaus in Dessau, founded in 1919, has been of key importance for the visual arts in the twentieth century, as the recent exhibition which has toured the major cities of Europe and America demonstrated. The Bauhaus parallels Piscator's theatrical experiments in the architectural field, 'seeking a new synthesis of art and modern technology' based on a study of the 'facts of human perception' and investigating 'the phenomena of form and space... to arrive at an objective means with which to relate individual creative effort to a common background'.[24] These architects and artists were not limited to industrial design. The stage offered a natural field for practical experimentation, and the Bauhaus founded its own theatre. Its director, Oskar Schlemmer, saw abstraction and mechanization as a dual 'emblem of our time' because these qualities separated components from an existing whole and reduced them to insignificance or revealed their potential. Alternatively they could result in 'the construction in bold outline of a new totality' through generalization. Moholy-Nagy, who later worked with Piscator, conducted 'creative experiments with *motion* and *sound*... action and tempo' through which he attempted to supplant the 'literary encumbrances' of logical sequences of action with an optical ballet, replacing man-the-actor by the fullest use of machinery – lights, mirrors, loudspeakers, gramophones and 'complex apparatus such as film, automobile, elevator, aeroplane'. The audience was to be involved in the action by loudspeakers under their seats, by suspended bridges extending the acting-space in all directions through the theatre above the heads of the stalls, and by 'platform stages built far into the auditorium'. The machinery was to be visible and its importance in a production was accentuated.

But the *Triadic Ballet*, the best known theatrical production of the Bauhaus, which was performed in 1922 and again in 1923, acts as another demonstration that there is no necessary relationship between specific techniques and effects. Like some of the details in Reinhardt's productions or Jessner's, although the Bauhaus dramaturgy as a whole was remarkably similar to Piscator's, the end-products were at opposite theatrical extremes because the aims were totally different. In Schlemmer's productions the machines were to be visible to the audience since they were seen as 'the most interesting aspect of the theatre' in our technological age, and the emphasis was to be on their 'peculiar and novel beauty, undisguised and as an end in itself'. The actor was to be completely absent because his range of movement was limited by natural laws and his presence encouraged an intellectual search for story-lines; or where his appearance was unavoidable an abstract costume turned his figure into a geometric form. This was a development of Gordon Craig's position. *The Dance of Gestures, The Dance of Form* and Moholy-Nagy's *Score Sketch for Mechanized Eccentrics* are typical of the Bauhaus experiments, and the titles illustrate the abstract nature of their work. There are similarities to both Wyndham Lewis' Vorticist play, *The Enemy of the Stars*, and to Marinetti's Futurist productions; and Schlemmer, who designed the set and the face-masks for Kokoschka's *Murder, Hope of Women*, believed that he was putting Craig's concept of the *Ueber-Marionette* into practice. The Bauhaus theatre was an integral part of the Cubist and Surrealist movements of the time: abstract, apolitical, a withdrawal from contemporary reality. Even though the theories of the Bauhaus theatre-specialists included all the dramatic elements that Piscator united in his art, their productions were deliberately 'without purpose' and unrepresentational: 'a clinically isolated concentration of action on the stage' in a building (only incidentally a theatre) which was seen solely as an 'architectonic-spatial organism'. What they created was in no sense concerned with contemporary society or politics, and as an abstract aesthetic experiment with a scientific purpose it had nothing to do with political theatre.

Brecht and Piscator

Bertolt Brecht, undeniably the most important playwright to have emerged in Germany since the First World War, is commonly acclaimed as the creator of a new type of drama: one appropriate to the modern age, capable of dealing with the political and economic aspects of life, impersonal yet still theatrical. Any 'epic' qualities in contemporary plays are associated with Brecht's work, and the various studies of his drama have assumed that his ideas were original. Brecht acknowledged his plagiarism of other authors, and critics, concentrating on the texts of his plays, have traced the influence of Kipling, Villon, the Bible, Büchner, Waley's translation of *Noh* dramas, the Asiatic, Elizabethan and early German theatres. His dramaturgy, however, is looked upon as his own; a unique, independent contribution to twentieth-century art. The literary sources for Brecht's techniques have often been emphasized since these are comparatively easy to document, while the only practical influences which have been considered are those that Brecht mentions himself – sporting events, market singers, silent films and Karl Valentin, the great Bavarian comedian. In particular the example of Piscator's experiments has been underestimated, and although scholars have been unable to ignore Piscator's activity during Brecht's formative years, only Helge Hultberg and Frederic Ewen have taken his influence seriously.[25] Both point out similarities between his practice and Brecht's theories, but neither make any detailed comparison, minimizing Piscator's importance in Brecht's development.

This is perhaps natural. Piscator's work looks undisciplined, over-rich in possibilities, and following contradictory lines. This apparent chaos, however, the false starts and occasional dead ends are the signs of a pioneer, blazing a new trail. Brecht's development is more logical and single-minded, but the contrast comes mainly from the fact that Piscator had already mapped out the terrain for him. Another explanation is that Brecht concentrated on refining a single style which, as Piscator had already demonstrated, was potentially adequate to deal with contemporary conditions, while Piscator, concentrating more on the material and the audience, was prepared to use any stylistic means to form new theatrical conventions.

It is easy to account for the view that Brecht alone is responsible for creating Epic Drama by the greater volume of Brecht's writings explaining and publicizing his work, the coherence of his achievements (which actually comes from their more limited nature and their reliance on the results of Piscator's experiments), and the wider distribution of his ideas available to an author in comparison to a director, who is restricted to his immediate audience. In addition, since material relating to Piscator's theatrical innovations has only recently been collected and made available for study, scholars concerned with Brecht have assumed that Piscator was an eclectic producer of mechanical stage effects, a mere technician. John Willett, for example, shows a basic misunderstanding of Piscator's work in his comment on Epic Theatre: 'The working out of a new apparatus on the basis of a new society is something...a good deal more radical than the particular technical methods for which Piscator had adopted the term.'[26] Yet 'the working out of a new apparatus on the basis of a new society' was the foundation of all Piscator's experiments, and his 'technical methods' cannot be divorced from his aim to adapt the theatre to modern conditions.

It is significant that Brecht's characteristic qualities – the linguistic concision and objectivity attributed to the influence of the *Noh* theatre, the loose sequences of scenes and geographical or chronological scope of action commonly put down to the example of the Elizabethan dramatists or Büchner, and the techniques of direct address by the author and interruption or commentary by the chorus which Willett and Ewen tentatively trace to Claudel's *Christophe Colombe* – were all present in Piscator's productions. It is overlooking the obvious to search so far afield for influences: *Christophe Colombe*, for instance, although performed in Berlin in 1930 only had 'epic' elements added in Barrault's 1953 version which did not reach Germany until 1962, long after Brecht's techniques had been fully developed. The relationship between Piscator and Brecht has also been discounted because most scholars, lacking detailed information about Piscator's experiments, follow Marxist critics who have political reasons for denying that the one Communist dramatist with an international reputation could owe anything to the 'petty-bourgeois radicalism of Erwin Piscator's theatre movement'.[27]

It might be possible to argue – as Piscator did when accused of plagiarizing from Meyerhold – that the similarities in their work were coincidental, expressing a common reaction to the pressures of their Weimar environment. Brecht and Piscator shared the same starting point: the war and the revolution which followed it. Each turned to Marxism as a credible interpretation of the economic and political confusion. *Neurealistisch* is a term that could be applied to the theatrical experiments of both. Their techniques were opposed to Naturalism which was too limited to deal with the breadth and complexity of modern conditions. Their common emphasis on objectivity was a reaction against the fervid patriotism that had marked the early stages of the war and a rejection of the pathetic emotionalism of the Expressionists. In this, as Piscator pointed out, they were representative: 'Our generation has set itself in conscious opposition to the over-emphasis, the over-evaluation of the emotions.'[28]

But Piscator adopted the Marxist viewpoint which provided the theoretical incentive for this 'realistic' practice earlier than Brecht, and he was already established in the Volksbühne by the time that Brecht took up residence in Berlin. Brecht acknowledged that

Piscator put on political theatre before the playwright [Brecht's impersonal way of referring to himself]. He had taken part in the war, whereas the playwright had not. The upheaval in 1918, in which both took part, had disillusioned the playwright and turned Piscator into a politician. It was only later through long study that the playwright came to politics.

But he asserted that both had separately and simultaneously discovered and developed the principles of 'epic' dramaturgy:

The supporters of Piscator disputed for a while with those of the playwright as to which of the two had discovered the epic style of performance. In fact they both evolved it at the same time in different cities; P. more in the staging, the playwright in the play.[29]

For Brecht there seems to have been little essential difference in their work. The basis of his claim to originality is that they each reached the same conclusion independently, working along parallel lines. Yet there can be no doubt that Piscator, whose major techniques had been established before 1928 and whose theories were coherently formulated by the publication of *The Political Theatre* in 1929, was ahead of his more famous colleague. As Willett noted, *The Flight over the Ocean* and the *Baden-Baden Cantata of Acquiescence* of 1929 marked the end of Brecht's early fantastic and cynical extravaganzas, and it was only with Brecht's own production of *Man is Man* in 1931 that his distinctive theatrical style emerged. Brecht conceded that Piscator had anticipated many of his characteristic practices, mentioning in particular the use of documentary film, the projection of captions and the moving stage, but limited Piscator's experiments to one aspect of what he considered he himself had achieved: 'Everything that goes by the name of topical theatre, or Piscator-stage, or educational drama [*Lehrstück*] belongs to the Epic Theatre.'[30] This statement, however, cuts both ways. If the *Lehrstück* is taken to be an extension of Agitprop theatre, then it was actually Piscator who had been responsible for the development of all three, and Piscator was therefore the true creator of Epic Theatre.

Brecht's own methods of production, always ready to discuss suggestions and alter his plays during rehearsal, gave the members of his troupe an unusually important place in the formation of his style, and actors from Piscator's collective, among them Ernst Busch, Leonhard Steckel and Alexander Granach, later joined Brecht's ensemble. Georg Grosz and John Heartfield also came to work with him, while Kurt Weill and Hanns Eisler, who provided him with scores from 1931 onwards, had composed the music for *Economic Competition* and *The Merchant of Berlin*. Even Caspar Neher, whose set designs provided the final form for the most characteristic of Brecht's later productions, served an apprenticeship with Piscator in 1929. The traffic was heavy, and it was all one way. Brecht himself worked closely with Piscator during the two years of the Piscator-Bühne, watching rehearsals, helping with script alterations and cooperating particularly in the important productions of *Schweik* and *Economic Competition*; but he had exerted no decisive influence upon Piscator: 'He came to all Piscator's rehearsals as an onlooker. It was only very seldom that he made any suggestions.'[31]

The essays in which Brecht first systematically outlined his theories only began to appear a year after the publication of *The Political Theatre*, when his association with Piscator had already ended. Günther Weisenborn, a close associate of Brecht's at this period, states that discussions about the adaptation of *The Mother* in 1930 first gave Brecht cause to define his concept of Epic Theatre,[32] and Willett remarks that *Man is Man*, commonly taken to be the first of Brecht's epic dramas, was 'formally no more epic than *Baal*...his whole picture of the "epic theatre" seems then [1931] to have been in a very sketchy state'.[33] Brecht's theories, impressive as they are, bear the same relationship to his plays as Piscator's book does to his productions. They indicate intention and provide criteria for measuring actual results. During the 1930s Brecht fought an acrimonious battle with Lukacs over Socialist Realism, defending his work against the ubiquitous charge of 'formalism'; and polemics led him to adopt extreme positions, so that Brecht – like Piscator – was later forced to modify his theories to account for his practices. Willett's comment that Brecht developed 'suitable theatrical methods which he was able to shuffle into an apparently coherent theory'[34] is reinforced by Piscator's sardonic observation: 'Above everything else Brecht had an extraordinary love for sticking a label on things, even before the contents had been determined.'[35] Abstract systems of thought fascinated Brecht, and this led him to define his theatrical principles as dogmatic absolutes. Where Piscator qualified his intentions: 'The theatre should no longer work *exclusively* on the onlookers' feelings...it should not *just* communicate impetus, enthusiasm, emotional excitement, but enlightenment, knowledge, perception'[36] – the change in function being primarily a shift of emphasis – Brecht tried to reverse the nature of drama in his theories, demanding a total exclusion of empathy from the actor/audience relationship – which, as the reaction to any of his plays demonstrates, is a practical impossibility. Yet this intellectual rigidity does lend his work an appearance of coherence and polish that was (sometimes only too obviously) lacking in Piscator's practical experiments.

The essence of the 'alienation effect', the keystone of Brecht's theatrical doctrine, can be seen as early as 1926 in Piscator's treatment of *The Drunken Ship*, where a clear distinction was made between the actors and the characters they represented in order to bring out the relevant issues in the play – a device repeated in *Tai Yang Awakes* – and any general description of Brecht's aims reveals a remarkable similarity to Piscator's approach. Both made out lists of the qualities that divorced their work from conventional theatre. In Piscator's list 'the extraordinary' was replaced by 'the typical', 'chance' by 'causality' (*Tendenz*), 'fantasy' by 'reality' and 'the decorative' by 'the constructive', so that the new drama he claimed to have created was 'rational' in the place of 'emotional' and its effect was 'pedagogic' instead of 'sensual'. This list, published by *Die Szene* in April 1929 is directly comparable to the list that Brecht appended to *Mahagonny* in 1931 to distinguish his own 'epic drama' from 'culinary opera'. The only difference is that Brecht's list is more detailed. Out of the nineteen qualities that he considered to be the basis of his plays nine are characteristic of Piscator's productions: 'Narrative/activates the onlooker [mentally]/global vision/intellectual structure (argument)/[the feelings] are forced into perception/tension arising from the events/Montage/the nature of society determines thought.' The others refer either to Brecht's particular concept of man as a variable and alterable entity or to the alienation of the audience.

Brecht narrowed the meaning of 'political theatre' to one facet of 'epic drama', while Piscator defined 'political' in a wider sense, perceiving that every aspect of twentieth-century existence was affected by public events and so related to politics. Since 1924 he had used the description 'epic' to distinguish his depiction of large-scale contemporary realities from the 'dramatic' illusion of personal conflict that was the normal subject matter of conventional plays, so that he applied the words 'epic' and 'political' as interchangeable synonyms.

The similarity in their work can be measured by the identical nature of their aims. The differences between them lie in their methods. Piscator's intentions, stated as early as 1920 when Brecht was still concerned with glorifying the anarchic individual in a lyrical manner, were to give theatre a social function by making it capable of portraying and commenting on the political realities of the age. This expresses Brecht's ideal exactly. Piscator had defended *Rasputin* on the grounds that 'we do not conceive of the theatre simply as a mirror of the age, but as a means to alter the age'.[37] And this sentence was echoed by Brecht: 'I wish to apply the maxim to the theatre that the point is not simply to interpret the world, but to alter it.'[38] The sentiment comes from Marx, and the difference between Brecht's deliberate distancing of the audience and Piscator's attempt to involve them while still appealing to rational objectivity can perhaps be traced to Lion Feuchtwanger's influence on Brecht. Feuchtwanger, who collaborated in the writing of *Edward II* and *The Visions of Simone Machard*, had modified Marx through the mouth of his autobiographical hero in *Success*:

Philosophers have explained the world, the point is to alter it. For myself, I believe that the only way to alter it is to explain it. If one explains it plausibly, then one alters it in a peaceful manner, through the spreading effects of reason. Only those who are unable to explain it plausibly attempt to alter it by force.

In aesthetic terms the difference between plausible explanation and force is precisely that between the dialectical exposition of Brecht's plays and Piscator's propaganda.

Brecht summed up the modern dramatist's problem as being the recognition that 'a reproduction of today's world' has become increasingly difficult. 'It was this perception which caused some of us playwrights and directors to set out on the search for a new means of artistic expression',[39] and at the beginning of his career he had perceived that

these things [the economy, modern conditions and processes, for instance food distribution] are not dramatic in our traditional sense, and if they are 'poeticized' then they are no longer true. Drama is no longer anything like that at all, and if it is thought that our contemporary world is no longer suitable for drama, then drama is no longer suitable for the world.[40]

This betrays an inability to resolve the paradox with the techniques to hand and the lack of a positive approach. From 1926 until the first of his didactic *Lehrstücke*, however, he worked with Piscator, whose experiments undoubtedly acted as an incentive and example. If it was true that 'the primacy of the theatrical apparatus is the primacy of the means of production. The theatrical apparatus resists any attempt to reconstruct it for other purposes in that when it comes into contact with the drama it immediately alters it...It "theatricalizes" everything'[41] – then the creation of a new type of production, new stage machinery and new techniques of communication were the preliminary and essential requisites for the 'epic' drama that Brecht envisaged. 'Without introducing innovations of a formal [i.e. technical] kind, no play-script can introduce the new material and the new viewpoints to the new classes of the audience.'[42] Piscator's placards and projections, film, treadmills and simultaneous acting areas provided the structure around which Brecht could build his plays and, at first, following Piscator, he associated 'epic' with 'documentary'.

Brecht acknowledged his debt to Piscator in a lecture to Scandi-

navian students in 1939: 'It turned out to be necessary to reconstruct the stage completely. It is not possible to detail here all
the inventions and innovations which Piscator used, together with
all the new achievements of technology, in order to bring the
immensity of modern material onto the stage' – and as late as 1936
Brecht's concept of 'epic' theatre was still an exact description of
Piscator's dramaturgy:

It was through technical achievements that the stage was made capable
of...integrating narrative elements into the dramatic presentation. The
possibility of projection, the increased flexibility of the stage through its
motorization, and the film: these completed the equipment of the
stage...In order to make the action comprehensible it became necessary
to represent the environment, in which men lived, in all its breadth and
'significance'...The stage began to narrate. No longer was the narrator
missing together with the fourth wall. It was not just that the background was brought into relationship with the action on the stage in that
other actions in other places were simultaneously called to mind on
large screens, but the speeches of the actors were illustrated or refuted by
projected documents, and concrete statistics gave tangible form to
abstract dialogues.[43]

Brecht's own testimony is backed up by evidence from members
of the Berliner Ensemble. His *Modelbücher* concentrate on the
actors and performances he directed gave the impression of a
bare stage, but one stage-hand commented 'in spite of that our
productions are extremely complicated technically',[44] and his stage
manager pointed out that Brecht used stage-machinery 'as a
dramaturgical means: for the travels of Grusche through the
mountains, for the journey of Mother Courage to the war; in other
words to indicate changes of place or the passing of time. It was no
doubt for this reason that the machinery was so important to him.'[45]
One function of Piscator's film, treadmills and revolves was identical.
Brecht took the adjective 'scientific', which critics had used to sum
up Piscator's work, to describe his own approach and, like Piscator's,
his Epic Theatre was intended to conform to the new standards of
technological media: the cinema and radio.

As examples of what the theatre could achieve, each of Piscator's
experiments was specifically intended to encourage contemporary
playwrights to handle sociologically relevant material. Brecht admitted taking part in them all, and his plays show that he not only

adopted Piscator's ideas but also exploited his distinctive techniques. *Edward II*, written a few months after Piscator's production of *Flags*, employed the same technique of silent-film scene-titles. At Brecht's suggestion Carl Ebert introduced film sequences into his Darmstadt production of *In the City's Jungle* a year after Piscator had effectively demonstrated the dramaturgical possibilities of film in *Tidal Wave*. This kind of parallelism can be traced in almost all Brecht's early work, and Piscator's influence can be clearly seen in *The Mother*, the *Lehrstück* Brecht used as a model for his epic dramaturgy. Here a simple simultaneous stage, almost an exact replica of the one Piscator had constructed for § *218* two years earlier, was designed by Caspar Neher, and Brecht commented that it was through the projection of texts and photographs that 'the stage *demonstrated*...the mighty spiritual movement within which the actions took place'.[46] The projections to scenes 11 and 14 were particularly reminiscent of *Rasputin*: 'Photographs of the war-leaders: the Czar, the German Kaiser, Poincaré, Wilson, Grey' and a film of 'documentary pictures from the October Revolution', accompanied by the projected text: 'In November 1917 the Russian Proletariat seized power'. In a later production of *The Mother* this film was replaced by another, synchronized with the final chorus. It 'portrayed...the progress of the revolutionary movement up to the present' – the very device that had caused the scandal about *Storm over Gottland* eight years earlier.

Piscator seems to have been justified in claiming that the origins of Brecht's style can be found in his stage experiments, and it is also true that the signs of his work are still present in Brecht's later dramas: 'Masks appeared [in *Schweik*] just as Brecht applies them in *The Caucasian Chalk Circle*; and in the same way Brecht owes the movement of *Mother Courage* to my invention of the treadmill even though he returns here once more to the far clumsier form of the revolving stage.'[47] Ernst Busch, Brecht's leading actor, goes further – 'everything that distinguishes Brecht's style he got from Piscator'[48] – and Brecht himself gratefully acknowledged Piscator's formative influence in an unpublished letter: 'No one in the whole of my productive period was as valuable for my artistic development as yourself.'[49] He also indicated his debt in a practical manner when he made more than one attempt to persuade Piscator to return to Berlin after the Second World War, offering him the opportunity to direct a production for the newly formed Berliner Ensemble and promising him (by proxy) a theatre of his own in East Berlin, 'since I find it hard to imagine a successful fight against provincialism, empty emotionalism, etc., and for great, politically mature theatre without you'.[50]

Brecht's reputation is beyond question, and it is certainly true that he modified Piscator's techniques, exactly as he did with his literary models, or when he transposed them directly he used Piscator's methods on a smaller and less obtrusive scale. Where Piscator set actors among the onlookers in *Tai Yang Awakes* and § *218* to involve them emotionally, Brecht placed choruses in the auditorium who deliberately stood apart and criticized the action of *The Mother*. His different approach to the audience created different functions for the machinery, and normally he used the techniques which Piscator had developed as narrative aids for his own purpose of breaking stage illusion. The most obvious difference between their work is that Brecht replaced Piscator's principle of direct confrontation with his own concept of alienation, but it should be noted that Brecht's regular practice did not always conform to even this central theory of dissociating the audience from the action. The close contact created by the informality of *Lehrstück* performances inevitably meant that every member of the audience was forced to participate, while the most characteristic of his illusion-breaking techniques related openly to the spectators: 'Prologue, songs between scenes during set-changes and occasional scene-titles, which were projected onto the curtain, established a direct contact with the public.'[51] Brecht rejected Piscator's concept of Total Theatre on the grounds that emotional involvement turned the audience into a 'passive (suffering) element of the synaesthetic art work'.[52] Yet in fact the opposite effect had been achieved in Piscator's productions where the onlookers, instead of having their potential for action dissolved by any form of artistic catharsis, were aroused to (sometimes even violent) civil disorder – so that actually Brecht's 'direct contact' is equivalent to Piscator's ideal of 'direct action'.

Brecht criticized Piscator's 'epic' machinery because, being 'inserted' not organic, it was 'at daggers drawn' with the actor: 'Yet even so Brecht could not have found his style without the epic machinery. His "little half-curtain" is a remnant of the documentary gauze and projection-screen for notices.'[53] Piscator's experiments with machinery and modern media were the basis of Brecht's 'theatre of the scientific age', and Piscator's solutions for presenting modern conditions on the stage recur throughout Brecht's work. In one sense his plays can be seen as the justification for Piscator's experiments, because they built on his 'examples' – and as Piscator wrote to Brecht, 'I believe, for my part, that no writer came closer to the conception I had of the theatre than you.'[54] But in fact he had to wait until the 1960s for the 'new drama', to which he so often referred, which could really be counted as a fulfilment of his practical work.

Even though Brecht borrowed Piscator's methods, the parable form he preferred is the opposite of documented contemporary drama, and his themes are moral paradoxes based on personal relationships, simplified and set in remote and grotesque worlds of the imagination in order to portray moral dilemmas clearly and interestingly. Both gained the distancing necessary to give particular material general significance, but while Brecht stripped down the essentials, withdrawing from the standards of actuality in his plays, Piscator gained universality through the global extension of his stage and the volume of documentation.

Piscator compared the difference between their approaches, from which the differences in their styles sprang, when he commented:

Brecht is my brother, yet our way of looking at affairs in general is different: Brecht reveals significant details of social life, while I attempt rather to give a view of political affairs in their totality...It is important for me to show the course of political realities. Brecht wishes to work obliquely through certain epochs, thus uncovering their structure: I would far prefer to show a continuous development.[55]

But both saw their work as complementary, and Brecht wrote: 'My idea is not that we should open a theatre together, even though I would always be at your disposal, as before, for projects which interested us both (i.e. for the majority of projects). One must work from at least two angles.'[56]

Critical misunderstandings

Few critics have been complimentary to Piscator, who was perhaps correct when he claimed that the novel elements of his productions were misunderstood in the Weimar years while those aspects which he considered important were ignored because the critics 'attempted to evaluate...something that at first was without comparison, for which no criteria were available, according to the artistic criteria that had been carried over from a past era'.[57] Critical support had been given to Piscator at first, even if his experiments were measured by inappropriate criteria and only Diebold and Jhering had approached his productions with open minds. But, apart from the technical faults in his work, as soon as Piscator's own maxim – that the theatre should act as a political tribunal – became widely accepted, even this approval was withdrawn. The party-political nature of his writings and the propagandist message of the plays he directed distracted attention from the dramaturgical significance of his experiments, dividing the critics down lines which had little to do with artistic considerations. To newspapers financed by the right wing his work was anathema, while the Communist press approved or criticized on dogmatic grounds according to ideological fluctuations. The political polarization of the 1920s, which Piscator himself had helped to create, deprived him of the wealthier sections of his public, the Communists withdrew their support because his complex experiments did not appear to have the immediate political value of Agitprop performances, and Jhering, looking on the spread of right-wing revanchism, despaired of the effectiveness of theatrical propaganda. The Piscator-Bühne went bankrupt, and although mismanagement and mechanical miscarriage played their part, the real reason for the failure of Piscator's attempt to reorganize the theatre in the twenties was the lack of attention paid to the dramaturgical aspects of his work. The value of any production was largely determined by the practical political application of the play.

A variation of the same approach, which did take his style into account but again in a political rather than artistic context, was the ideological criticism that Piscator's work lacked development because he failed to fill his 'political' style with the 'correct' revolutionary content. It was acknowledged that his dramaturgy provided an effective pole of opposition 'against bourgeois and social democratic theatre, which wished to remain unpolitical, i.e. counter-revolutionary'.[58] But from this standpoint the success of Piscator's productions removed the reason for their existence. They seemed progressively more pointless as their influence undermined traditional conventions – and, even though 'classical theatre' was resuscitated under the [Third Reich, since the leading Weimar directors all discarded illusionistic modes of representation Piscator was correct when he stated at the end of the decade: 'The art-theatre has begun to wither away. It is hardly still possible to hold to the line of pure art (the line of defence of political reactionaries). The public is no longer interested in it.'[59]

Depressingly, the major political criticisms recur after the emergence of Documentary Drama in the sixties. One line of approach condemns Piscator for ignoring dramatic art – aesthetic structure and distancing – in theatricalizing politics: 'He holds fast to the Dada slogan "Art is shit!".' The other is prepared to admit the value of his earlier experiments but dismisses his more complex methods of portraying the modern world on the grounds that he mistook the dialectical process of class history for a mechanical construction. More depressing still is the lack of attention to Piscator's work outside Germany. Piscator's influence has been ignored, and when 'political theatre' has been mentioned at all no effort has been made to comprehend it. Norman Marshall's book, *The Producer and the Play*, is a typical example. The few paragraphs on Piscator are limited to such inaccurate and superficial descriptions of his techniques as:

Sections of the stage rose, sank, revolved, slid; lantern slides and cinema-films were projected onto the backwall; above the proscenium Communist slogans blazed in lights; the gigantic shadows of machines were thrown onto gauzes behind which the actors went on with their performance; searchlights swept to and fro across the acting area; motor-cycles roared up and down steep ramps, and to add to the din there were the blaring of loudspeakers, the throbbing of machinery...amidst the rumble and turmoil of Piscator's productions the play was lost and the actor reduced to a non-entity

– and where he makes any attempt to evaluate Piscator's intentions, Marshall reveals ignorance of the nature of his experiments, confusing his work with the Bauhaus (and, incidentally, even misunderstanding that): 'In Germany Piscator was enforcing "un-individualistic acting" by dressing his actors in harsh, angular costumes which were deliberately at variance with the lines of the human body, so that the players seemed more like robots than human beings.' Similarly, Willett and Esslin mention Piscator in their books on Brecht only to dismiss him, while Garten, who has attempted the only survey of twentieth-century German drama in English, ignores him almost completely as a theatrical hack with second-hand ideas. Ewen is the only English-speaking scholar who has dealt with his work objectively, and he has restricted himself to repeating passages from Piscator's book.

Evaluation

Matthew Arnold once argued that in circumstances when the communication of cultural values has become impossible, then the task of the artist is criticism and his aim should be to re-formulate those values in order to produce a favourable climate for the creation of future poets. The First World War and the series of economic crises which followed had exposed a gulf between traditional art and the reality that the artist purported to portray – a dichotomy which was particularly obvious in Germany – and had called the traditional values of European civilization into question. Piscator's position is comparable to Arnold's, with the difference that former values appeared to have been finally discredited, so that rather than rejuvenating a time-honoured tradition his aim was to provide a means of expression which would be valid for the new conditions. His progress was a process of trial and error to make the theatre capable of dealing with the new dimensions of modern experience, and it has been claimed that even his 'mistakes and errors were normally more fruitful than the conventional virtues of others'.[60]

Piscator's experiments repeatedly questioned the premises and purposes of the theatre, and the character of his work can be seen by a glance at any programme of the New York Dramatic Workshop, which – significantly – was founded as an integral part of the New School for Social Research. 'The Dramatic Workshop should further modern research technique to meet the demands of the modern theatre.' A course on 'Contemporary Theatre and Film' was designed to demonstrate the stage's 'relation to the social and spiritual currents of our time'. Working on the principle that each period finds scenic forms evolved from its general culture, a course on 'Stagecraft' proposed 'to find the most appropriate and effective scenic means for our day'. Equally important, practising dramatists were drawn into the studies and given a practical grounding in the new stage techniques which were available to them. The pedagogic side of Piscator's work had already emerged and proved its value in the Studio that he founded for the Piscator-Bühne, and during his exile in America, where he taught among others Robert Penn Warren, Tennessee Williams, Robert Sherwood and Arthur Miller, he consolidated and passed on what he had already learnt. Piscator's ability to teach was no less important, if less spectacular than the new techniques of representation he evolved, for without his educative capability they would have had only limited influence and academic interest.

Creative direction can turn bad or dull plays into excellent entertainment – the classic example is Irving's production of *The Bells*, which turned a poor play into a vital and vivid performance. But an inventive (as opposed to interpretative) director is normally a menace to good drama because at one end of the scale he is solely interested in opportunities to display his own virtuosity, while at the other he is only concerned with the text in so far as it can be adapted for 'higher' (usually political) purposes. It is easy to dismiss Piscator as one of the second category on the basis of his record and the almost entirely political reaction to his productions in the Weimar era. But his work deserves more careful attention since his technical innovations had a dramaturgical purpose and his influence has determined the form of a major aspect of modern drama. As a director, he had to work with what materials were available to him – machinery and actors – and it must be remembered that until after the Second World War the plays he produced, with the exception of *The Robbers*, were of little dramatic or even literary value in themselves. There is some truth in Irving's remark that 'plays are made for the theatre and not the theatre for plays', and Piscator set about transforming the theatre at source – the stage.

In doing so he anticipated McLuhan's analysis of modern media, where the way in which a message is expressed is seen to be more important than the content because the medium determines the meaning. By this definition art transmits values in its manipulation of the means of expression, so that to alter the method of communication automatically changes cultural values as well as subject matter – and indeed, according to a slightly more established authority, creates a new art: 'If you can find in Nature a new material [media]...then you can say that you are on the high road towards creating a new art. For you have found that by which you can create it.'[61] Piscator's experiments changed the nature of the stage, and he was able to justify his textual alterations on the grounds that theatrical forms condition the type of play dramatists write. A conventional theatre is only capable of dealing with traditional subjects and the playwright therefore models his work on the techniques that he knows are available to him: 'In the final analysis he does not write his plays with a typewriter, but with the stage and its materials.'[62]

Piscator's rôle in encouraging the contemporary school of German documentary dramatists alone should have earned his work more attention than it has been given up to now since even unsympathetic critics have been unable to deny that 'Piscator... became the most important dramaturgical midwife for a new type of German drama'.[63] But his influence was not limited to his direct associates, Brecht, Hans Kirst, Leo Lania and Friedrich Wolf, nor to Hochhuth, Kipphardt, Weiss and their more recent followers, Tancred Dorst and Günther Grass. His Agitprop experiments, which determined the form of the English Theatre of Action and the American Living Newspaper as well as the German workers' theatre movement, have become widely accepted, and their indirect influence can be seen in productions as far apart as the Royal Shakespeare Company's *U.S.*, the Theatre Workshop's *Oh What a Lovely War* or Garson's *Macbird*. Joan Littlewood and Ewan McColl translated his version of *Schweik* in the 1930s and incidents from it recur in *Oh What a Lovely War*. His Total Theatre techniques are used in such different plays as *Dionysus in '69* and *Chicago '70*, and his documentary ideas are spreading. The impact of Hochhuth's plays is still being felt, and Piscator's New York version of *War and Peace*, which he later produced again in Berlin, was revived in Bristol after the war and has recently been adapted for B.B.C. television. Even his method of treating the Classics has been imitated – for instance in Roger Planchon's Marxist rendering of *Henry V*. Apart from his dominant influence in Germany, his years in New York had significant effects on drama in the U.S.A. not the least of which has been the rise of the underground stages which followed his successful foundation of two off-Broadway theatres; while Friedrich Wolf has even argued that all the left-wing plays of the professional theatre – whether an 'analytical' play like Wangenheim's *Mousetrap*, or one of the epic-informing plays of Brecht's, or one of my own plays – all these theatrical works in the 'great tradition' are inconceivable without the preparatory work of the Agitprop troupes, without the preparatory work of Piscator.[64]

Apart from specific influence, the significance of his work for the theatre as a whole is implied by a description of Brecht's, which deals with its general application:

Piscator's experiments at once produced a thoroughgoing chaos in the theatre. Just as they turned the stage into a machine-shop, so they turned the auditorium into a meeting-hall. For Piscator theatre was a parliament and the audience a legislative body. Before this body were visibly set the great public questions that demanded decisions. In place of speeches by delegates, concerning certain untenable conditions, we had an artistic reproduction of such conditions. The stage set itself the task of prodding the audience – the parliament – ...into making political decisions. Piscator's stage did not despise approbation, but it was more eager to arouse discussion. It did not aim only to provide a spectator with an experience, but wanted to make him draw practical conclusions, take hold on life and actively participate in living.[65]

It is a commonplace that the theatre depends on popularity for its existence – however much the social and political environment has changed Dr Johnson's statement remains true:

> The drama's laws the drama's patrons give
> And we that aim to please must please to live

– and whatever the faults of Piscator's productions, there can be no doubt that they were exciting. Tilla Durieux called his use of machinery 'electrifying', and what she has said about his production of *The Robbers* is true for his effect on modern theatre as a whole: 'He swept away the stale air, the pomposity, all that missed the essence.'[66] He gained an undeserved reputation for sensationalism from the stimulating novelty of his stage effects. He became notorious for his treatment of authors, for his involvement in contemporary political crises, and for the scandals that followed his premières. His experiments in the twenties have been described as

the most vitally alive productions in the lively theatrical centre of Berlin, which between revolution, inflation, stabilization and collapse...exactly mirrored their environment in cool, controlled and passionately shaped pictures...his plays and productions of the time, though frequently problematic in hindsight, corresponded to the era and its people. They set us on the stage and formulated our emotions and opinions...Their significance: substantiation and suppression, challenge and critical examination.[67]

His recent work in the Bundesrepublik, if less sensational, was of more lasting value. His innovations, anticipating McLuhan, established a new approach to reality as well as expanding the range of the theatre and transforming the stage into a competent instrument for dealing with our twentieth-century environment. As a creative influence Piscator ranks with Appia, Artaud, Gordon Craig and Meyerhold; but perhaps the highest praise is simply that his theatre was 'the most interesting stage in Europe'.[68]

Notes

CHAPTER 1

1. Piscator, letter to *Die Weltbühne*, Berlin 1928, No. 10.
2. Since the dramatist is the original creator, this is of course an illusion. He has far less immediate contact with his public than other artists and must rely on a chain of intermediaries for communication. But the audience have the impression that they are being directly spoken to, and for them the actors or the producer appear in the place of the artist.
3. Marinetti founded the Futurist movement which, although it shared many of the Dadaist characteristics, accepted the environment. The Futurists saw war as a spontaneous eruption of movements, as a simultaneous poem on a global scale or as a symphony of cries, shots and orders; and the majority found their way into Fascism.
4. Cf. Tristan Tzara, 'Dada Manifesto', in *Dada*, ed. Richard Huelsenbeck (Rowohlt, 1964), pp. 47f.
5. Tristan Tzara, 'Lecture to the Dada Congress' (1924), in *Dada*, p. 56.
6. Raoul Hausmann, 'Dada is more than Dada' (1921), in *Dada*, p. 39.
7. Raoul Hausmann, 'Pamphlet against the Weimar Philosophy' (1918), in *Dada*, p. 34. This association of Communism with simple Christian morality had a wide influence. Cf. Alfred Kerr, 'Bolshevism? It's called something else in all bibles...', cit. Piscator, *Das politische Theater* (Rowohlt, 1963), p. 102.
8. Here Dada approached Expressionism (cf. Stefan Zweig, 'The new pathos', in *Expressionismus*, ed. Paul Raabe (D.T.V., 1965), pp. 15f.), but their rejection of Expressionism as conventional and escapist was uncompromising (cf. Huelsenbeck, Foreword to *Dada*, p. 13).
9. The opening sentence of a 'Dada Manifesto', signed by Tzara, Grosz, Huelsenbeck, Hausmann, Franz Jung, Hugo Ball and Hans Arp, in *Dada*, p. 27.
10. *Die Aktion*, published by Franz Pfemfert, was the most radical of the Expressionist magazines. cf. *Expressionismus*, p. 144.
11. Piscator, *Schriften* (Berlin, 1968), vol. II, p. 279.
12. Piscator, *Das politische Theater*, p. 63 (my italics).
13. Even this was not original. Film had already been introduced to the theatre before the First World War in the French farce *A Million*, where the action on stage was interrupted and continued on the screen. A glass of water, raised to the lips by an actor, was drunk in the film. This, however, was merely a spectacular trick without functional significance, and there is no question of influence.
14. Piscator, *Das politische Theater*, p. 63.
15. Herbert Jhering, 'The new inquisition', in *Die Weltbühne*, 21 June 1932.
16. Piscator, 'Call to artists and men!', in *Der Freihaven*, Hamburg, 1921.

17. Cf. Piscator, *Das politische Theater*, pp. 55, 121, 122, and 224. See also, Piscator, *Rote Fahne*, Berlin, 6 September 1927.
18. Piscator, *Le Monde*, Paris, 4 May 1929. He repeated this in a lecture. Cf. *Schriften*, vol. II, p. 55.
19. Piscator, *Das politische Theater*, p. 39.

CHAPTER 2

1. Cf. Paper No. 1 from the Trades Union Council of the Moscow Department of Culture, 1924.
2. The first appeared in *Westermanns Monatshefte*, 1927.
3. Piscator, *Das politische Theater*, p. 238.
4. Peter Lind, 'Proletarisches Theater?', in *Neue Rheinland*, 1919–20, No. 8.
5. Piscator, *Das politishe Theater*, p. 22.
6. Reprinted in *New Red Stage*, London, June/July 1932.
7. The manuscript of *Russia's Day* (*Russlandstag*) is in the possession of the *Akademie der Künste*, East Berlin.
8. Cf. Piscator, *Das politische Theater*, pp. 47 and 48.
9. My italics.
9a. My italics.
10. Piscator, *Das politische Theater*, p. 49.
11. The ambivalent attitude of the Communist Party towards intellectuals is amply demonstrated in autobiographical accounts by André Gide, Louis Fischer, Arthur Koestler, Ignazio Silone, Stephen Spender and Richard Wright. Cf. *The God that Failed*, ed. R. Crossman (New York, 1964).
12. Piscator, 'Stage of the present and future', in *Rote Fahne*, 1 January 1928.
13. Piscator, in *Der Gegner*, Berlin, 1920–1, No. 4. This edition (ed. Wieland Herzfelde) was sold as a programme for the first performance of the Proletarisches Theater on 14 October 1920.
14. Cf. Piscator, in *Berliner Tageblatt*, 6 March 1927.
15. Cf. Karl Radek, cit. Malanowski, 'November 1918', in *Der Spiegel*, 25 November 1968.
16. *New Red Stage*, February 1932.
17. Piscator, *Der Gegner*, 1920, No. 4.
18. *New Red Stage*, June/July 1932.
19. Cf. 'Politisches Theater', in *Reallexikon der deutschen Literaturgeschichte* (1968), vol. III, pp. 191f.
20. Cf. Arthur Koestler, 'The initiates', in *The God That Failed*, pp. 41f.
21. Jewgeni Sanjatin, cit. Jürgen Rühle, *Literatur und Revolution* (Munich, 1963), p. 43.
22. Bertrand Russell, *The Practice and Theory of Communism* (London, 1954), p. 55.
23. My italics. Brecht's *Lehrstück*, *Die Massnahme* (1930), contains a paraphrase of this passage, which implies that it was both widely known and approved.
24. Cf. *Rote Fahne*, 14 October 1925.
25. Cf. editorial comment to Peter Kupke, 'Piscator and his political theatre', in *Theater der Zeit* (East Berlin, 1957), No. 5, p. 9.
26. 1923, the date given by Piscator (cf. Piscator, *Das politische Theater*, p. 55) refers to the actual buying of the Central-Theater. His first production opened on 29 September 1922, before the sale was completed.

Notes

CHAPTER 3

1. Herbert Jhering, *Von Reinhardt bis Brecht* (Berlin, 1961), vol. I, p. 288.
2. Cf. *Lexikon Sozialistischer deutscher Literatur* (Leipzig, 1964), p. 430.
3. Cf. Piscator, *Das politische Theater*, p. 153.
4. Ludwig Hoffmann, *Das deutsche Arbeiter-Theater* (Leipzig, 1957).
5. Piscator, *Das politische Theater*, p. 73 (my italics).
6. *Rote Fahne*, 11 July 1925.
7. Piscator, in *Vossische Zeitung*, Berlin, 5 September 1927.
8. Cf. Anatol Lunacharsky, *Die Revolution und die Kunst* (Dresden, 1962), pp. 54f.
9. Wilhelm Widmann, *Theater und Revolution* (Berlin, 1920), p. 84.
10. Friedrich Wolf, in *Das Arbeiter-Theater* (Berlin, 1928).
11. Mordecai Gorelik, in the pamphlet to Piscator's *Dramatic Workshop* (New York, 1942–3).
12. Piscator, *Das politische Theater* (journal), 1930, No. 1.
13. *Rote Fahne*, 26 October 1920.
14. Cf. *Sunday Worker*, 18 February 1926, 6 June 1926, 15 August 1926, 22 August 1926 and 5 September 1926.
15. Mark Chaney, 'Reflections of an old-stager', cit. L. A. Jones, *Zeitschrift für Anglistik und Amerikanistik* (Leipzig, 1966), p. 262.
16. Piscator, 'Supplément au Théâtre politique, 1930–1960', *Théâtre Populaire*, Paris, No. 47 (1962), 4.
17. Cf. Allardyce Nicoll, *The Theatre and Dramatic Theory* (London, 1962), p. 78.
18. Piscator, letter to *Die Weltbühne* (Berlin, 1928), No. 10.
19. Edmund Meisel, in the programme to *Hoppla, wir leben!*, Piscator-Bühne, September 1927, p. 4.
20. Karl Kraus, *Die Letzten Tage der Menschheit* (D.T.V., 1966), p. 5.
21. Rolf Hochhuth, *The Deputy* (trans. R. and C. Winston) (New York, 1964), p. 222.
22. René Lauret, *Le Théâtre Allemand d'Aujourd'hui* (Paris, 1934), p. 160.
23. Herbert Jhering, 'Erwin Piscator', in *Das Tagebuch* (Berlin, 1926), No. 47 (my italics).
24. Piscator, letter to Friedrich Wolf, dated 9 October 1930.
25. Piscator, postscript to 1968 ed. of *Das politische Theater*, in *Schriften*, vol. I, p. 265.
26. Piscator, *Das politische Theater*, p. 133.
27. Piscator, 'Über die Lehren der Vergangenheit und die Aufgaben der Zukunft', in *Das internationale Theater* (Moscow, 1934), No. 56.
28. Piscator, in *Berliner Börsen-Courier*, 25 December 1926 (reprinted as 'Grundsätzliches', in *Das politische Theater*, p. 94).
29. Piscator, 'Shall I go on the stage in time of war?' in the programme for the *Dramatic Workshop* (New York, 1942–3).
30. Piscator, *Schriften*, vol. II, p. 174.
31. Piscator, in *Das politische Theater* (journal), 1930, No. 1.
32. Programme to *Hoppla, wir leben!*, Piscator-Bühne (1927), p. 3.
33. Piscator, programme to *Hoppla, wir leben!*, p. 1, and also *Das politische Theater*, pp. 153–4.
34. Piscator, in *Le Monde*, Paris, 4 May 1929.
35. Piscator, *Das politische Theater*, p. 132, and also *Schriften*, vol. II, p. 52.

36. Berta Lask, 'Erwin Piscator: *Das politische Theater*', in *Die Linkskurve*, (Berlin, January 1930).
37. Piscator, in *Der Gegner*, Berlin, 1920–1, No. 4.
38. Piscator, *Schriften*, vol. II, p. 194.
39. Richard Wagner, *Oper und Drama* (Leipzig, 1910), p. 153.
40. Piscator, *Schriften*, vol. II, p. 176.
41. Piscator, postscript to 1968 ed. of *Das politische Theater*, dated March 1966, in *Schriften*, vol. I, p. 264.

CHAPTER 4

1. Arthur Eloesser, *Der Querschnitt*, October 1930.
2. Piscator, *Das politische Theater*, p. 130.
3. Piscator, in *Der Klassenkampf*, Berlin, 1927, No. 2, p. 47.
4. Piscator, *Das politische Theater*, p. 93.
5. Piscator, in *Theater Heute*, October 1964, p. 4.
6. Piscator, in *Berliner Börsen-Courier*, 31 March 1929.
7. Ehm Welk, cit. Piscator, *Das politische Theater*, p. 108.
8. See ch. 7, below.
9. Piscator, letter to the editor of the *New York Times*, dated 17 March 1943.
10. Hans Reimann, *Mein Blaues Wunder* (Munich, 1959), pp. 409f.
11. Piscator, *Das politische Theater*, p. 72.
12. See p. 87.
13. Herbert Jhering, *Von Reinhardt bis Brecht* (Berlin, 1961), vol. II, p. 331.
14. Paul Kornfeld, in *Das Tagebuch*, Berlin, 14 September 1929.
15. Bernhard Diebold, in *Frankfurter Zeitung*, 11 September 1929.
16. Piscator, in *Die Zeit*, Hamburg, 26 November 1965.
17. Piscator, *Das politische Theater*, p. 133.
18. Piscator, postscript to the 1968 ed. of *Das politische Theater*, *Schriften*, vol. I, p. 268.
19. Piscator, *Das politische Theater*, p. 48.
20. Piscator, in *Das internationale Theater*, 1934, No. 5.
21. Piscator, *Das politische Theater*, p. 33.
22. *Ibid.*, p. 71.
23. *Ibid.*, p. 194.
24. Leo Lania, in *Wiener Arbeiterzeitung*, 2 May 1924.
25. Piscator, *Das politische Theater*, p. 174.
26. *Ibid.*, p. 161.
27. Bernhard Diebold, in *Frankfurter Zeitung*, 20 November 1927.
28. *Münchener neueste Nachrichten*, 7 September 1927.
29. Ehm Welk, in an open letter 'An den Vorstand des Verbandes deutscher Volksbühne-Vereine', March 1927.
30. Piscator, *Das politische Theater*, p. 78.
31. Alfred Döblin, cit. Piscator, *Das politische Theater*, p. 62.
32. Erwin Kalser, cit. Wolfgang Drews, in the foreword to *Das politische Theater*, p. 10.
33. Piscator, *Das politische Theater*, p. 52.
34. Piscator, in *Das Kunstblatt*, Potsdam 1926, No. 7, p. 273.
35. Piscator, in *Der Klassenkampf*, 1927, No. 2, p. 47 – a point he thought important enough to repeat in *Die neue Bücherschau*, October 1927.
36. Programme to *Nachtasyl*, Volksbühne, 1926.

Notes

37. Edmund Meisel, programme to *Schweik*, Piscator-Bühne, 1928.
38. *Theatre Workshop Manifesto*, 1945.
39. Piscator, programme to *Tai Yang Erwacht*, Piscator-Bühne, 1930.
40. Max Reinhardt, *Ausgewählte Briefe*, (ed. F. Hadamowsky) (Vienna, 1963), p. 86.
41. Piscator, 'The American Theater', in the *New York Times*, 21 January 1940.
42. Piscator, *Das politische Theater*, p. 198.
43. Leo Lania, programme to *Konjunktur*, Piscator-Bühne, April 1928.
44. Piscator, *Das politische Theater*, p. 199.
45. Piscator, cit. Günther Stark, in *Der Freihaven*, Hamburg, 1926, No. 9.
46. *Vossische Zeitung*, 24 January 1928.
47. Piscator, *Das politische Theater*, p. 73.
48. *Ibid.*, p. 136.
49. *Ibid.*, p. 124.
50. *Ibid.*, p. 170.
51. *Ibid.*, p. 133.
52. *Ibid.*, p. 175.
53. Piscator, 'Justification', *Schriften*, vol. II, p. 51.
54. This was a frequently repeated statement. Cf. Piscator, *Das politische Theater*, pp. 41, 134, 158, 185 and 228.
55. Walter Stang, 'National Socialism and theatre', in *Süddeutsche Monatshefte*, April 1934, No. 7.
56. Paul Kornfeld, 'Political theatre', in *Das Tagebuch*, Berlin, 14 September 1929.
57. Piscator, 'Stage of the present and future', in *Rote Fahne*, 1 January 1928.
58. Marshall McLuhan, *The Medium is the Massage* (Penguin, 1967), p. 146.
59. Piscator, *Schriften*, vol. II, p. 232.

CHAPTER 5

1. Piscator, *Schriften*, vol. II, p. 31.
2. Leo Lania, 'Drama and History', programme to *Rasputin*, Piscator-Bühne, January 1928.
3. Piscator, in *Das Theater-Tagebuch*, Emsdetten, 1953, No. 4.
4. Bernhard Diebold, 'Critical analysis: the Piscator-drama', in *Frankfurter Zeitung*, 20 November 1927.
5. Piscator, *Schriften*, vol. II, p. 192.
6. Piscator, *Das politische Theater*, p. 88.
7. *Ibid.*, p. 124.
8. Montage through simultaneous stages was a natural development of the realistic principle which underlay the Dada art forms – Bruitism, Simultaneity and Collage. See ch. 1, above.
9. Bernhard Diebold, in *Frankfurter Zeitung*, 20 November 1927.
10. Piscator, in *Der neue Weg*, Berlin, 1926, No. 8, p. 148.
11. Cf. *Die Linkskurve*, Berlin, 1929, Nos. 2 and 3 (Andor Gabor), where the productions of *Economic Competition*, *The Last Kaiser*, *What Price Glory?* and *The Merchant of Berlin* are criticized. This magazine, founded as the mouthpiece of the Association of Proletarian-Revolutionary Authors, took *Arbeiterliteratur* as synonymous with 'Marxist Literature' and viciously fought all left-wing liberal workers, including Toller, Plievier and Tucholsky, all of whom worked with Piscator, 'and tolerated the real enemy...Hitler. So the Communist literary journal accurately reflected the rôle that the

Communist Party played in the destruction of the German democracy'. Jürgen Rühle, *Literatur und Revolution*, pp. 144f.

12. Arnold Hauser, *Sozialgeschichte der Kunst und der Literatur* (Munich, 1953), cit. Piscator, in *Bühnentechnische Rundschau* (October, 1959).

13. Piscator, *Schriften*, vol. II, p. 145.

14. Brecht, in *Der Freihaven*, 1928, No. 4.

15. Exactly the same technique has been borrowed by Joan Littlewood, and proved its effectiveness in the 1963 Theatre Workshop production of *Oh What a Lovely War*.

16. See ch. 7, below.

17. Piscator, *Schriften*, vol. II, p. 204.

18. *Ibid.*, p. 163.

18a. *Ibid.*, p. 163.

19. Leo Lania, 'Drama and history', cit. (unacknowledged) Piscator, *Das politische Theater*, p. 161.

20. *Rote Fahne*, 12 April 1925.

21. Piscator, 'Technology – an artistic necessity for the modern theatre', in *Bühnentechnische Rundschau*, October 1959, pp. 10f.

22. Piscator, *Das politische Theater*, p. 85.

23. *Ibid.*, p. 123.

24. Hans Reimann, *Mein blaues Wunder*, pp. 401f.

25. Piscator, *Schriften*, vol. I, p. 65. Here I have returned to the reading of the 1929 ed. because it reveals Piscator's intentions more clearly.

26. Piscator, *Das politische Theater*, p. 130.

27. *Ibid.*, p. 190.

28. *Ibid.*, p. 231.

29. *Ibid.*, p. 210.

30. Vsevolod Meyerhold, 'Ideology and technology in the theatre', in *Theater Heute*, February 1963.

31. Piscator, *Schriften*, vol. II, p. 76.

32. *Rote Fahne*, 17 January 1931.

33. The Communists exploited even the most unlikely elements of the theatre for propaganda, including ballet. Jean Weidt's performances were mimed dances on social themes: e.g. 'A soldier's complaint' or 'A peasant's story'. He performed solo, but dance was an integral part of many Agitprop productions, and is found for example in Brecht's work or in Joan Littlewood's curious Expressionistic play of 1939, *John Bullion* ('a ballet with words'). Piscator was also involved in this type of political ballet through his wife, Maria Ley-Piscator, who taught dancing at the New York Dramatic Workshop, and whose routines reflected either typical subjects of Socialist Realism ('3 hymns in praise of work', 'At the anvil' etc.) or Expressionist themes on the lines of Auden's *Dance of Death* ('Decaying society', 'Capital makes a few deals', 'Images of jingo patriotism' etc.).

34. Piscator, 'Objective acting', in *Actors on Acting* (ed. Cole and Chinoy) (New York, 1949), p. 287.

35. Piscator, 'Political theatre', in *Die neue Bücherschau*, Berlin, 1927, No. 4.

36. Herbert Jhering, in *8-Uhr Abendblatt*, 4 April 1930, and Monty Jacobs, in *Vossische Zeitung*, 29 November 1930.

37. Herbert Jhering, *Von Reinhardt bis Brecht*, vol. III, p. 54.

38. Herbert Jhering, *Berliner Börsen-Courier*, 29 November 1930.

39. Piscator, in *Actors on Acting*, p. 289.

40. Piscator, *Das politische Theater*, p. 151.
41. Piscator, *Das politische Theater*, p. 131. Brecht shared this opinion, cf. *Über Realismus* (Leipzig, 1968), pp. 41f.
42. Erich Heller, *The Disinherited Mind* (Penguin, 1961), p. 217.
43. Karl Kraus, foreword to *Die letzten Tage der Menschheit* (1919) (Munich, 1966), p. 5.
44. Professor Paul Holzhausen, 'The war on the stage', in *Hochland*, Munich, 1915–16, No. 1, p. 757.
45. Piscator, *Das politische Theater*, p. 175.
46. *Ibid.*, p. 131.
47. *Ibid.*, p. 132.
48. Piscator, *Schriften*, vol. II, p. 52.
49. Erich Schlaikjer, 'Historical figures on the stage', in *Berliner Kämpfe*, 1901.
50. Leopold Jessner, in *Die Zukunft der deutscher Bühne* (Berlin, 1917).
51. Piscator, in *Das internationale Theater*, 1933, No. 3, p. 11.
52. Béla Balázs, in *Das Wort*, Moscow, 1938, No. 5.
53. Peter Hacks, in *Neue deutsche Literatur*, East Berlin, 1957, No. 10.
54. Bertrand Russell, *The Practice and Theory of Bolshevism*, p. 95.
55. Piscator, *Das politische Theater*, p. 132.
56. *Ibid.*, p. 152.
57. *Rote Fahne*, 25 January 1928, and 16 March 1928.
58. Hans Reimann, *Mein blaues Wunder*, pp. 407f.
59. Piscator, *Das politische Theater*, p. 187 (my italics).
60. *Ibid.*, p. 166.
61. Ludwig Hoffmann, *Das deutsche Arbeiter-Theater*, p. 116.
62. *Dresdner Generalanzeiger*, 18 January 1931.
63. The dashes indicate where sentences or complete paragraphs have been cut, and the brackets indicate Piscator's insertions into the text.
64. René Lauret, *Le Théâtre Allemand d'Aujourd'hui* (Paris, 1934), p. 163.

CHAPTER 6

1. Bernhard Diebold, 'Drama of the moment', in *Frankfurter Zeitung*, 11 September 1929.
2. Piscator, 'Supplément au théâtre politique, 1930–1960', *Théâtre Populaire*, No. 47 (1962), 4.
3. Piscator, cit. Günther Stark, in 'Piscator's intentions in the *Tidal Wave* production', in *Der Freihaven*, 1926, No. 9.
4. Piscator, in *Die Volksbühne*, Berlin, 1926, No. 3, pp. 1–2.
5. Piscator, cit. Günther Stark, in 'Piscator's intentions in the *Tidal Wave* production', in *Der Freihaven*, 1926, No. 9.
6. Piscator, in *Das Theater-Tagebuch*, 1953, No. 4, p. 2.
7. Programme to *Hoppla!*, Piscator-Bühne, September 1927, p. 1.
8. Piscator, *Schriften*, vol. II, p. 272.
9. Piscator, in *Das Internationale Theater* (Moscow, 1933), p. 11.
10. Piscator, *Schriften*, vol. I, p. 264.
11. Piscator, programme to *Krieg und Frieden*, Schiller Theater, Berlin, 1954–5.
12. Piscator, *Schriften*, vol. II, p. 147.
13. Allardyce Nicoll, *The Theatre and Dramatic Theory* (London, 1962), p. 70. See also W. Kerr, *How not to write a Play* (London, 1955), p. 74, and Somerset Maugham, *The Summing Up*, p. 135.
14. Jakob Altmeier, cit. Piscator, *Das politische Theater*, p. 66.

15. Kurt Pinthus, in *8-Uhr Abendblatt*, Berlin, 4 April 1930.
16. L. W., 'Drama and public meeting', in *Die Literatur*, Berlin, 1929–30, p. 498.
17. Ludwig Hoffmann, *Das Deutsche Arbeiter-Theater, 1918–1933*, p. 113.
18. L. F. G., 'Piscator's years in New York', in the *American-German Review*, New York, June/July 1966.
19. Walter Gropius, cit. Piscator, *Das politische Theater*, p. 128.
20. Béla Balázs, 'Theatre for the people', in *Die neue Schaubühne*, Dresden, July 1919.
21. Piscator, in *Der Gegner*, 1920–1, No. 4.
22. Somerset Maugham, *The Summing Up*, pp. 131–2.
23. E. D. Martin, *The Behaviour of Crowds* (London, 1920), p. 26.
24. Gustav le Bon, *The Crowd* (London, 1897), p. 58.
25. Julius Bab, *Das Theater im Lichte der Soziologie* (Leipzig, 1931), p. 118.
26. Piscator, cit. L. F. G., in the *American-German Review*, June/July 1966.
27. Walter Gropius, cit. Piscator, *Das politische Theater*, p. 126.
28. Piscator, *Das politische Theater*, p. 86.
29. *Rote Fahne*, 12 April 1921. In fact this point was intended as evidence of Piscator's objectivity, and he cited it as such. Cf. Piscator, *Das politische Theater*, p. 54.
30. George Grosz, cit. Piscator, *Das politische Theater*, p. 192.
31. Piscator, 'Technology – an artistic necessity for the modern theater', in *Bühnentechnische Rundschau*, Berlin, October 1959, No. 5, pp. 1of.
32. Piscator, 'Totaltheater und totales Theater', in *World Theatre*, Brussels, 1966, No. 1, pp. 6–7.

CHAPTER 7
1. Günther Rühle, *Theater für die Republik*, p. 43.
2. Franz Baumgarten, 'Theatre and circus', in *Das grosse Schauspielhaus*.
3. Friedrich Hedler, in *Die neue Literatur*, Berlin, April 1933.
4. Hanns Johst, in *Ostwart-Jahrbuch* (Breslau, 1926).
5. Hans Zeigler, in *Völkischer Beobachter*, Berlin Edition, 4 April 1932.
6. Walter Stang, in *Süddeutsche Monatshefte*, April 1934, No. 7.
7. Piscator, *Das politische Theater*, p. 229.
8. Friedrick Wolf, letter to Pollatschek, cit. Ludwig Hoffmann, *Das deutsche Arbeiter-Theater*, p. 111.
9. Paul Fechter, *Deutsche Allgemeine Zeitung*, Berlin, 7 September 1929.
10. Piscator, *Das politische Theater*, p. 167.
11. Piscator, in *Bühnentechnische Rundschau*, Berlin, October 1959, pp. 1of.
12. Piscator, in an open letter to *Die Weltbühne*, 1928, No. 10.
13. Piscator, in *World Theatre*, 1956, No. 4, pp. 291f.
14. Piscator, in *Das Theater-Tagebuch*, 1953, No. 4.
15. Piscator, in *Die Volksbühne*, 1926, No. 3, p. 1.
16. Piscator, in *Berliner Tageblatt*, 6 April 1927.
17. Piscator, in *Die Volksbühne*, 1926, No. 3, p. 1.
18. Piscator, in *Berliner Tageblatt*, 6 April 1927.
19. Walter Gropius, introduction to *The Theatre of the Bauhaus*, O. Schlemmer, L. Moholy-Nagy and F. Molnas, trans. A. S. Wensinger (W.U.P., Connecticut, 1961), pp. 12 and 14.
20. Piscator, undated typescript, in the Akademie der Künste, West Berlin.
21. Piscator, in *Berliner Tageblatt*, 6 April 1927.

22. Piscator, *Schriften*, vol. II, p. 170.
23. Piscator, in *Berliner Tageblatt*, 7 January 1928 (my italics).
24. Piscator, in *Das politische Theater* (journal), Berlin, 1930, No. 1, p. 9.
25. Piscator, in *Bühnenblätter*, Nationaltheater, Mannheim, 1954–5, No. 2.
26. Piscator, in *Die Zeit*, 26 November 1965.
27. Henning Rischbieter, in *Deutsches Theater Heute* (Hannover, 1967), p. 199.
28. Piscator, in *Bühnenblätter*, Nationaltheater, Mannheim, 1954–5, No. 2.
29. *Ibid.*
30. Piscator, *Schriften*, vol. II, pp. 206–7.
31. Piscator, 'In conversation', *Bühnenblätter*, Nationaltheater, Mannheim, 1954–5, No. 2.
32. Max Reinhardt (1902), cit. Arthur Kahane, *Tagebuch des Dramaturgen* (Berlin, 1928), pp. 118–19.
33. Brecht, in *Berliner Börsen-Courier*, 25 December 1926.
34. Piscator, programme to *Hoppla!*, Piscator-Bühne, 1927.
35. Piscator, *Das politische Theater*, p. 132.
36. Herbert Jhering, *Von Reinhardt bis Brecht*, vol. II, pp. 223f.
37. Maria Ley-Piscator, radio script, 13 December 1940.
38. Piscator, *Schriften*, vol. II, pp. 220f.
39. *Ibid.*
40. *Ibid.*
41. Piscator, in *Die Literatur*, Berlin, 1929–30, No. 6, p. 381.
42. Piscator, in *Die Zeit*, 26 November 1965.
43. Piscator, in *Das Theater-Tagebuch*, Emsdetten, 1953, No. 4.
44. Piscator, in *Blätter der Piscator-Bühne*, 15 January 1931.
45. Piscator, *Das politische Theater*, p. 233.
46. Piscator, *Schriften*, vol. II, p. 252.
47. Piscator, *Das politische Theater*, p. 78.
48. Herbert Jhering, *Von Reinhardt bis Brecht*, vol. II, p. 323.
49. *Bronx Home News*, New York, 22 May 1942.
50. *Herald Tribune*, New York, 22 May 1942.
51. Piscator, *Das politische Theater*, pp. 78–9.
52. Piscator, in *Rote Fahne*, 1 January 1928.
53. Max Brod, in *Die Weltbühne*, 4 September 1929.
54. *Ibid.*
55. Piscator, in *Bühnentechnische Rundschau*, October 1959.
56. Piscator, foreword to *Der Stellvertreter* (Rowohlt, 1963), p. 7.
57. Cf. Eric Bentley (ed.), *The Storm over the Deputy* (New York, 1964).
58. Piscator, in *Das politische Theater* (journal), 1930, No. 1.
59. Piscator, *Schriften*, vol. II, p. 214.

CHAPTER 8

1. Cf. Adolf Behne, 'Lyrical or architectonic stage?' in *Die neue Schaubühne*, Dresden, March 1919.
2. Cf. Stefan Zweig, 'The New Pathos' (1909), in *Expressionismus. Der Kampf um eine literarische Bewegung*, ed. Paul Raabe (D.T.V., 1965), pp. 15 and 21.
3. *Ibid.*, p. 17.
4. Piscator, *Das politische Theater*, p. 149.
5. Carl Vollmoeller, 'An account of the development of the big theatre', in *Das Grosse Schauspielhaus*, Berlin, 1920.

6. Kurt Pinthus, 'The possibility of a future people's theatre', in *Das Grosse Schauspielhaus.*
7. Piscator, *Das politische Theater,* pp. 73 and 74.
8. Max Reinhardt, 'Concerning actors', in *Gesammelte Schriften,* ed. F. Hadamowski (Vienna, 1963).
9. Heinz Herald, cit. Jürgen Rühle, *Theater und Revolution,* pp. 128–9.
10. Max Reinhardt, 'Concerning actors', in *Gesammelte Schriften,* ed. F. Hadamowski.
11. Piscator, *Schriften,* vol. II, p. 189.
12. Arnold Zweig, 'Theatre, mass, man', in *Das Grosse Schauspielhaus.*
13. Alfred Kerr, 'Young Germany', in *Expressionismus. Der Kampf um eine literatische Bewegung,* p. 121.
14. Siegfried Jacobsohn, in *Die Weltbühne,* Berlin, 1918.
15. Kurt Pinthus, 'The future of the theatre?', in *Das deutsche Theater der Gegenwart,* ed. Max Krell (Leipzig, 1923).
16. Wolfgang Drews, in *Theater Heute,* 4 April 1962.
17. See ch. 2, above.
18. Jürgen Rühle, 'Agitprop und Spieltheater', in *Theater Heute,* February 1963.
19. Herbert Jhering, in *Aktuelle Dramaturgie,* Berlin, 1924, p. 22.
20. Herbert Jhering, *Von Reinhardt bis Brecht,* vol. III, p. 56.
21. Piscator, postscript to U.S.S.R. ed. of *Das politische Theater* (Moscow, 1933), reprinted in *Schriften,* vol. II, pp. 101–9.
22. Piscator, in *Rote Fahne,* 1 January 1928.
23. Piscator, in *Das politische Theater* (journal), 1930, No. 1, p. 10.
24. *The Theatre of the Bauhaus,* O. Schlemmer, L. Moholy-Nagy and F. Molnas, introduced by W. Gropius, trans. A. S. Wensinger (W.U.P., Connecticut, 1961), p. 7.
25. Cf. Frederic Ewen, *Bertolt Brecht, His Life, His Art and His Times* (New York, 1967), pp. 148f., and Helge Hultberg, *Die Aesthetischen Anschauugen Bertolt Brechts* (Copenhagen, 1962), pp. 54f.
26. John Willett, *The Theatre of Bertolt Brecht,* p. 170.
27. Ernst Schumacher, *Die dramatischen Versuche Bertolt Brechts* (Berlin, 1955), p. 125.
28. Piscator, *Das politische Theater,* p. 85.
29. Brecht, *Bertolt-Brecht-Archiv,* Folder 127, p. 22.
30. Brecht, *Schriften zum Theater,* Bibl. Suhrkamp 1957, vol. XLI, pp. 61f.
31. Ernst Busch, in conversation, 28 March 1969.
32. Günther Weisenborn, *Der gespaltene Horizont* (Munich, 1964), pp. 240–1.
33. John Willett, *The Theatre of Bertolt Brecht,* p. 174.
34. *Ibid.,* p. 86.
35. Piscator, *Das politische Theater,* p. 181.
36. *Ibid.,* p. 40 (my italics).
37. *Ibid.,* p. 175.
38. Brecht, *Schriften zum Theater* (Berlin, 1964), vol. VII, p. 153.
39. Brecht, *Schriften zum Theater,* Bibl. Suhrkamp, vol XLI, p. 7.
40. Brecht, cit. Elizabeth Hauptmann, 'Working notes', 26 July 1926, in *Erinnerungen an Brecht,* ed. H. Witt (Leipzig, 1964), p. 52.
41. Brecht, *Schriften zum Theater,* Bibl. Suhrkamp, vol. XLI, pp. 29–30.
42. Brecht, *Schriften zum Theater* (Berlin, 1964), vol. III, pp. 116–17.
43. Brecht, *Schriften zum Theater,* Bibl. Suhrkamp, vol. XLI, pp. 62–3.

44. G. Horst, in *Erinnerungen an Brecht*, p. 229.
45. S. Gerhardt, *ibid.*, pp. 226–7.
46. Brecht, *Schriften zum Theater*, Bibl. Suhrkamp, vol. XLI, p. 38.
47. Piscator, *Schriften*, vol. II, p. 214.
48. Ernst Busch, in conversation, 25 March 1969.
49. Brecht, letter to Piscator, dated Santa Monica, March 1947.
50. *Ibid.*, February 1947.
51. *Theaterarbeit*, ed. Helene Weigel (Berlin, 1967), p. 20.
52. Brecht, *Schriften zum Theater*, Bibl. Suhrkamp, vol. XLI, p. 21.
53. Piscator, *Schriften*, vol. II, p. 171.
54. Published by Piscator in 'Supplément au Théâtre politique, 1930–60', *Théâtre Populaire*, No. 47 (1962), 4.
55. Piscator, *Schriften*, vol. II, p. 207.
56. Brecht, letter to Piscator, dated Santa Monica, February 1947.
57. Piscator, *Das politische Theater*, pp. 158–9.
58. Berta Lask, in *Die Linkskurve*, January 1930.
59. Piscator, *Das politische Theater*, p. 226.
60. Friedrich Wolf, in *Berliner Zeitung*, 3 September 1947.
61. Gordon Craig, *On the Art of the Theatre*, p. 73.
62. Piscator, *Schriften*, vol. II, p. 261.
63. Henning Rischbieter, in *Deutsches Theater Heute*, p. 199.
64. Friedrich Wolf, unpublished essay, 'The creative problem of the Agitprop theatre'.
65. Brecht, *Schriften zum Theater* (Berlin, 1964), vol. III, 86–7.
66. Tilla Durieux, in *Theater Heute*, 4 April 1962.
67. Wolfgang Drews, *Theater*, Munich 1961, pp. 138f.
68. *Die Arbeiter Internationale Zeitung*, Berlin, 1928, No. 7.

Chronological Table
of Piscator's major work and other productions relevant to his development

Work and date	Producer and points of interest	Theatre
1918		
Reinhard Goering, *Seeschlacht*	Max Reinhardt (*Kriegsexpressionismus*)	Deutsches Theater, Berlin
Ernst Toller, *Die Wandlung*	Karlheinz Martin (*Stationen* structure)	Die Tribüne, Berlin
1919 PISCATOR–DAS TRIBUNAL		
Aeschylus, *Orestie*	Max Reinhardt ('Mass theatre')	Opening of Grosses Schauspielhaus, Berlin
Herbert Kranz, *Freiheit*	Karlheinz Martin (*Proletkult*)	Proletarisches Theater, Philharmonie, Berlin
August Strindberg, *Gespenstersonata*	Piscator (Expressionism)	Das Tribunal, Königsberg
1920 PISCATOR – PROLETARISCHES THEATER		
K. A. Wittfogel, *Der Krüppel* Ladislaus Sas, *Vor dem Tore* Lajos Barta, *Russlands Tag*	Piscator. Design: John Heartfield (Agitprop)	Proletarisches Theater, Berlin (Workers' Halls)
Schiller, *Wilhelm Tell*	Leopold Jessner (break in academic tradition)	Staatliches Schauspielhaus, Berlin
1921		
Franz Jung, *Die Kanaker*	Piscator (Agitprop)	Proletarisches Theater, Berlin (Workers' Halls)
Ywan Goll, *Der Unsterbliche*	Ywan Goll (?) (film, masks and *Verfremdung*)	Dresden
Anton Chekov, *Onkel Wanja, Drei Schwestern*	Moscow Art Theatre, Stanislavski	(?) Berlin (guest appearance)

Chronological Table

Work and date	Producer and points of interest	Theatre
1922 PISCATOR–CENTRAL-THEATER		
Ernst Toller, *Die Maschinenstürmer*	Karlheinz Martin	Grosses Schauspielhaus, Berlin
Maxim Gorki, *Die Kleinbürger*	Piscator (Naturalism)	Central-Theater, Berlin
Triadisches Ballett, Bauhaus	L. Moholy-Nagy/Oscar Schlemmer (Mechanism and Abstraction)	Landestheater, Stuttgart
1923		
Romain Rolland, *Die Zeit wird kommen* Leo Tolstoi, *Die Macht der Finsternis*	Piscator (Naturalism)	Central-Theater, Berlin
Scribe, *Adrienne Lecouvreur* Racine, *Phaedre* Oscar Wilde, *Salome*	Tairoff, Moscow (conventional production)	(?) Berlin (guest appearance)
1924 PISCATOR–VOLKSBÜHNE		
Alfons Paquet, *Fahnen*	Piscator (slide-projection and scene-titles on placards)	Volksbühne, Berlin
Brecht, *Edward II*	Brecht. Design: Caspar Neher (influence of Piscator's *Fahnen* production)	Kammerspiele, München
Erwin Piscator/ Felix Gasbarra, *Revue Roter Rummel*	Piscator. Music: Edmund Meisel (cabaret structure and compère/commère figures: 'Agitation Programme')	Berlin (Workers' Halls)
1925		
Berta Lask, *Die Befreiung*	Piscator (Agitprop)	(Arbeiterspielgruppe), Berlin
Rudolf Leonhard, *Segel am Horizont*	Piscator. Design: Traugott Müller (stage-construct)	Volksbühne, Berlin
Politische-satirische Abende	Piscator (Agitprop)	Berlin (Workers' Halls)

220

Work and date	Producer and points of interest	Theatre
Arnolt Bronnen, *Rheinische Rebellen*	Leopold Jessner (influence of *Fahnen*: captions and use of flags)	Staatliches Schauspielhaus, Berlin
Erwin Piscator/ Felix Gasbarra, *Trotz Alledem!*	Piscator. Design: John Heartfield (use of documentary film and arena stage: 'Historical Revue')	Grosses Schauspielhaus, Berlin
1926		
Alfons Paquet, *Sturmflut*	Piscator Film: Hübler-Kahla (narrative and scenic use of film)	Volksbühne, Berlin
Paul Zech, *Das Trunkene Schiff*	Piscator. Design: George Grosz (*Verfremdung*)	Volksbühne, Berlin
Schiller, *Die Räuber* (adapted by Piscator)	Piscator. Music: Edmund Meisel (modern costume and textual alterations)	Staatliches Schauspielhaus, Berlin
Maxim Gorki, *Nachtasyl* (adapted by Piscator)	Piscator (expansion of stage dimension)	Volksbühne, Berlin
Shakespeare, *Hamlet*	Leopold Jessner (influence of Piscator's *Räuber* production)	Staatliches Schauspielhaus, Berlin
1927 PISCATOR-BUHNE		
Ehm Welk, *Gewitter über Gottland* (adapted by Piscator)	Piscator (film and textual alteration)	Volksbühne, Berlin
Brecht, *Im Dickicht der Städte*	Carl Ebert (influence of Piscator's *Fahnen* production)	Hessisches Landestheater, Darmstadt
Ernst Toller, *Hoppla, wir leben!* (adapted by Piscator)	Piscator. Design: John Heartfield and Traugott Müller (simultaneous stages and film)	Opening of Piscator-Bühne I, Theater am Nollendorfplatz, Berlin
Alexei Tolstoy, *Rasputin* (adapted by Piscator/ Lania/Gasbarra/Brecht)	Piscator. Design: Traugott Müller (simultaneous stages, *Verfremdung*, epic use of film, *Globus-Bühne*)	Piscator-Bühne I

Chronological Table

Work and date	Producer and Points of interest	Theatre
(?)	Blaue Blusen Ensemble, Moscow (Russian Agitprop)	Theater am Nollendorfplatz (guest appearance)
1928		
Max Brod/Hans Reimann, *Die Abenteuer des braven Soldaten Schweik* (adapted by Piscator/ Lania/Gasbarra/Brecht)	Piscator. Design: George Grosz, Film: Hübler-Kahla (treadmills – expansion of stage dimension, masks, puppets and cartoons)	Piscator-Bühne I
Leo Lania, *Konjunktur*	Piscator. Music: Kurt Weill (constructive scenery and newspaper technique)	Piscator-Bühne I, Lessing-Theater
J. R. Bloch *Der letze Kaiser*	Karlheinz Martin (influence of Piscator's use of film)	Piscator-Bühne I
Brecht/Weill, *Die Dreigroschenoper*	Erich Engel	Theater am Schiffbauerdamm, Berlin
Erich Mühsam, *Sacco und Vanzetti*	Leopold Lindtberg (influence of Piscator's Documentary Drama)	November Studio (Alexander Granach), Berlin
1929 SECOND PISCATOR-BÜHNE		
Maxwell Anderson, *Rivalen* (adapted by Carl Zuckmayer)	Piscator. Design: Caspar Neher	Theater in der Königgratzer Strasse, Berlin
Friedrich Wolf, *Cyankali*	Hans Hinrich (influence of Documentary Drama)	Lessing-Theater, Berlin
Walter Mehring, *Der Kaufmann von Berlin*	Piscator. Design: L. Moholy-Nagy. Music: Hanns Eisler (over-complex stage machinery)	Piscator-Bühne II, Theater am Nollendorfplatz
PISCATOR-KOLLEKTIV		
Karl Credé, *§ 218 (Frauen in Not)*	Piscator (involvement of the audience)	Apollotheater, Mannheim, and on tour
H. J. Rehfisch, *Die Affäre Dreyfus*	Heinz Kenter (influence of Documentary Drama)	Volksbühne, Berlin

Work and date	*Producer and points of interest*	*Theatre*
1930		
Theodor Plievier, *Der Kaisers Kulis* (adapted by Piscator)	Piscator. Design: Traugott Müller. Music: Edmund Meisel (epic form gained from dramatizing a novel)	Lessing-Theater, Berlin
Gogol, *Der Revisor* Tretjakov, *Brülle China!* Ostrovski, *Der Wald*	Meyerhold, Moscow (judged by critics to be behind German theatrical development)	Theater am Nollendorfplatz (guest appearance)
Bill-Bjelozerkovski, *Mond von Links*	Piscator (Agitprop)	Wallnertheater, Berlin
1931		
Friedrich Wolf, *Tai Yang erwacht*	Piscator. Design: John Heartfield. Choreography: Jean Weidt (simplicity of style and involvement of the audience)	Wallnertheater, Berlin
Bertolt Brecht, *Mann ist Mann*	Brecht. Design: Caspar Neher (first principles of Brecht's Epic Theatre)	Volksbühne, Berlin
1932 PISCATOR IN THE U.S.S.R.		
Bertolt Brecht, *Die Mutter*	Brecht (development of 'epic' theories and influence of Piscator: film from *Rasputin* and *Gewitter über Gottland*)	Komödienhaus, Berlin
Film (1932–4) *Aufstand der Fischer von St Barbara* (after Anna Seghers)	Piscator (mass crowd effects and attention to naturalistic details)	Moscow Film Co.
Benito Mussolini, *Hundert Tage*	Franz Ulbrich (first significant Fascist production in Germany)	Nationaltheater, Weimar
1933		
Hanns Johst, *Schlageter*	Franz Ulbrich (Nazi Documentary Drama)	Staatliches Schauspielhaus, Berlin
1936 PISCATOR IN PARIS		
1938 PISCATOR IN THE U.S.A.		

Chronological Table

Work and date	Producer and points of interest	Theatre
1939 Piscator/Brecht, *The Good Soldier Schweik* (trans. Ewan McColl)	Joan Littlewood (evidence of Piscator's influence outside Germany)	'Theatre of Action', Manchester
1940 Shakespeare, *King Lear*	Piscator (modernization of Classics)	Dramatic Workshop, Studio Theatre, New York
1942 Erwin Piscator/ Alfred Neumann, *War and Peace*	Piscator (adaption of a novel)	Dramatic Workshop, Studio Theatre, New York
1945 Bertolt Brecht, *The Private Life of the Master Race*	Piscator. Music: Hanns Eisler	Pauline Edwards Theatre, New York
1946 Michael Pogodin *The Aristocrats*	Piscator (use of film and projection)	Dramatic Workshop, New York
1948 Robert Penn Warren, *All The King's Men* (adapted by Piscator)	Piscator (adaptation of a novel)	President Theatre, New York
1949 Wolfgang Borchert, *The Outsider*	Piscator	President Theatre, New York
Bertolt Brecht, *Mutter Courage und ihre Kinder*	Brecht (influence of Piscator's techniques: machinery of expansion)	Deutsches Theater, Ost-Berlin
Heinz Herald, *The Burning Bush* (adapted by N. Langley)	Piscator ('Living Newspaper' style)	Dramatic Workshop, Studio Theatre, New York
1950 Franz Kafka, *The Scapegoat* (adapted by Piscator)	Piscator (return to Total Theatre techniques)	President Theatre, New York
1951 Shakespeare, *Macbeth*	Piscator (first use of the term 'living theatre')	President Theatre, New York

Work and date	*Producer and points of interest*	*Theatre*
1952 PISCATOR IN THE BUNDESREPUBLIK		
Lessing, *Nathan der Weise*	Piscator (techniques of expansion)	Schauspielhaus, Marburg
1954		
Bertolt Brecht, *Der kaukasische Kreiderkreis*	Brecht, Design: Caspar Neher (influence of Piscator's *Schweik* production: masks and techniques of expansion)	Theater am Schiffbauerdamm, Ost-Berlin
1955		
Erwin Piscator/ Alfred Neumann, *Krieg und Frieden*	Piscator (introduction of the *Lichtbühne* and use of the *Schicksalsbühne*)	Schillertheater, West-Berlin
1956		
Büchner, *Dantons Tod*	Piscator. Design: Caspar Neher	Schillertheater, West-Berlin
1957		
Schiller, *Die Räuber*	Piscator (contrast with earlier production)	Nationaltheater, Mannheim
1959		
Max Frisch *Bredermann und die Brandstifter*	Piscator (Total Theatre techniques)	Nationaltheater, Mannheim
Schiller, *Don Carlos*	Piscator (absence of mechanical effects)	Kammerspiele, München
1962		
Paul Claudel, *Christophe Colombe*	J-L. Barrault ('total theatre')	Essen
Bertolt Brecht, *Flüchtlingsgespräche* (adapted by Piscator)	Piscator	Kammerspiele, München
Bertolt Brecht, *Die Tage der Commune*	J. Tenschert. Design: Caspar Neher	Theater am Schiffbauerdamm
PISCATOR – FREIE VOLKSBÜHNE		
Gerhardt Hauptmann, *Die Atriden-Tetralogie* (adapted by Piscator)	Piscator (fidelity to the author's intentions)	Freie Volksbühne, West-Berlin

Chronological Table

Work and date	Producer and points of interest	Theatre
1963		
Rolf Hochhuth, *Der Stellvertreter*	Piscator (first of the new Documentary Drama)	Freie Volksbühne
Romain Rolland, *Robespierre* (adapted by Piscator/ Gasbarra)	Piscator (adaptation of a novel)	Freie Volksbühne
1964		
Heinar Kipphardt, *In der Sache J. Robert Oppenheimer*	Piscator (new Documentary Drama)	Freie Volksbühne
1965		
Peter Weiss *Die Ermittlung*	Piscator (the extreme of Documentary Drama)	Freie Volksbühne
1966		
H. H. Kirst/Erwin Piscator, *Aufstand der Offiziere*	Piscator (re-use of the *Globus-Bühne*)	Freie Volksbühne
Günther Grass, *Die Plebejer proben den Aufstand*	H. Utzerath (influence of new Documentary Drama)	Schillertheater, West-Berlin
1967		
Rolf Hochhuth, *Die Soldaten*	Hans Schweikart (dedicated to Piscator)	Freie Volksbühne
1968		
Tancred Dorst, *Toller*	Peter Palitzsch (evidence of Piscator's continuing influence)	Würtembergische Staatstheater, Stuttgart

This is not intended to be a complete list of either Piscator's productions or all the significant theatrical developments that have occurred during the period covered. The only productions that are mentioned are those which have been discussed above. A fuller list of Piscator's productions in Germany can be found at the end of Piscator, *Schriften*, ed. Ludwig Hoffmann (Berlin, 1968), vol. II.

Bibliography

This is not intended to be a complete bibliography. At the time of writing neither the material in the Piscator Centre, Akademie der Künste, West Berlin, nor that recently acquired by the Centre for Soviet and East European Studies, Southern Illinois, has been catalogued. The only works listed are those of direct relevance to Piscator's career or those referred to above which are unpublished. Readers interested in general theory, theatrical history or aesthetics should refer to:

Cheshire, David. *Theatre. History, Criticism and Reference*, London, 1967.

Works by Piscator

Das politische Theater, Schultz Verlag, Berlin, 1929; Rowohlt Verlag, Reinbek bei Hamburg, 1963 (trans. into Russian, 1933, and Czechoslovak, 1962).
Schriften, 2 vols. (ed.) Ludwig Hoffmann, Henschelverlag, East Berlin, 1968.
'Denk an seine Bleisoldaten' (poem), in *Das Aktionsbuch* ed. Franz Pfemfert (Berlin, 1917).
'Über die Aufgaben der Arbeiterbühne', in *Das Arbeiter-Theater* (ed.) D.A.T.B. (Berlin, 1928).
'Objective acting', in *Actors on Acting* (ed.) Cole and Chinoy, New York, 1949.
Foreword, Rolf Hochhuth, *Der Stellvertreter*, Rowohlt Verlag, Reinbek bei Hamburg, 1963.
Foreword, Ernst Toller, *Hop La, Nous Vivons!*, Paris, 1966.
Diary covering the years 1952, 1956, 1958, with various excerpts (typescript) from other diaries, and incomplete correspondence for the years 1945, 1946, 1949–50, 1954, 1955, 1957, 1958–9, 1961, 1962 (unpublished). In the possession of the Akademie der Künste, West Berlin.
'Amerika – the Dramatic Workshop' (typescript). Akademie der Künste, West Berlin.
'Ankunft in New York' (typescript). Akademie der Künste, West Berlin.

'Piscator in Schuldturm' (concerning the Piscator-Bühne situation in 1930) (typescript). Akademie der Künste, West Berlin.
'Die Rolle des Fernsehens in der amerikanischen Gesellschaft' (typescript). Akademie der Künste, West Berlin.

Newspaper articles by Piscator

Baukunst und Werkform, Nürnberg, 1957, No. 8.
Berliner Börsen-Courier, 25 December 1926; 31 March 1929.
Berliner Tageblatt, 6 April 1927, 7 January 1928.
Blätter der Piscator-Bühne, Berlin, 15 January 1931.
Bühnentechnische Rundschau, Berlin, 1959, No. 5.
Der Freihaven, Hamburg, 1921, No. 3.
Der Gegner (ed.) Wieland Herzfelde, Berlin, 1920–1, No. 4.
Hamburger Abendblatt, 23 November 1957.
Das Internationale Theater, Moscow, 1933, No. 3; 1934, Nos. 5 and 6.
Das Kunstblatt, Potsdam, 1926, No. 7.
Le Monde, Paris, 4 May 1929.
Moskauer Rundschau, 5 October 1930; 1933, No. 336.
Nachrichtblatt der Volksbühne, Berlin, March 1924.
Nationaltheater Mannheim Bühnenblätter, 1954–5, No. 2; 1955–6, No. 9.
Die neue Bücherschau, Berlin, October 1927.
Das Programme, Tübingen, 1954–5, No. 6.
Die rote Fahne, Berlin, 29 November 1924; 6 September 1927; 1 January 1928.
Das Schönste, München, 1961, No. 2.
Das Stichwort, Essen, 1959–60, No. 10; 1960–1, No. 13.
Theater Heute, Hannover, October 1964.
Théâtre populaire, Paris, Nos. 16 (1955), 19 (1956), 47 (1962).
Theater der Zeit, Berlin, 1958, No. 7.
Volksbühnen-Spiegel, Berlin, 1958, No. 8.
Welt am Abend, Berlin, 17 July 1925; 11 February 1931; 17 December 1932.
Die Weltbühne, Berlin, 1928, Nos. 5, 6, 10; 1930, No. 23.
Die Zeit, Hamburg, 15 December 1961; 26 November 1965.
Other newspaper articles by Piscator have been reprinted in *Schriften*, vol. II.

Plays – director's copies belonging to Piscator

These range from copies with marginal annotations to specially bound, interleaved copies. In some the alterations are limited to pencilled cuts in the speeches, some have comments in different hands, while in others the additions are all in Piscator's handwriting. A few (the books for

Hoppla, wir leben!, the 1955 production of *Krieg und Frieden* and the 1957 production of *Die Räuber*) have typewritten acting directions, notes and sketches as well as typewritten alterations to the text, and for one production (the 1926 version of *Die Räuber*) there are several surviving copies in different stages of emendation. The following, with others of lesser interest, are held by the Piscator Centre, Akademie der Künste, West Berlin.

Brecht, Bertolt, *Flüchtlingsgespräche* (1962) adapted by Piscator.

Büchner, Georg, *Dantons Tod* (1956).

Hauptmann, Gerhart, *Die Atriden-Tetralogie* (1962) adapted by Piscator.

Hochhuth, Rolf, *Der Stellvertreter* (1963).

Kipphardt, Heinar, *In der Sache J. Robert Oppenheimer* (1964).

Lessing, G. E., *Nathan der Weise* (1952).

Piscator, Erwin and Kirst, Hanns Helmut, *Aufstand der Offiziere* (1966).

Piscator, Erwin and Neumann, Alfred, *Krieg und Frieden* (1955, 1956, 1957).

Rolland, Romain, *Robespierre* (1963) adapted by Piscator.

Sartre, Jean Paul, *The Flies* (1947).

Schiller, Friedrich, *Don Carlos* (1959).

Shakespeare, William, *King Lear* (1940), *Macbeth* (1951), adapted by Piscator.

Weiss, Peter, *Die Ermittlung* (1965).

In the possession of the Akademie der Künste, East Berlin:

Toller, Ernst, *Hoppla, wir leben!* (1927) adapted by Piscator.

For certain other productions, although the director's copies are missing, acting-scripts survive in various stages of completeness:

Barta, Lajos, *Russlands Tag* (1920), complete typescript, Akademie der Künste, East Berlin.

Piscator, Erwin; Brecht, Bertolt and Lania, Leo, *Die Abenteuer des braven Soldaten Schweik* (1928), complete typescript, Bertolt-Brecht-Archiv, East Berlin.

Piscator, Erwin and Gasbarra, Felix, *Trotz Alledem!* (1925), full synopsis with typewritten description of various scenes, Akademie der Künste, East Berlin.

Play programmes relating to Piscator's productions, etc.

Dramatic Workshop Programme, New York, 1940–1, 1942–3, spring/summer 1951, Akademie der Künste, West Berlin.

Piscator-Bühne, *Hoppla, wir leben!*, Berlin, 1927; *Der Kaufmann von Berlin*, Berlin 1929–30; *Konjunktur*, Berlin, 1928; *Rasputin*, Berlin,

1927; *Rivalen*, Berlin, 1929; *Schweik*, Berlin, 1928; *Tai Yang erwacht*, Berlin, 1930, Akademie der Künste, West Berlin.
Piscator-Kollektiv, § *218*, Berlin, 1930, Akademie der Künste, West Berlin.
Schiller Theater, *Krieg und Frieden*, Berlin, 1954–5, Akademie der Künste, West Berlin.
Studio Theatre, *War and Peace*, New York, 1942, Akademie der Künste, West Berlin.
Volksbühne, *Nachtasyl*, Berlin, 1926, Akademie der Künste, West Berlin.
Ley-Piscator, Maria, radio scripts (typescript), 12 December 1940; 13 December 1940, Akademie der Künste, West Berlin.

Secondary literature relating to Piscator's work

Bab, Julius, *Die Chronik des deutschen Dramas*, vol. v, Berlin, 1926.
  Das Theater der Gegenwart, Leipzig, 1928.
  Das Theater im Lichte der Soziologie, Leipzig, 1931.
Carter, Huntley, *The New Spirit in the European Theatre, 1914–1924*, London, 1925.
Cole, Toby and Chinoy, Helen (eds.), *Actors on Acting*, New York, 1949.
  Directors on Directing, New York, 1954.
Deutscher-Arbeiter-Theater-Bund (ed.), *Das Arbeiter-Theater*, Berlin, 1928.
Esslin, Martin, *Brecht, a Choice of Evils*, London, 1959.
Ewen, Frederic, *Bertolt Brecht, His Life, His Art and His Times*, New York, 1967.
Gassner, John, *Masters of the Drama*, New York, 1954.
Grosz, Georg, *Ein kleines Ja und ein grosses Nein. Sein Leben von ihm selbst erzählt*, Reinbek bei Hamburg, 1955.
Heartfield, John, *Photomontagen zur Zeitgeschichte* I, Zürich, 1945.
Hoffmann, Ludwig (ed.), *Deutsches Arbeiter-Theater (Schriften zur Theaterwissenschaft*, vol. IV), Berlin, 1961.
Hultberg, Helge, *Die Aesthetische Anschauungen Bertolt Brechts*, Copenhagen, 1962.
Jhering, Herbert, *Aktuelle Dramaturgie*, Berlin, 1924.
  Der Kampf ums Theater, Dresden, 1922.
  Von Reinhardt bis Brecht, 3 vols., West Berlin, 1958–61.
Kahane, Arthur, *Tagebuch des Dramaturgen*, Berlin, 1928.
Krell, Max (ed.), *Das deutsche Theater der Gegenwart*, Leipzig, 1923.
Lauret, René, *Le Théâtre Allemand d'Aujourd'hui*, Paris, 1934.
Ley-Piscator, Maria, *The Piscator Experiment*, New York, 1967.
Marshall, Norman, *The Producer and the Play*, London, 1962.
Reimann, Hans, *Mein blaues Wunder*, München, 1959.
Rohmer, (ed.), *Das sozialistische Berufstheater in Berlin*, Berlin, 1933.

Rühle, Günther, *Theater für die Republik, 1917–1933*, Frankfurt, 1967.
Rühle, Jürgen, *Theater und Revolution*, D.T.V., 1963.
Schumacher, Ernst, *Die dramatischen Versuche Bertolt Brechts*, East Berlin, 1955.
Weisenborn, Günther, *Der gespaltene Horizont*, München, 1964.
Willett, John, *The Theatre of Bertolt Brecht*, London, 1967.

Newspaper Articles Relating to Piscator's Work

8-Uhr Abendblatt, Berlin, 4 April 1930.
Die Aktion, (ed.) Franz Pfemfert, Berlin, 1919.
Akzente, München, 1966, No. 3.
American–German Review, June/July 1966.
Das Argument, West Berlin, March 1968, Nos. 1–2.
Arbeiterbühne und Film, Berlin, March 1929, May 1931.
Die Arbeiter Internationale Zeitung, Berlin, 1928, No. 7.
Bayerische Staatszeitung, München, 20 October 1959.
Berliner Börsen-Courier, 25 February 1921, 11 December 1923, 23 February 1926, 25 December 1926, 5 September 1927, 24 January 1928, 3 March 1929, 29 November 1930, 16 January 1931.
Berliner Kämpfe, 1901.
Berliner Tageblatt, 6 November 1920, 4 September 1927, 26 November 1929, 16 January 1931.
Berliner Zeitung, 3 September 1947.
Blätter des deutschen Theaters, Berlin, 1921–2, No. 17.
Das blaue Heft, Berlin, 15 March 1926.
Bronx Home News, New York, 22 May 1942.
Bühnentechnische Rundschau, Berlin, 1959, No. 5.
Dada, Malik Verlag, Berlin, April 1920.
Deutsche Allgemeine Zeitung, Berlin, 7 September 1929.
Deutsche Blätter für Philosophie, Berlin, 1929–30, No. 3.
Deutsche Bühne, Frankfurt, 1919.
Deutsche Rundschau, Berlin, 1957, No. 2; Baden Baden, 1958, No. 1.
Deutsches Theater Heute, Hannover, 1967.
Deutsches Volksblatt, Stuttgart, 13 February 1963.
Dresdner Generalanzeiger, 18 January 1931.
Encounter, London, April 1955.
Die Fackel, Berlin, 13 September 1926.
Frankfurter Zeitung, 20 November 1927, 1 April 1929, 11 September 1929.
Der Freihaven, Hamburg, 1926, No. 9.
Gewerkschaftsrat, Moscow Department of Culture, 1924, Paper No. 1.
Herald Tribune, New York, 22 May 1942, 23 May 1942.
Die Hilfe, Berlin, 1927, Nos. 19, 23.
Hochland, München, 1915–16, No. 1.

Das Jahr der Bühne, Berlin, 1920–1.
Jungsozialistische Blätter, Berlin, 1927, No. 11.
Der Kämpfer, Berlin, 10 September 1927.
Die Linkskurve, Berlin, February 1929, March 1929, January 1930, July 1930, November 1932, December 1932.
Die Literatur, Berlin, 1928–9, No. 9; 1929–30, No. 6.
Magazin für Alle, Berlin, 1931, No. 2.
Münchener neueste Nachrichten, 7 September 1927.
Neue deutsche Literatur, East Berlin, 1957, No. 10.
Die neue Literatur, Berlin, April 1933.
Der neue Merkur, Berlin, 1921, No. 1.
Neue Rheinland, 1919–20, No. 8.
Neue Rundschau, Frankfurt, 1962, No. 73.
Die neue Schaubühne, Dresden, January 1919, March 1919, July 1919, September 1919, November 1920, January 1925.
Die neue Volkszeitung, New York, 30 May 1942.
Der neue Weg, Berlin, 16 April 1926.
New Masses, New York, 19 March 1946.
New Red Stage, London, February 1932, June 1932, July 1932.
New York Post, 22 May 1942.
New York World Telegram, 17 December 1949.
Nürnberger Zeitung, 22 February 1949.
Das politische Theater, Berlin, 1930, No. 1.
Pravda, Moscow, 21 August 1946.
Der Querschnitt, Berlin, January 1926, February 1926, March 1926, October 1930.
Rheinische Merkur, 9 October 1959.
Die rote Fahne, Berlin, 26 October 1920, 6 December 1920, 12 April 1921, 8 December 1924, 12 April 1925, 14 June 1925, 11 July 1925, 14 July 1925, 14 October 1925, 25 January 1928, 5 April 1930, 12 April 1930, 17 January 1931.
Roter Stern, Berlin, 1928, No. 5.
Schwabisches Tageblatt, Tübingen, 19 July 1960.
The Sentinel, New York, 9 May 1942.
Sommerkurs, Goethe Institut, 1966.
Steglitzer Anzeiger, Berlin, 1 July 1922.
Süddeutsche Monatshefte, München, April 1934, No. 7.
The Sun, New York, 22 May 1942.
The Sunday Worker, London, 18 February 1926, 6 June 1926, 1 August 1926, 15 August 1926, 22 August 1926, 5 September 1926, 29 August 1928.
Die Szene, Berlin, 1928.
Der Tag, Berlin, 13 March 1920, 22 May 1926, 25 January 1928; West Berlin, 22 February 1963.

Das Tagebuch, Berlin, November 1926, No. 46, 14 September 1929, 19 September 1929.
Die Tat, Berlin, October 1922.
Tempo, Berlin, 4 April 1930.
Theater Heute, Hannover, April 1962, February 1963, October 1965, 1965 (Sonderheft).
Das Theater Tagebuch, Emsdetten, 1953, No. 4.
Theater der Zeit, East Berlin, 1957, No. 5.
The Times, London, 16 March 1968.
The Twentieth Century, clxix, 1961.
Völkischer Beobachter, Berlin ed., 4 April 1932.
Die Volksbühne, Berlin, 1926, No. 3.
Vossische Zeitung, Berlin, 25 January 1924, 5 September 1927, 24 January 1928, 29 November 1930, 16 January 1931.
Welt am Abend, Berlin, 24 January 1928, 1931, No. 13.
Die Weltbühne, Berlin, 1920, No. 4, 23 January 1927, 4 September 1929, 21 June 1932.
Westermanns Monatshefte, 1927, No. 10.
Wiener Arbeiterzeitung, 2 May 1924.
Das Wort, Moscow, 1938, No. 5.
Zeitschrift für Anglistik und Amerikanistik, Leipzig, 1966.

Background studies relevant to Piscator's work

Angress, Werner, *Stillborn Revolution, The Communist Bid for Power in Germany, 1921–1923*, Princeton, 1963.
Ballusek, Lothar von, *Dichter im Dienst, der sozialistische Realismus in der deutschen Literatur*, Wiesbaden, 1963.
Bithell, Jethro, *Modern German Literature, 1880–1950*, London, 1959.
Brecht, Bertolt, *Schriften zum Theater*, 7 vols., Suhrkamp Verlag, 1963–4.
   Ueber Realismus, Leipzig, 1968.
Dorst, Tancred and Neubauer, Helmut, *Die Münchner Räterepublik. Zeugnisse und Kommentar*, Suhrkamp Verlag, 1966.
Erlich, Victor, *Russian Formalism: History, Doctrine*, The Hague, 1965.
Garten, H. F., *Modern German Drama*, London, 1959.
Hauser, Arnold, *Sozialgeschichte der Kunst und der Literatur*, München, 1953.
Heiber, Helmut, *Die Republik von Weimar*, D.T.V., 1968.
Huelsenbeck, Richard (ed.), *Dada, Ein Dokumentation*, Rowohlt, 1964.
le Bon, Gustav, *The Crowd*, London, 1897.
Lersch, Heinrich, *Mann im Eisen*, Berlin, 1924.
Lunacharsky, Anatoli, *Die Revolution und die Kunst*, Dresden, 1962.
Martin, E. D., *The Behaviour of Crowds*, London, 1920.

Bibliography

Mehring, Walter, *Berlin Dada. Eine Chronik mit Photos und Dokumentation*, Zürich, 1959.
McLuhan, Herbert Marshall, *Understanding Media: the Extensions of Man*, New York, 1964.
McLuhan, Herbert Marshall and Fiore, Quentin, *The Medium is the Massage*, Penguin, 1967.
Raabe, Paul (ed.), *Expressionismus. Der Kampf um eine literarische Bewegung*, D.T.V., 1965.
Motherwell, Robert (ed.), *The Dada Painters and Poets*, Documents of Modern Art, vol. 8, New York, 1951.
Rühle, Jürgen, *Literatur und Revolution*, Köln-Wien, 1960.
Russell, Bertrand, *The Practice and Theory of Bolshevism*, London, 1962.
Schöne, Albrecht, *Ueber politische Lyrik im zwanzigsten Jahrhundert*, Göttingen, 1965.
Sokel, Walter, *The Writer in Extremis: Expressionism in Twentieth Century German Literature*, Stanford, 1959.
Sontheimer, Kurt, *Antidemokratisches Denken in der Weimarer Republik*, München, 1968.
Schwartz, Albert, *Die Weimarer Republik*, Konstanz, 1958.
Vollmoeller, Karl (ed.), *Das grosse Schauspielhaus*, Berlin, 1920.
Weigel, Helene (ed.), *Theaterarbeit*, East Berlin, 1967.
Wensinger, A. S. (ed.), *The Theatre of the Bauhaus*, Connecticut, 1961.
Widmann, Wilhelm, *Theater und Revolution*, Berlin, 1920.
Witt, Huber (ed.), *Erinnerungen an Brecht*, Leipzig, 1964.
Wolf, Friedrich, *Aufsätze über Theater*, Berlin, 1952.

Unpublished works

Anon., *The Fire Sermon* (typescript), in the possession of Mr Clive Barker, Birmingham University.
Anon., *Where's that Bomb?* (acting copy), in the possession of Mr Clive Barker, Birmingham University.
Chaney, Mark, *Reflections of an Old Stager*, in the possession of Mr L. A. Jones, Leipzig University.
Littlewood, Joan and McColl, Ewan, *Exchange Visit* (typescript), in the possession of Mr Clive Barker, Birmingham University.
The Good Soldier Schweik (acting copy), in the Theatre Workshop, Theatre Royal.
John Bullion (typescript), in the possession of Mr Clive Barker, Birmingham University.
The Sleepwalker (typescript), in the possession of Mr Ewan McColl.
The Strange Case of Sigismund McHess and the Weird Sisters (typescript), in the possession of Mr Clive Barker, Birmingham University.

Index

Index

(Dates in brackets refer to dates of performance by P. or his colleagues)

Absurd drama 8; *see also* Dorst, Tancred; clown/tramp figures 122

Acting structures 4, 65, 70, 76, 78–9, 83–4, 86–8, 98–101, 104–5, 109–10, 112–16, 125, 132–3, 139–40, 149, 158–62, 176, 184, 186, 193, 197, 220; as images 87–8, 98, 100, 116, 184; 'global stage' 70–1, 84, 88, 105, 111, 158, 200, 221, 226; 'light-stage' (*die Lichtbühne*) 7, 160–71, 173, 175, 225; revolving stage 84, 89, 101, 114, 134, 139, 160, 185, 196–8, 202; simultaneous stages 4, 51–2, 84, 99–102, 103–4, 119, 139, 150, 167, 181–2, 186, 196, 198, 221; 'Stage of Fate' (*Schicksalsbühne*) 7, 104–5, 163, 173, 225; 'treadmill' (*laufendes Band*) 4, 70–2, 81, 83, 87, 89, 100, 113, 134, 158, 160, 175, 198, 222; *see also* Actor; Costumes; Film; Music; Scenery; Stage-machinery

Acting collective, *see* Studio of the Piscator-Bühne

Actor: rôle of 1–2, 4, 6, 24–6, 32, 46, 48, 54, 66–7, 78, 98, 100, 107–20, 121, 125, 136–40, 144, 147–50, 162, 164, 170, 174, 189, 194, 199, 202, 204; training of 5, 7, 42, 68–9, 74, 80, 115–17, 119–20, 152

Actuality, key concept of P. 1, 10, 15, 43, 57–63, 72–4, 76, 85, 102, 107, 109–10, 113, 131, 171, 173, 177–8, 200; *see also* Documentary Drama, standards

Aeschylus 58, 150; *Orestie* (1919) 219

Agitprop Theatre 2–3, 6, 22, 23–40, 41–65, 74, 80, 98, 119, 135, 153, 155, 184–5, 193, 201, 205–6, 219–20, 223; agitation 23–4, 27, 29–30, 32, 43–7, 55, 57, 62, 65, 136, 185, 220; comedy in 34–5; *see also Red Revue, The*; parody 23, 26–7, 32–5, 50–1;

propaganda 3, 22, 23–5, 27–40, 42–7, 48, 51–2, 56–7, 61–3, 65, 117 n.33, 135–6, 155, 201; religious aspects 28–9, 35–9; revue 3–4, 39, 41–65; simplicity 26–8, 31, 33, 37, 52, 98; in England 24, 26, 35–6; in Scotland 34; in U.S.A. 36; in U.S.S.R. 23–4, 26, 36, 185, 222; *see also Before the Door*; Blue Shirts; *Cripple, The*; Proletarian drama; Propaganda plays; *Russia's Day*

All-Union Congress of Soviet Writers 75; *see also* Radek, Karl

Anderson, Maxwell, *Rivalen* 222

Anouilh, Jean 57; *Ardèle* 89

Antheil, Georges, Futurist 93–4

Apollotheater, Mannheim 222

Appia, Adolph 66, 207

Aragon, Louis, and Dada 13

Aristotle 63–4, 103, 121, 136; unity of action 86, 100

Arnold, Matthew 203

Arp, Hans, founder of Dada 12–13; *see also* Dada

Artaud, Antonin 1, 25, 207

Artistic forms, abandonment of 8, 15–16, 24–5, 54, 73, 80, 131–2, 163; *see also* Dada

Association of Proletarian-Revolutionary Authors 102 n.11

Atreus Trilogy (Hauptmann, 1962) 57, 169, 225

Audience: influences on 18–20, 33, 36–7, 42, 44, 47–8, 51, 54, 57, 67, 76, 89, 103, 113, 120, 132–3, 163, 165, 170, 176; informing of 51, 74, 194; involvement of 29, 31, 34, 39, 46, 48, 50, 54, 65, 79, 81, 86–8, 95–6, 119, 134–51, 159, 167, 177, 182–3, 185, 188, 194–5, 199, 206, 222–3; and crowd 143–5; provoking of 142, 177; rôle of 2, 8, 21, 23–6, 32, 190–1, 199

Index

Baader, Johannes, and Dada 14; *see also Green Corpse, The*
Baden-Baden Cantata of Acquiescence (Brecht) 192
Balázs, Béla 54, 140–1, 144, 149; *see also* Agitprop Theatre
Ball, Hugo, founder of Dada 12–13; *see also* Dada
Barrault, Jean-Louis, produces *Christophe Colombe* (Claudel) 151, 191, 225
Barrie, J. M. 20; *see also* English Workers' Theatre Movement
Barta, Lajos, *Russia's Day* 27–32, 34–7, 219
Bauhaus 202, 220; choreography 116; formalized abstraction 1, 94, 162, 188–9, 220; influence on P. 139, 147–8, 162, 188–9; *see also* Schlemmer; *Triadic Ballet*
Becher, J. R., *Workers, Peasants, Soldiers* 54
Beckett, Samuel, *Play* 100, 148
Before the Door, Agitprop play 27, 47–8
Bentley, Eric, critic 107
Bergner, Ludwig, director 181
Berlin: Agitprop first seen in 24; influence on P. 18, 76, 206–7
Berlin Kolonne Links 55
Berliner Ensemble 148, 197, 199; *see also* Brecht; *Modellbücher*
Bernhardt, Sarah, and rôle of actor 67
Bible, influence on Brecht 10, 190
Bill-Bjelozerkovski, *Mond von Links* (1930) 223
Bloch, J. R., *The Last Kaiser* 69, 71
Blue Shirts, first Agitprop troupe 23–4, 222
Borchert, Wolfgang: *The Outsider* (1949) 156, 224
Brahm, Otto, naturalist producer 16, 21, 83, 165–6
Brando, Marlon 7
Brecht, Bertolt 8, 10, 16, 17, 68–9, 86, 116, 117, n.33, 148, 150, 166, 176, 183, 185, 189–200, 202, 206; collaboration with P. 7, 158, 172, 174–5, 193, 196, 200, 220–2, 234; contrast to P.'s epic theatre 106, 117–18, 190, 192, 199–200, 223; development 190–6; influenced by P. 2, 190–200, 205, 220–1, 223–5; 'parable-plays' (*Lehrstück*) 39, 179, 196, 198–200; and politics 1, 7, 17,

126, 141, 156, 190, 192, 195–6; theatrical alienation 106, 134, 194–5, 199; plays: *Baden-Baden Cantata of Acquiescence* 192; *In the City's Jungle* (1927) 198, 221; *Die Tage der Commune* (1962) 7, 225; *The Caucasian Chalk Circle* (1955) 198, 225; *Edward II* 195, 198, 220; *The Flight over the Ocean* 192; *Flüchtlingsgespräche* (1962) 225; *Drums in the Night* 41; *Mahagonny* 195; *Man is Man* (1931) 192–3, 223; *Mother Courage* (1949) 198, 224; *The Mother* (1932) 193, 198–9, 223; *The Private Life of the Master Race* (1945) 224; *The Threepenny Opera* (1928) 222; *see also* Epic Theatre; Theater am Schiffbauerdamm
Breton, André, and Dada 13
Brod, Max 68, 70, 126, 174–5, 222; *see also Good Soldier Schweik, The*
Bronnen, Arnolt, *Rhineland Rebels* (1925) 91–2, 221
Brook, Peter 142, 168–9
Bruckner, *Criminals* (1928) 131
Buchner, Georg 107, 156, 190–1; *Danton's Death* (1956) 182–4, 225; *Woyzeck* 103, 121
Busch, Ernst, actor 193, 198
Byron, Lord George, *Manfred* 66

Cabaret Voltaire, Zürich, and Dada 13–14, 44
Caucasian Chalk Circle, The (Brecht, 1954) 198, 225
Central-Theater 3–4, 40 n.26, 41, 58, 164, 220; *see also* Rehfisch; Volksbühne closed 6
Chaplin, Charles, films of 10, 125, 188
Chaplinade, The 17; *see also* Goll, Ywan
Characters: on film 109–12, 113; on stage 42, 108–10, 112–13, 121–3; identification with 134; P.'s use of on stage 7, 69, 79, 100–1, 104–8, 114–15, 119–20, 125–8, 138, 152, 163–4, 170, 173; stereotyping of 99, 107, 123–30, 173, 178; *see also* Agitprop Theatre, parody; Hero-figure; Individual
Chekov, Anton 41, 148, 150, 164; *Onkel Wanja* 219; *The Three Sisters* 41, 219
Chicago '70 205

Classical Theatre 8, 16, 96, 108, 142, 152, 155–6, 164–71, 201–2, 205, 224; ignores reality 10, 60; oriental 148
Claudel, Paul, *Christophe Colombe* 151, 191, 225
Cocteau, Jean 171
Commedia del'Arte, improvisations at 66, 121
Commentary: in Agitprop plays 24, 46–8, 54; in P.'s plays 131, 152, 177, 179, 191; *see also* Epic Theatre; Programme; Revue
Costumes: Bauhaus view of 189; Party view of 55–6; P.'s use of 3, 27, 118, 151, 165–6, 188, 202; *see also* Acting structures; Stage-machinery
Corrie, Joe 34
Court Theatre, Munich, P. works at 3, 16
Craig, Gordon 25, 91, 207; artist-director 66–7, 189; concept of *Ueber-Marionette* 189
Credé, Karl 154; *§218* (1929) 6, 74, 101, 105, 119, 135, 137–8, 140, 154, 198–9, 222
Cripple, The (*Wittfogel*, 1920), Agit-prop play 27, 47, 219; *see also* *Russia's Day*
Cubist movement 189; *see also* Bauhaus

Dada 9–10, 12–16, 21, 44, 54; Abstraction 13–14, 21, 115; artistic forms 15–13, 24, 100 n.8; criteria 1–3, 13–14; Fascism 13; Marxism 3, 14–15, 18–19, 54; in Berlin 14–16; in Switzerland 13–14, 44; influence on P. 3, 5–6, 16–18, 202; *see also* Arp, Hans; Ball, Hugo; Huelsenbeck, Richard; Panderma; Tzara, Tristan
Dalberg, w. von, producer 168
Dance of Form, The 189; *see also* Bauhaus
Dance of Gestures, The 189; *see also* Bauhaus
Danton's Death (Büchner, 1956) 182–4, 225
Das Tribunal, Königsberg 3–5, 20–1, 58, 219
De Tocqueville 122
Deputy, The (Hochhuth, 1963) 7–8, 59 n.21, 156, 160, 175–7, 225
Despite All! (*Trotz Alledem!* 1925),

revue 3–4, 42, 49–51, 54–5, 65, 77, 81, 87, 109–10, 126, 143, 221; *see also* Revue
Deutches Theater, Berlin 219; Ost-Berlin 224
Dialogue, importance of 4, 77–81, 82, 85, 96, 98, 100, 114, 124, 147, 164, 170, 185; interruption of 138; *see also* Documentary Drama
Die Aktion, Expressionist magazine 17
Diebold, Bernhard, critic 71, 72–3 & n.15, 108, 132, 150–1, 159, 201
Dionysus in '69 205
Director, as innovator 2, 60–1, 66–9, 82–3, 100, 112, 117, 123, 145, 164–5; influence of P. on 5; rôle of 20, 133, 151, 164, 166, 168–9, 191, 204
Döblin, Alfred, critic 103
Documentary Drama 2, 4–5, 8, 65, 66–96, 97–8, 107, 131–2, 134, 141, 150, 152–3, 157, 171, 176, 178–80, 187, 196, 200, 202, 205, 222, 226; approach 120–2, 125; documentation 18, 65, 72, 73–81, 85–6, 89, 97, 99, 110, 113, 131–2, 149, 163, 171–3, 176–9, 185, 197, 200; machinery 66–73, 78, 80, 81–9, 91–6, 142; *see also* Stage-machinery; relation to journalism 60, 72, 74, 79–81, 86, 91, 98–9, 132, 153, 157, 186, 222; standards: actuality 43, 72–4, 76, 85, 95, 102, 131, 177–8, 200; immediacy 18, 49, 51, 57–8, 69, 72–5, 81, 89, 95–6, 102; objectivity 37, 42, 46, 51, 63–5, 69, 72, 73–7, 81, 89, 92, 97–9, 110, 118, 129, 131, 134–6, 153, 176, 178; use of film 4, 17–18, 69, 71–3, 77–8, 81, 88–92, 99, 110, 178, 193, 198–9, 202, 221; visual nature 68, 77–80, 85–6, 88, 90, 100, 147, 148, 170–1; *see also* Generalization; Symbolism
Dorst, Tancred 205; *Toller* (1968) 8, 157, 159, 226; *see also* Absurd drama
Dramatic Workshop of New School for Social Research (New York), P. worked at 7, 68–9, 113, 139, 152, 203, 224; P.'s wife worked at 117 n.33
Drawing-room comedy 10, 155
Dreiser, Theodore, *American Tragedy* (1943), 102, 105
Drums in the Night (Brecht) 41; *see also* Realism, 'brutal'

Drunken Ship, The (Das Trunkene Schiff, Zech, 1926) 81, 101, 118, 188, 194, 221
Duchamps, Marcel, art of 98
Durieux, Tilla, actress 106, 172, 206
Duschinsky, *The Unemployed* 131
Duse, Eleanora 67

Ebert, Friedrich, moderate leader 19
Ebert, Carl, producer 198, 221
Eckhart, Dietrich, *Lorenzaccio* 155
Economic Competition (Lania, 1928) 5, 79–81, 85–6, 88, 102 n.11, 156–7, 172–3, 193, 222; *see also* Documentary Drama, relation to journalism
Edward II (Brecht) 198, 220
Eisenstein, Albert, *Battleship Potemkin* 30, 187–8
Eisler, Hanns 193, 222, 224
Eliot, T. S. 10, 103, 142
Eluard, Paul, and Dada 13
'Emergency Relief Association for the Actors of the Piscator-Bühne' 119; *see also* Studio of the Piscator-Bühne
Empson, William 103
Engel, Erich, producer 222
Epic Theatre 7–8, 46, 97–130, 131, 150, 152, 157, 172–3, 175, 183, 190–200, 206, 223; abstraction 97–9, 112–15, 129, 132, 185; alienation effect 18, 103, 106, 118, 134, 172–3; dramatic structure 99–102, 110–12, 116; means of commentary 102–7, 182; commentators 46–7, 103, 105–6, 131, 177, 179; film 17–18, 44, 104, 107–12, 113, 119, 125, 128–30, 138–40, 177, 196–8, 202, 221; placards 17–18, 65, 77, 89, 104, 106, 112, 114, 118–19, 140, 149, 159, 167, 185, 196; projection 17–18, 42, 44–5, 77, 103–4, 106–7, 114, 119, 159, 167, 177, 196–9, 202; simultaneous stages 4, 99–102, 103–4, 119, 196, 198, 221; and the novel 8, 102–3, 152, 157, 172, 174–5, 223–4, 226; structural principle 99; *see also* Acting structures; Brecht; Film; Generalization; Stage-machinery
Esslin, Martin, critic 202
Everding, director 178; *see also* Joel Brand
Ewen, Frederic, critic 190–1, 203

Exile of P. from Germany 37, 68, 112, 156, 159, 161
Existentialism: *en-soi* 115, 164; 'limit-situation' 122
Expressionism 13 n.8, 17, 20–1, 49, 79, 181, 183–5, 192; authors 21, 41, 97; influence on P. 17, 22, 44, 80, 161–2, 181, 183, 187, 219; New Pathos 181; plays 3, 12, 20–1, 32, 44, 50, 97, 117 n.33, 128; *see also Die Aktion*; Strindberg; Young Germany Movement

Fascism 62, 154–6, 169; culture 13, 20, 91, 155–6; and Futurism 13 n.3; plays 155–6, 168, 223; and theatre of involvement 92
Fehling, Jürgen, director 68, 181
Felsenstein, produces Britten's *Midsummer Night's Dream* 89; produces Offenbach's *Barbe-bleue* 89
Feuchwanger, Lion, influence on Brecht 195–6
Film 4–5, 17–18, 42, 49–52, 62, 71–2, 88, 103, 107–10, 119, 133, 159–60, 166–7, 169, 171–3, 177, 185, 187–8, 198, 202, 219, 221–3; as commentary 104, 106, 107–10; as correlative for modern age 4, 72, 81–2, 203; as documentation 4, 69, 77–8, 81, 104, 107, 109–10, 172, 178, 193; as expansion of action 4, 44–5, 89–90, 104, 107, 150, 173; as expansion of stage 4, 51–2, 72, 81, 84, 90–1, 101–2, 110, 125, 128, 133, 139, 141–2, 161, 173, 197; integration of with stage 102, 110–12, 116, 142; as means of involvement 65, 72, 134, 150–1, 159; as method of generalization 86, 90–2, 95, 97–102, 128–30
Flags (Fahnen, Paquet, 1924) 17–18, 41, 44, 77, 79, 81, 91, 103–5, 112, 153, 198, 220–1
Flight over the Ocean, The (Brecht) 192
Flüchtlingsgespräche (Brecht, 1962) 225
'Formalism' 25, 52–3, 56, 61, 72, 117, 160–4, 194
Free Thälmann, Agitprop play 55
Freie Volksbühne, P. director of (1962) 7, 156, 175, 178, 225–6
Frisch, Max, *The Fireraisers* 140, 225
Funarov, *The Fire Sermon* 36, 94
Functionalism 61, 131, 151, 160–4, 181, 184, 194

Futurism 9–10, 93–4, 189; and Dada 13 & n.3; *see also* Fascism; Marinetti

Garrick, David, actor 165, 168
Garson, Barbara, *Macbird* 205
Garten, H. F., critic 202–3
Gasbarra, Felix, Communist author 38, 41–2, 50, 68, 126, 152, 220–2, 226
Generalization 50, 86–92, 97, 127–30, 188; of characters 124, 200; of speeches 68, 99, 167
Goebbels, Josef 91, 156
Goering, Reinhard, *Naval Encounter* (*Seeschlacht*, 1918) 183–4, 219
Goethe and drama 11, 60, 142
Gogol, Nicholai, *Der Revisor* (1930)
Goll, Ywan: theatrical techniques of 17–18, 219; *Der Unsterbliche* (1921) 219
Good Soldier Schweik, The, Adventures 223
of (1928, 1939), 4–6, 49, 58–9, 70 79, 81–3, 89, 102, 110, 113, 125, 157–8, 161, 174–5, 188, 193, 198, 224–5; Brod/Reimann version 68, 70, 126, 174–5, 222; epic structure 83, 85, 87, 175; Grosz cartoons 6, 18, 89, 115, 126, 159, 161, 174, 222; hero-figure, *below*; influence 205, 224; political aspects 126, 175; puppets 79, 82, 100, 115, 129, 222

Gorki, Maxim 68, 124; *The Lower Depths*, P. adapts (1926) 18, 59, 68, 221 *Die Kleinburger* (1922) 220
Graff, S., *The Endless Street* 131
Granach, Alexander, actor 127, 193, 222
Grass, Günther 205; *The Plebians Rehearse the Uprising* (1966) 8, 226
Gray, Terence, and rôle of director 66
Green Corpse, The 14; *see also* Baader; Dada
Grieg, Nordal: *The Defeat* 7; *see also* Brecht, *Die Tage der Commune*
Gropius, Walter, director of Bauhaus 139, 145, 150, 180; *see also* Bauhaus; Total Theatre
Grosses Schauspielhaus, Berlin 219–21
Grosz, Georg 193; and Dada 14; and P. 17–18, 115, 148, 159, 221–2; *see also Good Soldier Schweik*

Grotowski and ritualism 1

Hallup 54; *see also* Agitprop Theatre
Handke, Peter, *Abuse of the Audience* 142, 177
Hašek, Jaroslav, *see Good Soldier Schweik*
Hasenclever, Walter 57
Hauptmann, Gerhart 123; *Atreus Tetralogy* (1962) 57, 169, 225; *Before Sunrise* 73; *The Weavers* 123; revival of plays of 41
Heartfield, John 41, 49, 193; and Dada 15; influence on P. 3, 17, 41, 219, 221, 223; *see also* Herzfelde, Wieland
Heller, Erich 121
Herald, Heinz, *The Burning Bush* (1949) 224
Hero-figure 45, 92, 110, 114, 121–2, 127–30, 151, 155; Communist 114–15, 122–7; *see also Good Soldier Schweik*, hero-figure; *Hoppla*
Herzfelde, Wieland: *see* Heartfield, John
Herzog, Wilhelm, *The Dreyfus Affair* 153; *see also* Rehfisch
Hessisches Landestheater, Darmstadt 221
Hindenberg, Paul von 50, 172
Hinrich, Hans, producer 222
Hitler, Adolf 27, 35, 92, 155–6, 169, 176
Hochhuth, Rolf 59, 175–6, 178, 180, 205; plays of 2, 171, 179; *The Deputy* (*Der Stellvertreter*, 1963) 7–8, 59 n.21, 156, 175–7, 226; *The Soldiers* (1967) 8, 226; *see also* Total Theatre
Hoffman, Abbie, and drama 1
Hofmannsthal, Hugo von, and rôle of director 67
Hölz, Max, revolutionary 45
Hoppla, we are alive! (Toller, 1927) 5, 18, 49, 70–1, 74, 78, 81, 85, 88, 90, 94–5, 99–102, 110–11, 127–30, 135–6, 145, 221; acting-structure 158, 161, 163, 172, 188; *see also* Generalization; Hero-figure
Horvath, *Sladek* 131
Hübler-Kahla, Johann 109–10, 221–2; *see also* Studio of the Piscator-Buhne
Huelsenbeck, Richard, founder of Dada 12–14, 17; *see also* Dada
Hultberg, Helge, critic 190

Index

Ibsen, Henrik 1, 20, 41, 108; *Ghosts* 108

Immortal, The 17–18; *see also* Goll, Ywan

Improvisation: in acting 66, 74, 113, 121; textual 6, 68, 74, 79–81, 98–9, 152, 158, 166–7, 169, 174–5, 193, 205, 221; *see also* Agitprop Theatre; *Commedia del' Arte*; Welk, Ehm

In the City's Jungle (Brecht, 1927) 198, 221

In the Matter of J. Robert Oppenheimer (Kipphardt, 1964) 157, 177, 179, 226

Individual 11, 20, 60, 121, 124, 127–30, 141, 143–5, 152, 169, 173, 195; interest moves from, to society 31, 63, 103, 105–6, 110, 114, 116, 118, 121–5, 129, 135, 140–1, 180; in P.'s productions 104–5, 111–12, 116, 118–19, 122–3, 125, 127–30, 140–2, 145, 163–4, 170, 176, 180, 202; *see also* Characters; Hero-figure

International Revolutionary Theatre Association (1934) 6, 62; *see also* Agitprop Theatre

International Workers' Theatre Organization (1930) 52–3, 55

Investigation, The (Weiss, 1965) 157, 171, 177–9, 226

Irving, Henry, *The Bells* 204

Jelagin, J., biographer of Meyerhold 186

Jessner, Leopold, Expressionist director 20, 49, 68–9, 91–2, 108, 124, 165, 181, 189, 219, 221; influence on P. 184–5, 187; resigns from Staatstheater 154

Jhering, Hebert, critic 71, 117, 119–20, 153–4, 168, 186, 201

Joel Brand (Kipphardt) 177–8

Johnson, Samuel 206

Johst, Hans, *Schlageter* (1933) 92, 223

Jonson, Ben, 'Comedy of Humours' 121

zöuvet, Louis, and rôle of director 67

Joyce, James, and 'stream of consciousness' school 146

Jung, Franz: *Die Kanaker* (1921) 219; and P. 17

Junge Volksbühne organization 155

Kabuki Theatre 117–18

Kafka, Franz, *The Scapegoat* (1950) 224

Kaiser, Georg 20

Kaiser (Weilhelm II) 51, 169, 19 attacks on 122, 165; and *Rasputin* 6, 77, 132, 198

Kaiser's Coolies, The (Plievier, 1930) 102, 105–6, 222–3

Kammerspiele, München 220, 225

Kästner, Erich, and revue 44

K.D.P. (German Communist Party) 24, 48, 55, 64–8, 91, 123, 126, 154, 172; control over P.'s Agitprop plays 38–9, 42, 50, 61; and elections of 1924 & 1932 42–5, 50, 56, 141; rejection of Weimar Republic 27

Kenter, Heinz, producer 222

Kerr, Alfred, critic 56, 71, 131, 158

Kipling, Rudyard, influence on Brecht 190

Kipphardt, Heinar 2, 8, 180, 205; *In the Matter of J. Robert Oppenheimer* (1964) 157, 177, 179, 226; *Joel Brand* 177–8

Kirst, H. H., *The Officers' Uprising* (1966) 71, 105, 205, 226

Kokoschka, Oscar, *Murder, Hope of Women* 189

Komödienhaus, Berlin 223

Kornfeld, Paul, critic 72 & n.14

Kranz, Herbert, *Freedom* (1919), 184, 219

Kraus, Karl 59, 122, 148; *The Unconquered* (1929) 131

Kürfurstendamm 48; and Dada 21

Landestheater, Stuttgart 220

Langley, N. 224

Lania, Leo 54, 76 & n.24, 126, 152, 174–5, 205, 221–2; *Economic Competition (Konjunktur*, 1928) 5, 85–6, 222

Lask, Berta 54, 63 n.36; *Die Befreiung* (1920) 220; *see also* Agitprop Theatre

Last Kaiser, The (Bloch, 1928) 69, 71, 71, 102, n.11, 112, 160, 162, 222

Lazlo, Carl 16; *see also* Dada; Panderma

Lenin, N. 28, 31, 38, 45, 50, 127; in *Rasputin* 126–7, 139

Leonhard, Rudolf, *Sail Ahoy* (1925) 77, 220

Lessing, G. E. 11, 156; *Nathan the Wise* (1952) 91, 225

Lessing-Theater, Berlin 222

Levine, E., revolutionary 15, 21, 176
Lewis, Wyndham, *The Enemy of the Stars* 189; *see also* Vorticism
Ley-Piscator, Maria 117 n.33
Liebknecht, Karl, murder of 3, 18, 38, 42, 45, 50–1, 126; *see also Despite All!*; Luxemburg, Rosa; Spartacus
Lindtberg, Leopold, producer 222
Littlewood, Joan 20, 35, 61, 67, 74, 82, 104 n.15, 205, 224; influenced by P. 2, 224; *John Bullion* 117 n.33; *Oh What a Lovely War* 104 n.15, 205; *The Sleepwalker* 35; *The Strange Case of Sigismund McHess and the Weird Sisters* 35; *see also* Theatre Workshop
Living Newspaper 55; American 2, 26, 74, 205, 224; in U.S.S.R. 24, 26; *see also* Agitprop Theatre; Proletarian drama
'Living Theatre' 160–4, 224
Loudspeakers, use of 77, 81–2, 84, 89–90, 94, 98, 110, 114, 133, 139, 149, 188, 202; *see also* Documentary Drama, machinery; Stage-machinery
Lower Depths, The (Gorki, 1926) 18, 59, 82, 84, 221
Ludendorff, Erich 172
Ludwig, Emil 107
Lukács, G., literary theoretician 125, 194
Lunacharsky, Anatoli, Commissar for Culture 52–3; *see also* Marxism, ideology and art
Luxemburg, Rosa, murder of 3, 18, 38, 45, 50–1, 110, 126; *see also* Liebknecht; Spartacus

McColl, Ewan 205, 224
McLuhan, Marshall 2, 94–6, 204, 207
Machine-Wreckers, The (Toller, 1922) 41–3, 220
Mahoganny (Brecht) 195
Man is Man (Brecht, 1931) 192–4, 223
Mann, Thomas 20
Mannerism in P.'s work 82; *see also* Realism
Marc, Franz, theories on colours 185
Maria Stuart (Schiller), as image 177

Marinetti, Filippo: and Dada 13, 15, 18; and Futurism 13 & n.3, 189
Marshall, Norman, *The Producer and the Play* 202
Martin, Karlheinz, Expressionistic director 20–1, 68–9, 181, 219–20; 220; *see also* Proletarisches Theater; Tribune, The
Marxism 14, 122, 124, 176, 192; approach to art 20–1, 38, 80–1, 84, 93, 102 n.11, 187; hero-figures 122–30; ideology and art 6, 25, 33–5, 37–40, 47–9, 51–7, 61, 63–5, 69, 75, 91, 114–15, 119, 126, 134–5, 140–1, 172, 191, 201; influence on P. 3, 6–7, 18–19, 25, 30–1, 38, 63–4, 91–2, 96, 119, 123, 157, 176, 187, 191–2, 201; materialist philosophy 30, 37, 52, 64, 123; 'proletarian art' 25, 27–30, 35, 52, 56, 75–6, 92; support for theatre 24, 26, 38–9, 42–3, 50, 53–6, 144, 184; *see also* Dada
mass-media 53, 95, 98, 142–3, 159, 197, 204–5; on stage 2, 51, 72, 81, 116, 133, 150–1, 152, 157, 159, 200; *see also* Film; Loudspeakers; Projection; Radio
Maugham, W. Somerset 144
Mayakovsky, V., *Mysterium Buffo* 186
Medieval drama 10, 24, 36, 101; influence on Brecht 190–1
Mehring, Walter: and Dada 15, 17–18, 44; and P. 17, 88; *The Merchant of Berlin* (1929) 6, 18, 49, 70–1, 222; *see also* Political Cabaret
Meisel, Edmund 186; and P. 18, 44, 58, 82, 135, 220–1, 223; *see also Good Soldier Schweik*
Melchinger, Siegfried, critic 109
Melodrama 103, 172; in Agitprop 27, 45; nineteenth-century 32
Merchant of Berlin, The (Mehring, 1929) 6, 18, 49, 70–2, 75, 81, 88, 102 n.11, 113, 148, 154, 158, 160, 193, 222
Meyerhold, Vsevolod 81–2, 86–7, 91, 94, 207, 223; 'Biomechanics' 116–17; influence on P. 185–7, 191; and politics 1, 61, 123–4; *see also* October Theatre
Miller, Arthur, 'anti-heroes' of 121, 204
Mime 118, 166, 171

Modellbücher 147, 197; *see also* Berliner Ensemble; Brecht

Moholy-Nagy, designer 148, 188–9, 220, 222; and Fascism 13; *Score Sketch for Mechanized Eccentrics* 189; *see also* Bauhaus

Molière, satire of 121, 142

Montage, use of 15, 49–50, 79, 116, 149, 177, 181, 187–8, 195; *see also* Acting-structures; Documentary Drama; Revue

Moscow Art Theatre 41, 52, 147, 219; *see also* Stanislavski

Mother, The (Brecht, 1932) 193, 198–9, 223

Mother Courage (Brecht, 1949) 198, 224

Mühsam, Erich 126, 176; *Eleven Executioners* 44; *Reasons of State* (*Sacco und Vanzetti*, 1928) 153–4, 222

Müller, Traugott 58, 88, 220–2

Music: for P.'s productions 5, 44, 58, 82, 114, 133, 135, 137, 151, 166, 170, 193; 'revolutionary' 53, 62, 185–6; *see also* Eisler; Marinetti; Meisel; Weill

Music hall, convention of 43–4; *see also* Revue

Mussolini, Benito, *Hundred Days* (1932) 155, 223

Nationalism 6, 154, 192

Nationaltheater, Weimar 223

Nationaltheater, Mannheim 225

Naturalism 1, 66, 74–5, 83, 88, 103, 107–8, 120, 138, 165, 192; P. tries 4, 89, 164, 177–8, 220, 223; revival of 41, 58–9, 73, 155

Naumann, Bernard, critic 179

Neher, Caspar, designer 184, 193, 198, 220, 222–3, 225

Neue Sachlichkeit movement 4, 58, 131

Neumann, Alfred: P. works with 7, 224–5; *Krieg und Frieden* (1955) 225

'New Drama' 69, 130, 151–80 *passim*, 200

Nicoll, Allardyce, 107

Noh Theatre 108, 116–17, 190–1; *see also* Bauhaus; Brecht; Meyerhold, 'Biomechanics'

November Revolution 14, 50, 122, 176; influence on P. 18–19; *see also* Berlin; Spartacus

November Studio, Berlin 222

Nuremberg trials portrayed on stage 176

Objectivity 37, 42, 46, 51, 63–5, 69, 72, 73–7, 81, 89, 92, 97, 99, 129, 131, 134–6, 153, 155, 172, 176, 178, 191–2, 195; of acting-technique 98, 118–19, 135

October Revolution 36, 86–7, 198

October Theatre 61, 86–7, 186; *see also* Meyerhold

Off-Broadway theatres 7, 205

Officers' Uprising, The (Kirst, 1966) 71, 105, 226

On the Waterfront 109

'Open Theatre' 103; *see also* Büchner

Oppenheimer, portrayed on stage 176–7; *see also In the Matter of J. Robert Oppenheimer*

Osborne, John, *Look Back in Anger* 142

Ostrovski, A.; *Der Wald* 223; *How the Steel was Tempered* 185–6

Palitzsch, Peter, producer 157, 159, 226

Pallenberg, Max, actor 5, 115; *see also Good Soldier Schweik*

Panderma 9–10, 16; *see also* Dada; Lazlo, Carl

Paquet, Alfons: *Flags* (*Fahnen*) 17–18, 41, 44, 81, 103, 220; *Tidal Wave* (*Sturmflut*, 1926) 4, 81, 125, 127, 171, 173, 221

Pauline Edwards Theatre, New York 224

Picabia, Francis, and Dada 13

Picasso, Pablo 70; *Guernica* 39

Pinthus, Kurt, critic 135

Pirandello, Luigi 156

Piscator-Bühne, first 5–6, 49, 51, 56, 61, 69–71, 74–5, 83, 85, 87, 101, 104, 112–13, 116, 119–20, 126, 131, 157, 159–60, 170, 175, 193–4, 201, 221–2, 224; second 6, 49, 154, 222; *see also* 'Emergency Relief Association for the Actors of the Piscator-Bühne'; Studio of the Piscator-Bühne

Planchon, Roger, producer 67; influenced by P. 2, 205

Playwright 27, 34, 82–3, 123, 152–80 *passim*, 197, 206; influences on 5, 7–8, 20, 68, 152, 154, 158, 169–70, 203–5; rôle of 2, 66–8, 78, 93, 100, 153, 157, 165, 171, 177; *see also* Actor; Director; Stage-machinery

Plievier, Theodor 102 & n. 11; *The Kaiser's Coolies* (1930) 102, 222–3

Pogodin, Michael, *The Aristocrats* (1946) 224

Poetry in drama 93, 155, 157, 171, 178

Political Cabaret, Berlin 15, 44; *see also* Dada; Mehring, Walter

Political theatre 6–7, 11, 21, 25, 36, 48, 52–4, 61–5, 70, 75–6, 84, 114, 120, 132, 137–8, 140–2, 149, 153–4, 157, 163–4, 168, 170, 176, 181, 185, 189, 192, 195, 200–2, 206

Political Theatre, The (Piscator) 56, 63, 70, 163, 177, 187, 192–4, 203

Prampolini, Enrico, Futurist 94

President Theatre, New York 224

Prévert, *Les Enfants du Paradis* 89

Private Life of the Master Race, The (Brecht, 1945) 224

Programmes for Piscator's productions 47–50, 71, 75, 77, 126, 135–6, 141–2, 148

Projections 17–18, 42, 48, 61, 84, 91, 101, 103–4, 106–7, 119, 150, 193, 202, 220; as correlative for modern age 81–2, 89, 94, 100–1; as documentation 77–8, 81; as extension of stage 50–2, 86, 111–12, 114, 161–2, 167, 198; as means of involvement 44–5, 159–60; *see also* Epic Theatre

Proletarian drama 21–2, 27–9, 35, 42, 44–7, 54, 56, 76, 125–7, 140, 184, 205; determining factors 23–6

Proletarisches Theater, Berlin 3, 21–2, 24–7, 34, 41, 48, 52, 57, 65, 68, 145, 219; of Karlheinz Martin 21, 219; *see laos* Martin, Karlheinz; *see also* *Russia's Day*

Propaganda plays 19–20, 23, 74, 142, 184, 201; Communist 2, 11, 23–4, 48, 51–4, 56–7, 61–2, 64, 69, 77, 84, 91, 117 n.33, 124, 126, 142, 153, 172; of P. 3, 6, 8, 22, 24, 27–40, 43–7, 56, 62, 69, 94, 126, 154–5, 196, 201; *see also* Agitprop Theatre; Revue

Rabelais and political satire 43–4

Racine, *Phaedre* 220

Radek, Karl, revolutionary 31, 75

Radio, use of on stage 81–2, 90; *see also* Documentary Drama, machinery; Stage-machinery

Rasputin (Alexei Tolstoy, 1927) 5–6, 49, 68, 75, 85, 102, 113, 125, 135–6, 141, 145, 171–2, 195, 221, 223; Acting structure 70–1, 79, 84, 88, 90–1, 104–6, 110–11, 158, 186, 198; and Kaiser 6, 77, 132; Lenin portrayed in 126–7

Rathenau, Walter, assassination of 42–3, 72

Rauschenberg, art of 98

Realism 9–10, 12, 18, 39–40, 75–6, 83, 98, 106–11, 116, 121–2, 125, 154, 177–80, 185, 189; 'brutal' 41; *see also* Brecht, *Drums in the Night*; in P.'s work 4, 6, 8, 25, 32, 37, 40, 57–63, 64–5, 73–4, 76–82, 84, 90, 93, 112, 127, 149–50, 152, 157, 171, 174–5, 180, 192, 194–5, 200, 207, *see also* Symbolism; theatrical 37, 42, 57–63, 73; *see also* Neue Sachlichkeit; Socialist Realism

Rebel Players, Hackney 55

Red Flag, The, Communist newspaper 11, 45, 51, 54, 57, 126, 135

Red Megaphone, Salford 55

Red Revue, The (1924) 3–4, 42, 43–7, 48, 50, 54–6, 105, 129, 220; *see also* Programmes; Revue

Rehfisch, Hans José 3; *The Dreyfus Affair* (1929) 153, 222; *see also* Herzog; Volksbühne

Reichstag 48; K.P.D. seats on 43; National Socialist seats on 154

Reimann, Hans 68, 70, 113, 126, 174–5, 222

Reinhardt, Max 16, 68, 154, 184, 189, 219; *Danton's Death* 182–4; influence on P. 170, 182–3, 187; innovations 83, 108, 165–6, 182–3; Theatre of the Five Thousand 21, 42, 140, 182, *see also* audience; *see also* Vollmoeller, *Miracle*

Renaissance court masques 66; innovations 82–3

Revue 39, 41–65, 87, 137, 150, 153, 181; 'Agitation programme' 43–7; 'compère' figures 46–7, 105, 137, 220, *see also* Epic Theatre, means of commentary; 'historical revue' 49–51, 55, 61, 65, 221; influence 54–7; political nature 3, 42–7, 55, 153; versatility 43–6, 47; *see also* Agitprop Theatre; *Despite All! Red*; *Revue, The*

Index

Robbers, The (Schiller, 1926 & 1957) 85, 99, 165–70, 185, 188, 204, 206, 221, 225; Lenin portrayed in 127

Rolland, Romain: *Robespierre* (1963) 102, 226; *Die Zeit Wird Kommen* (1923) 220

Royal Shakespeare Company, *U.S.* 205

Russell, Bertrand 37–8, 125

Russia's Day, Agitprop play (1920) 27–32, 34–7, 41–2, 45, 50, 219; *xee also* Barta, Lajos; Heartfield, John

Sail Ahoy (Leonhard) 77, 88, 109, 220

Sartre, Jean-Paul 57; *Iron in the Soul* (1953) 102

Sas, Ladislaus, *Vor dem Tore* (1920) 219

Saxe-Meiningen, Duke of 66, 120; *see also* Naturalism

Scenery: abolition of 58, 162; by Heartfield 41, 49; P.'s use of 41, 70–2, 84, 87–8, 109, 114, 132–4, 139, 151, 162, 175; rôle of 2, 4, 117, 184; simplicity in Agitprop and Revue 27, 42, 49; *see also* Acting structures; Stage-machinery

Schauspielhaus, Marburg 225

Schiller 5, 11, 53, 60, 68, 156, 177; *Don Carlos* (1959) 225; *Maria Stuart* 177; *The Robbers* (*Die Rauber*, 1926, 1957) 68, 165–8, 170, 221, 225; *Wallenstein* 177; *Wilhelm Tell* 219

Schillertheater, West Berlin 225–6

Schlageter (Johst, 1932) 92, 223

Schlemmer, Oscar, Bauhaus director 188–9, 220

Schweikart, Hans, producer 226

Scottish Community Drama Association 34

Schwitters, Kurt, and Fascism 13

Scribe, *Adrienne Lecouvreur* (1923) 220

Sehgers, Anna, *The Revolt of the Fishermen*, filmed by P. 6, 87, 223

Shakespeare, W. 143, 150, 156, 165, 183; *Hamlet* (1926) 165–6, 221; *Henry V* 109, 205; *King Lear* (1940), 168, 224; *Macbeth* (1951) 162, 165, 224; *Richard II* 58

Shaw, G. B. 20, 156

Sherwood, Robert 204

Simplicity, theatrical 26–8, 31, 33, 37, 52, 73, 87–8, 93, 98–9, 103, 114–15, 117, 119, 128, 179, 200, 223; *see also* Acting structures

Socialist Realism 54, 73–7, 117 n.33, 124, 194; in P.'s work 4, 8, 25, 32, 40, 74; *see also* Documentary Drama, objectivity; Realism

Spartacus, German left-wing party 18–19, 43; Spartacist revolt 3, 50; *see also* Liebknecht, Karl; Luxemberg, Rosa

Staatliches Schauspielhaus, Berlin 185, 219, 221, 223

Staatstheater 154

Stage-machinery 2, 12, 17–18, 25, 37, 41–2, 44, 66–73, 88, 98, 103, 105, 113–14, 116–20, 131–3, 137, 142, 145, 156–62, 169–71, 174–5, 184–6, 188–9, 191, 196–7, 202, 204, 206, 222, 225; as correlative for modern age 4–5, 70, 80–5, 89, 91–5, 152, 160–1, 189, 200, 207; and documentation 81; as expansion of stage 68, 72–3, 78, 86–7, 91, 97–8, 140, 147, 149, 157, 197; function of 32, 92–6, 97, 99, 134, 149, 162–3, 199; and realism 57–8; romanticization of 73–4, 88, 94; *see also* Acting structures; Loudspeakers; Radio

Stalin, Joseph 35, 52–3, 56, 124, 244; *see also* Agitprop Theatre, propaganda; Propaganda plays

Stanislavski, K. 41, 147, 164, 219; 'Method' 118; *see also* Chekov; Naturalism; *Three Sisters, The*

Steckel, Leonhard, actor 193

Stein, Gertrude, and 'stream of consciousness' school 146

Stoppard, Tom, *Rosencrantz and Guildenstern are Dead* 109

Storm over Gottland (Welk, 1927) 6, 65, 68–9, 78, 90, 99, 127, 158, 161, 185, 188, 198, 221, 223

Strindberg, A. 20, 41, 68; *Ghost Sonata* (1919) 3, 219; *see also* Expressionism

Studio of the Piscator-Bühne 5–6, 69, 109–10, 115–17, 119–20, 141, 152, 163, 193, 204, 222–4; *see also* Actor, rôle of; 'Emergency Relief Association for the Actors of the Piscator-Bühne'; Hübler-Kahla

Studio Theatre, New York 71, 224

Subscribers' Club 145; *see also* Proletarisches Theater

Sunday Worker 55

Surrealism 13, 189; *see also* Dada; Bauhaus

Symbolism 108, 118, 121, 123, 126–
7, 141, 151, 184–5; in P.'s work 79,
83–5, 88, 99–100, 115, 125, 149, 160,
171–4, 176; *see also* Documentary
Drama, visual nature; Realism

Tage der Commune, Die (Brecht, 1962)
225
Tai Yang Awakes (Wolf, 1931) 110,
112, 117–19, 127, 130, 140–1, 158,
194, 199, 223
Tairoff, Alexander, producer 186, 220
Taylor, John Russell, *Dictionary of
the Theatre* 150
'Teaching' plays 39, 54; *see also*
Brecht, 'parable plays'
Tempo 31, 46, 49, 72–3, 77, 107, 133–
6, 149, 184, 188; *see also* Total
Theatre
Tenschert, J., producer 225
Theater am Nollendorfplatz, Berlin
83, 116, 221–3
Theater am Schiffbauerdamm, Berlin
7, 116, 222, 225; *see also* Brecht
Theatre, the: amateur, of P. 24–7, 32,
39–41; of affirmation 64; as an art
form 1, 87, 106, 119, 137, 150, 154,
165, 202; as educational institution
11, 123, 193; as 'entertainment' 1, 3,
11, 18, 42, 47, 83, 93, 136, 156, 170;
functions of 1, 4–5, 8, 9, 11–12, 18,
25, 30, 70, 103, 136; in Germany
9–12, 19–22, 39, 59–60, 67, 108, 117,
124, 155–6, 165, 179, 205; professional, of P. 3, 24, 32, 40–1, 43, 46,
52, 56, 58, 63, 69, 80
Théâtre complet 151; *see also* Total
Theatre
Théâtre engagé 122–3; influenced by
P. 2
Theatre of Action, Manchester 53–5,
205, 224
Theatre of the Five Thousand 21, 42,
49, 140, 143, 182; *see also* Reinhardt,
Max
Theatre Workshop 20, 74, 92, 104
n.15; *Oh What a Lovely War* 104
n.15, 205; *see also* Littlewood, Joan
Third Reich, the 169, 176; and art 124,
155–6, 202
Three Sisters, The (Chekov) 41, 219;
see also Naturalism; Stanislavski
Threepenny Opera, The (Brecht/Weill,
1928) 222

Tidal Wave (*Sturmflut*, Paquet, 1926)
4, 81, 89–90, 110, 125, 127, 133,
161, 171, 173, 176, 198, 221
Toller, Ernst 21, 102 n.11, 152, 176;
Die Wandlung (1918) 219; *Hoppla,
we are alive!* 5, 18, 49, 70–1, 78, 94–5,
99–100, 127–30, 221; *The Machine-
Wreckers* 41–3, 220, *see also* Heartfield, John; *Transfiguration* 4
Tolstoy, Alexei 156–7; *Rasputin* 5–6,
49, 68, 70–1, 221
Tolstoy, Leo 132; *The Powers of
Darkness* (*Die Macht der Finsternis*,
1923) 41, 220; *War and Peace
(Krieg und Frieden),* 1942, 1955 7,
59, 71, 173, 224–5
'Topical theatre' 8, 65, 92, 102, 131–2,
138, 149, 153, 193; *see also* Piscator-
Bühne
Total Theatre 2, 4–5, 7–8, 65, 84, 92,
120, 131–51, 152, 161, 180, 182, 199,
205, 225; anti-literary nature 114,
147–9, 182; definitions 149–51;
Gropius-theatre 139–40, 145–9, 150,
180, *see also* Gropius, Walter;
Synaesthetic art 8, 66–7, 133–4,
148–9, 199; tempo 31, 46, 49, 72–3,
77, 107, 133–6, 149, 184; 'theatre of
involvement' 8, 65, 92, 134–49, 159,
182, 199, *see also* audience; theoretic
justification 133–5, 140–1, 149,
151
Tretjakov, Sergei, *Brülle China!* 223
Triadic Ballet 188–9, 220; *see also*
Bauhaus
Tribunal, Das, Berlin 20–1, 219
Tribune, Die, Berlin, 20, 219
Troppenz 55; *see also* Agitprop
Theatre
Tucholsky, Kurt 102 n.11; and revue
44
Twelfth Night (Shakespeare) 113; *see
also* Dramatic Workshop
Tzara, Tristan, founder of Dada 12–
14; *Coeur à Gaz* 13; *see also* Dada

Ulbrich, Franz, Fascist producer
223
Utzerath, H., producer 226
'Utilitarian theatre' 8, 51–4, 57, 61–3;
see also Revue

Valentin, Karl, influence on Brecht 190
Villon, and political satire 43–4, 190

Volksbühne, Berlin 3, 21, 185, 223; P. guest director at 4–6, 41, 65, 69, 77, 101, 192, 220–2; dismissed 6, 68–9; *see also* Central-Theater; Junge Volksbühne; Rehfisch
Vollmoeller, Carl, *Miracle* 42, 183; *see also* Reinhardt, Max
Vorticism, English 93, 109; *see also* Lewis, Wyndham

Wachtangov, producer 123
Wagner, Richard 64, 148, 155; *Gesamtkunstwerk* 66
Waley, A., translator of *Noh* dramas 190
Wallenstein (Schiller), as image 177
Wallnertheater, Berlin 223
Wangenheim, G. von 17; *Mousetrap* 206
War and Peace (Tolstoy, 1942), P. produces 7, 59, 71, 79, 102, 105–6, 173, 205, 224
Wedekind, Frank 20, 44
Warren, Robert Penn 204; *All the King's Men* (1948) 102, 224
Weidt, Jean, 'the Red Dancer' 117 & n.33, 118, 223
Weill, Kurt, composer 193, 222; *see also Threepenny Opera, The*
Weimar Republic 9–22 *passim*, 39, 53, 56, 108; disintegration of 153–5; drama in 5, 8, 19, 57, 67, 117, 159, 176, 180, 183, 191, 200–2, 204; P.'s influence during 152–3, 200–1, 204; in P.'s productions 88; rejection of by K.P.D. 27, 43, 56
Weisenborn, Günther 193
Weiss, Peter 2, 8, 171, 180, 205; *The Investigation* (1965) 157, 178–9, 226
Welk, Ehm 78–9; *Storm over Gottland* (*Gewitter über Gottland*, 1927) 6, 65, 68–9, 78, 221

Wesker, Arnold, 'anti-heroes' of 121
What Price Glory? 70–1, 102 n.11, 107, 134, 184 (*Rivalen*, 1929), 222
Where's that Bomb? 33
Whip, The, at Drury Lane: treadmill stage 83
Wilde, Oscar, *Salome* 220
Willet, John, critic 191–4, 202
Williams, Tennessee 7, 171, 204
Wittfogel, K. A.: *The Cripple* (*Der Krüppel*, 1920) 27, 47, 219
Wolf, Friedrich 17, 55, 152, 158, 205–6, 223; *Cyanide* (1929) 131, 222; *Sailors of Cattaro* 188; *Tai Yang Awakes* (1931) 110, 112, 117–19, 127, 130, 140–1, 158, 199, 223; *see also* Agitprop Theatre
Workers' Educational Confederation 49–50
Workers' Theatre Movement, English 20, 26, 33; *see also* Propaganda plays; *Where's that Bomb?*
Workers' Theatre, United States 26
Workers' theatre groups, Germany 24, 153
Würtembergische Staatstheater, Stuttgart 226

Yeats, W. B., and rôle of theatre 25, 147; *Plays for Dancers* 137
Young Germany Movement 12, 183–4; *see also* Expressionism; Reinhardt, Max

Zech, Paul, *The Drunken Ship* (*Das Trunkene Schiff*, 1926) 81, 118, 221
Ziegel, Erich, producer 165
Zola, Emile 153
Zuckmayer, Carl 222
Zweig, Stefan 181